Fig. 3
William Clayton
From *Iron Workers, Tredegar, Wales*
1865

The photographs were taken in response to a debate surrounding the role of women in industry. One letter writer in the *Merthyr Telegraph*, 1865, pointed out that 'working men complain that their wives are of very little use to them as help-meets. They can't make their children's clothes and they can't cook...' Another expressed concern over the impact of physical work on reproductive health: 'The employment of the physically weak in labours demanding great physical exertion, tends to lessen the capacity of throwing off diseases, and gradually dwarfs the physical frame... when these females become the mothers of the succeeding generation, we find the offspring debilitated by the weakness of the parent.'

Their attempts to add a femininity to their appearance is notable in its marked contrast to the harsh labour they are performing.

'The bonnet or hat, for it is difficult to discern to which of these classes this head-dress belongs, is bedecked with beads, brooches and feathers, the latter addition in a way imitating the Prince of Wales plume. In this dress, with faces black with dust and smoke, it is difficult, when elevated 50 or 100 yards, to discern the sex to which these objects belong; and a gentleman, who evidently had never witnessed such a sight before, on visiting the town of Tredegar recently, expressed his astonishment at making mountains on mountains and inquired what animals those were he saw moving about on the top? In the tempest and the storm, in rain and in snow, in the sun and heat, exposed to all weathers, women and girls are employed on the tips in South Wales.' — *Bristol Mercury*, 29 April 1865

Fig. 4
William Clayton
From *Iron Workers, Tredegar, Wales*
1865

Fig. 5
William Clayton
From *Iron Workers, Tredegar, Wales*
1865

Fig. 6
John Martin
The Destruction of Sodom and Gomorrah
1852

Thirteen years earlier, John Martin was also depicting the anxieties of the age in his masterpiece *The Destruction of Sodom and Gomorrah*, a painting as much about the mid-Victorian period as the distant ancient world it depicts. It serves as a warning about the potential implosion of society, as the city destroys itself under the weight of its sin and disease – two problems that, for many Victorians, were inextricably linked. The industrial boom of the early 1800s had caused an unprecedented exodus of the rural poor to urban centres; by 1851, for the first time in human history, more people in the nation were living in cities than in the countryside. The population of London was 2.6 million and this rapid urbanisation caused huge infrastructural problems. Water, which had previously been drawn from wells and streams, was now a bringer of death. Polluted by factory waste-products and sewage, the river Irwell in Salford went purple and foamed with noxious gases.

Fig. 7
John Martin
The Destruction of Sodom and Gomorrah (detail)
1852

Two years before *The Destruction of Sodom and Gomorrah* was completed thousands had died in the 1848–49 London cholera epidemic – a man-made near-apocalypse. Martin would have been well aware of this: he was obsessed with the sewage problem faced by the largest city in the world and for over 20 years had been lecturing, publishing plans and lobbying parliament on the subject. In 1845 he formed the joint-stock Metropolitan Sewage and Manure Company, tasked with creating a system that would remove the waste to the rapidly industrialising farmland of the South East. As well as being needed to boost production and cope with the population increase, it was also envisaged that the public works would put the unemployed to better use than the workhouse: a punitive parody of the factory. This only served to enhance his visionary credentials, but his ambitious schemes invited much public ridicule, with *Punch* magazine commenting, in 1843, that he was 'positively pathetic about having devoted a long and arduous life to the sewers and cesspools of his native city, 14 long years had he laboured to enlarge the subterranean ways and water courses of the modern Babylon'. Martin was vindicated shortly after his death with the construction of a large-scale sewage system in London, which bore a resemblance to his own plan and its ambitions.

Fig. 8
John Martin
Plan for Preventing the Pollution of the Water of the Thames
1834

'Plan for preventing the pollution of the water of the Thames and preserving the sewage for agricultural purposes, by means of Grand Sewers running parallel with each bank, into which all the minor drains should fall. Wharfs should be so constructed as to form the roof of the sewer; with a grand public walk forming a roof to the wharf, the three combined objects would cost little more than either of the three separate; whilst the utility, grandeur and proportionate value of the property would be greatly increased.'
— John Martin, 2 June 1834

Fig. 9
G. Greatbach
The Black Country, Near Bilston
1869

H. Warren. R.A.

HE BLACK COUNTRY.

(NEAR BILSTON)

A fellow engineer also saw industrial chaos in similarly epic terms:

'The Black Country is anything but picturesque. The earth seems to have been turned inside out. Its entrails are strewn about; nearly the entire surface of the ground is covered with cinder heaps and mounds of scoriae. The coal, which has been drawn from below ground, is blazing on the surface. The district is crowded with iron furnaces, puddling furnaces and coal pit engine furnaces. By day and by night the country is glowing with fire, and the smoke of the ironworks hovers over it. Workmen covered with smut, and with fierce white eyes, are seen moving about amongst the glowing iron and dull thud of forge-hammers.

Amidst these flaming, smoky, clanging works, I beheld the remains of what had once been happy farmhouses, now ruined and deserted. The ground underneath them had sunk by the working out of the coal, and they were falling to pieces. They had in former times been surrounded by clumps of trees but only skeletons of them remained, dilapidated, black and lifeless. The grass had been parched and killed by the vapours of sulphurous acid thrown out by the chimneys; and every herbaceous object was a ghastly grey – the emblem of vegetable death in its saddest aspect. Vulcan had driven out Ceres.' — James Nasmyth, Engineer, *An Autobiography*, 1883

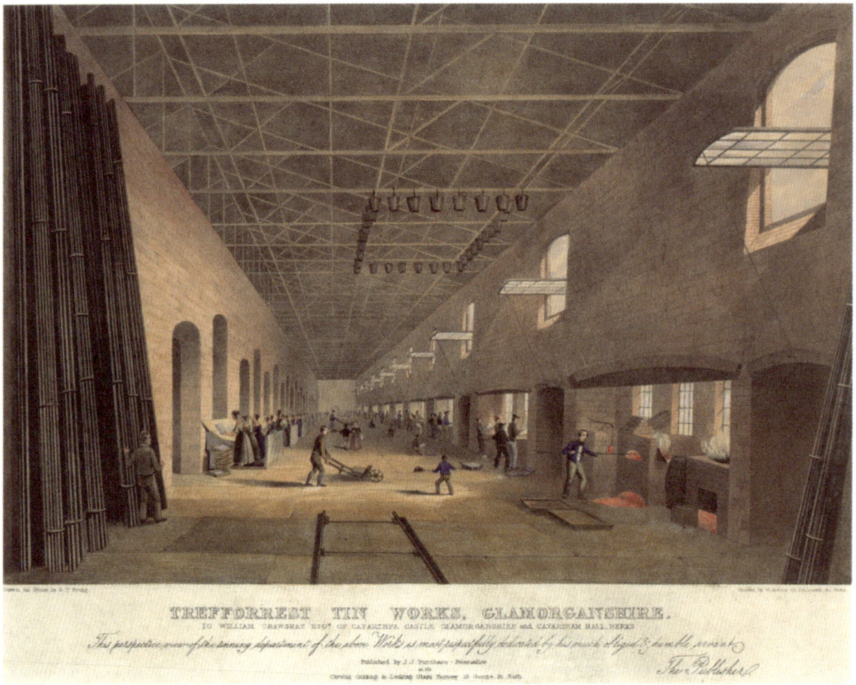

Fig. 10
G. F. Bragg
Treforest Tin Works, Glamorganshire
c. 1840

Fig. 11
Gavin Watson
Slough Centre, End of the Night
1989

Factories were a new world of moral chaos, extraordinary places, full of danger, where the youth of both sexes were often in heated proximity, deafened by the noise of the machines that shook the buildings and their bodies. Just the kind of experiences sought out and replicated in clubs and warehouse parties – parties that, for a short time in the late 1980s, took place in the same buildings where the machines and workers (possibly ancestors of the party's attendees) once laboured. The following passage reads like a tabloid editorial for the mid-Victorian era:

'The contagion of vicious example and impure conversation... compelled to make one of a society which is continually exhaling the miasma of vice... breathing its pollution every moment... The restless motion of the machinery has begun; the continual clack of the several wheels... There reigns in the work-rooms a Babel of confused sounds – the irreverent laugh, the open blasphemy, the licentious conversation... anger is stirred into acts of tyranny... In the heart of the factory – an assemblage of the vile of human beings, a fermenting mass of sin and vice, such as we may well doubt was ever before concentrated in one burning focus. It seems as if the mighty capacities of steam had lent an impetus, not only to the industry and ingenuity of man, but an equal impetus to all his faculties and contrivances of vice.'
— H. Worsley, *Juvenile Depravity*, 1849

Fig. 12
Newman & Co
Penrhyn Slate Quarries, Near Bangor, Wales
1842

Fig. 13
Salt Mine, Cheshire
1814

Not all visions of the age were so negative or troubling. The epic interventions into nature by heavy industry were a gift to Romantic landscape artists. This was a moment when a salt mine became a temple and the Penrhyn Slate Quarry a Welsh Grand Canyon.

Fig. 14
Photograph of
James Sharples
Date unknown

Fig. 15
James Sharples
Sketch of Forearm for The Forge
Date unknown

Factory life too was celebrated in the work of the self-taught artist James Sharples, posing on the previous page as an industrial worker. Sharples worked as a smith's boy in a foundry in Bury from the age of ten; at the age of 19 he began a painting entitled *The Forge* (1859), which he subsequently engraved, having spent ten years learning the technique. The print was a sensation: an industrial nativity scene, celebrating the birth of a piece of iron.

Sharples himself is an example of the 'self-help' philosophy popular with the emerging middle class of the time, which expounded that every man was the writer of his own destiny and that industry was a self-regulating pseudo-science that, left to itself, would ensure a harmonious balance for worker and factory/forge-owner alike. Despite this notion, and the print's popularity, he was never able to fully capitalise on his talent and had to remain in industry. He died a pauper in 1892.

Fig. 16
James Sharples
The Smithy
(reproduced after Sharples' death)
1894

With an iconography little changed from that exhibited in Sharples' work, Britain's post-war industrial rebirth was announced in *Steel* (1945). It was filmed by Jack Cardiff, a cinematic artist of light and shade, a John Martin or Joseph Wright for the twentieth century. Industry had never looked so good and would never look so good again. In the closing minutes, the stirring voiceover rallies a nation with its invocation of a shared industrial identity; poignant but for the wrong reasons:

'Britain is proud of her steel industry from the great record of output, quality and close understanding between workers and management has grown her name as producer of the world's finest steel. Making of this steel is something more than a skilled craft to the Jim Browns of Sheffield, the Jock McDonalds of Clydeside and the Bryn Evanses of South Wales. To them it is part of a long tradition, worthy of generations of craftsmen who have dedicated their life to steel, tough as these men who make it. An inspiration to the coming generation who will carry the flaming torch of Britain's steel industry. Making steel for the ships that plough the seven seas, steel for the planes that race across the skies, steel for the bridges and houses of a world at peace once more… Steel for the new life of tomorrow, that will reward the people of today.'

Fig. 17
Ronald Riley (director),
Jack Cardiff (cinematographer)
Steel
1945

Thomas Hornor, an engineer, also understood the glamour of heavy industry. His depiction of the *Rolling Mills, Merthyr Tydfil* (1819) offers the kind of light show that would be emulated 160 years later by heavy metal bands. A music genre and a live experience that barely subconsciously celebrates an industry and culture through its sound and ritual. 'Metal' is both a re-enactment of an industrial process and a requiem for its loss. The music, like the industry, is in the blood – literally. Noddy Holder's family tree, for instance, is itself a history of the Black Country with relatives who were chain-makers, tong-filers and blacksmiths.

It has become something of a cliché to associate industrial sounds and rock music, but as this description of Birmingham from 1852 makes clear, it is an idea that has been around for 160 years:

'The people live in an atmosphere continually vibrating with clamour… it would seem as if their amusements had caught the general tone, and that the noises of the place, grown part of customary existence to its people – inwrought as it were, into the very staple of their lives – exerts over them some such unmarked influence as that exerted on the sleeper by the foundry; and that, when they relax from their labours, they seek to fill up the void by modulated noises, first caught up, like the song of the bird beside the cutler's wheel or coppersmith's shop, in unconscious rivalry of the clang of the hammers and engines.' — Hugh Miller, *First Impressions of England and its People*, 1847

Fig. 18
Thomas Hornor
Rolling Mills, Merthyr Tydfil
1819

Fig. 19
Judas Priest
Unleashed in the East
1979

Bands like Judas Priest offered up a new form of masculinity to the de-industrialised youth of the UK – a look that would not have been out of place in a John Martin painting. For rock bands, the rigour of touring is a public declaration of their work ethic, turning something creative into a proper job.

The timed discipline of industrial work has musical implications, not only in terms of personal dedication, but also in the very heart of its regular, repetitive beat. When asked about how his sound related to his native Manchester, the record producer Martin Hannet recalled: 'I was struck years ago by a room full of air compressors in the Ferranti factory that were banging out this astonishing, four-in-the-bar bass-drum rhythm – I just stood in the centre of the room for hours.'

Fig. 20
REX/
Andre Csillag
Judas Priest – K K Downing, Dave Holland, Rob Halford, Ian Hill and Glenn Tipton, London
1981

The sounds of mining are more mysterious, appropriate for an industry that mainly takes place out of sight. Miners of the nineteenth century were a breed apart – the industrial elite. Theirs was a tight-knit culture that pre-dated the Industrial Revolution. The image above shows a miner going to work – he would be unrecognisable on his return trip. The dangerous, subterranean working environment ensured better labour organisation with a stronger sense of their own worth than labourers in the newer industries; blackleg workers were dealt with harshly, even fatally on some occasions. Mining was harsh to an almost parodic degree; the following accounts of child labour are barely believable to a twenty-first-century reader.

Fig. 21
G. Jameson
A Pitman Going to Work
c. 1811

'I have worked at this pit going two years. Coming to work at eight or before, but I set off from home at seven. I walk a mile and a half to my work, both in winter and summer. I get porridge for breakfast before I come, and bring my dinner with me – a muffin. When I have done about 12 loads I eat it while at work; I run 24 corves [coal wagons] a day; I cannot come up till I have done them all. If I want to relieve myself I go into any part of the pit. Sometimes the boys see me when they go by. My father slaps me sometimes upon the head, or upon the back, so as to make me cry.

'A very ignorant child (commented Mr. Scriven, the Sub-Commissioner), she stood shivering before me from cold. The rag that hung about her waist was once called a shift, which is as black as the coal she thrusts, and saturated with water, from the dripping of the roof and shaft. During my examination of her the banksman whom I had left in the pit came to the public-house and wanted to take her away, because, as he expressed himself, it was not *decent* that she should be (her person) *exposed* to us; oh no! It was criminal above ground; and like the two or three other colliers in the cabin, he became evidently mortified that these deeds of darkness should be brought to light.' — *Parliamentary Papers*, 1842, quoted in E. Royston Pike, *Human Documents of the Industrial Revolution in Britain*, 1970

Fig. 22
Girl with Belt-and-Chain Dragging Coal Tubs Underground
Published in *Parliamentary Papers*
1842

Fig. 23
Miner with Candle, Climbing Ladder
c. 1805

Fig. 24
Adrian Street
Bodybuilding
1975

Fig. 25
Adrian Street as Teddy Boy (second from right), *Wales* c. 1957

If James Sharples tried to leave a life of industrial toil by documenting it, Adrian Street (b. 1940) transcended it in a more spectacular fashion. When Street started work in a mine in 1955, children had been replaced by pit ponies, but the conditions at Brynmawr Colliery had not changed substantially. A keen bodybuilder, he left Wales for London at the age of 16, with the sound of jeering from his workmates and father ringing in his ears. Hanging around the Soho underworld he found success initially with body building and modeling. Seventeen years later he returned with his championship wrestling belts – part prodigal son, part prophet from the future, enlightening the coal serfs as to how the world would look in a post-industrial UK. The imagery is pure William Blake: the prophecy of Jerusalem has come to life as a shining Adrian lands to deliver us from industrial toil.

Fig. 26
Dennis
Hutchinson
Adrian Street
with his Father
at the Pithead
of Brynmawr
Colliery, Wales
1973

As with many pioneers, Street made up his destiny as he went along, influencing glam rock, fashion and, of course, his chosen trade, which he still occasionally indulges in. In 1980, wrestling was taken off TV in the UK, so Street left for the US where his outrageousness was amplified. Though shorter than most US wrestlers, he soon became a top attraction, introducing spandex and sexual ambiguity to the ring. He now has a cottage industry making costumes for wrestlers including all of those used in the film *The Wrestler* (2008). One of the few things that his profession had in common with factory life was the sound of the bell.

Fig. 27
Adrian Street at a US Airport with Valet, Miss Linda
Mid-1980s

Fig. 28
Adrian Wrestling in the UK
c. 1973

For the newly-industrialised Victorian factory worker, the fragmentation of time, coupled with what Friedrich Nietzsche called 'the endless repetition of the same' (first mentioned in *The Gay Science*, 1882), must have been a brutal shock to the system. No longer was time measured by the seasons and the rising and setting of the sun – 'time is nature' – now it was split into units of production, as humans became just another, potentially unreliable, part of a mechanical process.

Fig. 29
Towers Yard Bell
1835

'In reality there were no regular hours: masters and managers did with us as they liked. The clocks at the factories were often put forward in the morning and back at night, and instead of being instruments for the measurement of time, they were used as cloaks for cheatery and oppression. Though this was known amongst the hands, all were afraid to speak, and a workman then was afraid to carry a watch, as it was no uncommon event to dismiss any one who presumed to know too much about the science of horology.' — Anon, *Chapters in the Life of a Dundee Factory Boy*, 1887

There were even clocks made that measured productivity as time: the two-faced timepiece shown here was connected to a watermill at a silk factory in Preston, and would show 'lost' time if the wheel did not turn quickly enough – this time would have to be made up at the end of the working day. Similar rules were not unusual in other factories: Crowley Ironworks had a rulebook that stretched to 100,000 words.

Fig. 30
E. Hartley
Double-Dial Longcase Clock from Green Silk Mill
1810

'In all these ways – by the division of labour; the supervision of labour; fines; bells and clocks; money incentives; preachings and schoolings; the suppression of fairs and sports – new labour habits were formed, and a new time-discipline was imposed…' — E. P. Thompson, *Work-Discipline and Industrial Capitalism*, 1967

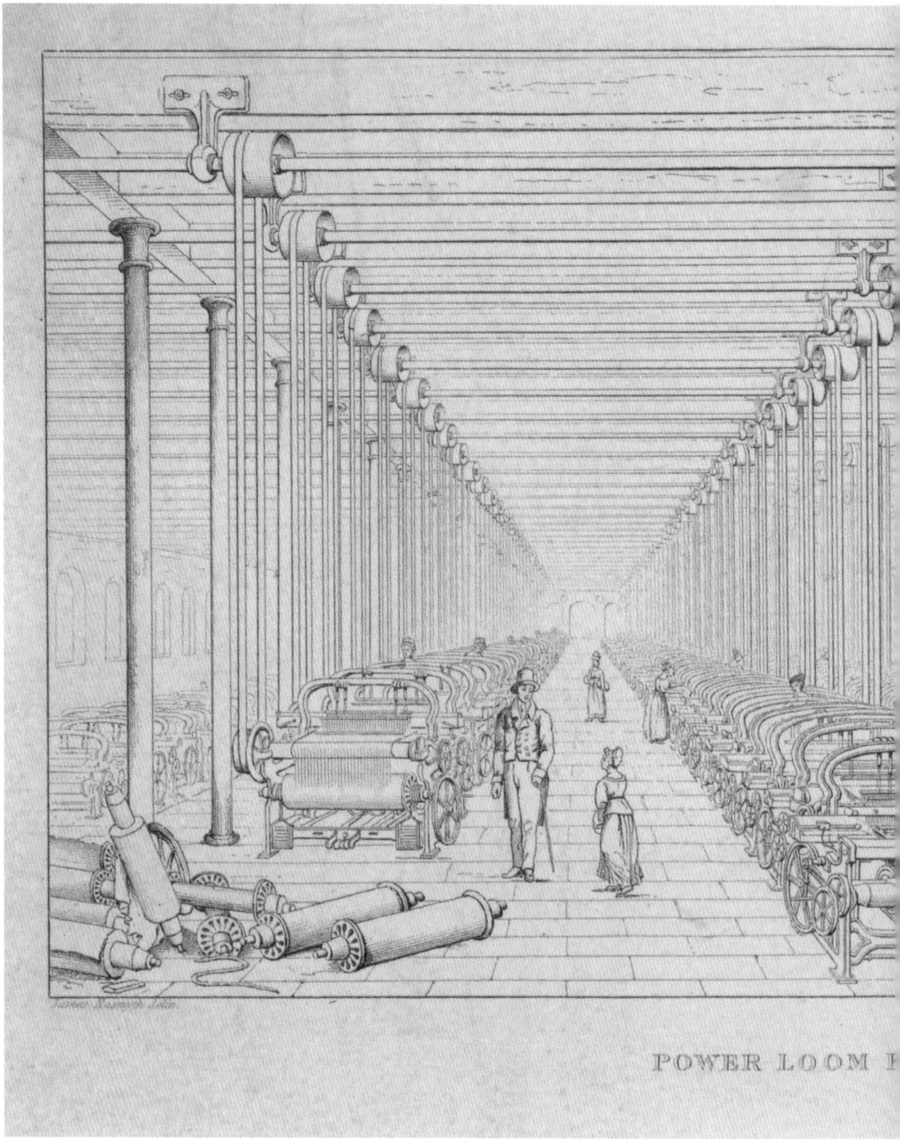

Fig. 31
J. W. Lowry
Power Loom Factory of Thomas Robinson Esq., Stockport
1849–50

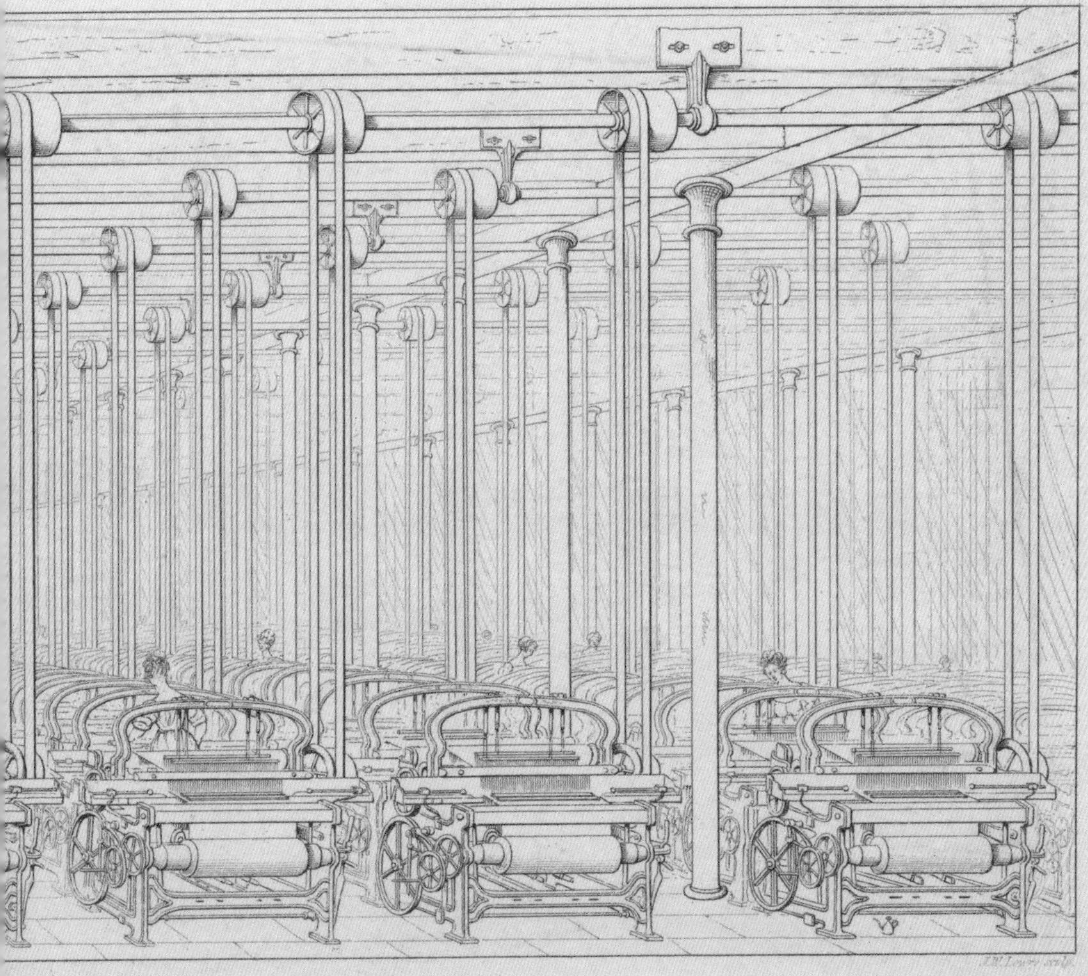

J.W. Lowry sculp.

OF THOMAS ROBINSON ESQ^R.

OCKPORT.

Time discipline was often enforced with a complicated system of rules and fines, vividly illustrated in this poster from Thomas Ainsworth & Sons Mill in Preston. Many rules are based around subservience to the machine and its running, which, like the two-faced clock, is the true measure of time (Rules 3 and 4).

The 'necessary' in Rule 8 refers to the toilet, often a place of danger for women, as they were vulnerable to assault whilst there. Rule 9 forbids taking scraps of cotton into the toilet to use as loo roll. Trade unions were banned, which explains how Rule 1 could be enforced, whereby the worker had to give a least one month's notice, but could be sacked on the spot – another form of time discipline.

In 1853, a general strike amongst power-loom workers spread between mills in the North of England. 'The Preston Lockout' remained in place for the better part of eight months, during which time an estimated 20,000 to 26,000 workers were out of employment, half of them women and children. The strike was sparked by the disparity between the rising cost of living and pay, which was judged by strikers to be due a ten per cent increase.

The cartoon overleaf from the lock-out shows blackleg workers, known as 'knobsticks', being delivered and upacked for work. During the dispute, workers were banned from meeting in groups in the town and from singing protest songs, so would have meetings on the outskirts and sing songs like 'The Preston Steam Loom Weaver' and the rousing 'Ten Per Cent!' into the city:

'Come all you men of freedom, wherever you may be,
I pray you give attention, and listen unto me.
It's of this strike in Preston town, their courage being good,
I do believe they stand firm whilst they have life and blood
So now my boys, don't daunted be, but stand out to the fray:
We ne'er shall yield nor quit the field, until we've won the day.'

Fig. 32
Thomas Ainsworth & Sons
Rules to Be Observed in this Factory, Church Street Mills, Preston
c. 1830

RULES

TO BE OBSERVED

And kept by the People

EMPLOYED IN THIS FACTORY.

1st.

EACH Person employed in this Factory engages to serve THOMAS AINSWORTH and SONS, and to give one Month's Notice, in writing, previous to leaving his or her employment, such notice to be given in on a Saturday, and on no other day; but the Masters have full power to discharge any Person employed therein without any previous Notice whatsoever.

2nd.

THE hours of attendance are from Six o'clock in the Morning until half-past Seven at Night, excepting Saturday, when work shall cease at half-past Four; half an hour allowed for Breakfast, and one hour for Dinner; and any Person not coming to work at the stated periods shall for every offence, forfeit Sixpence, and be deducted for the time they are absent.

3rd.

ALL Wages (to be calculated according to the time the Steam Engine may have run) shall be due and payable on each Saturday, in the Afternoon, one hour after the same shall have been demanded at the Counting-house, by the Person or Persons entitled thereto; and in no case whatsoever shall they be due or payable at any other time; and any Person leaving his or her employment without notice, shall forfeit all wages due at the time at which he or she left such employment.

4th.

ANY Spinner whose wheel or wheels are standing either for want of Piecers or from any other cause whatsoever, during the time the Steam Engine is going, or not keeping them employed at their usual and proper speed, shall, for every hour, pay sixpence.

5th.

EACH Spinner shall keep his or her wheels and wheel-house clean swept and fluked, or in default thereof, shall forfeit One Shilling.

6th.

IF any waste, rovings, utensils, or machinery of any kind be misused, spoiled, damaged, lost, or carelessly misplaced, the Person so misusing, spoiling, damaging, losing, or carelessly misplacing the same, shall forfeit and pay One Shilling; and also pay the value thereof, if lost, spoiled, or damaged.

7th.

ANY Person altering in any way whatever the wheels or other machinery at which he or she is employed, or permitting the same to be done (without leave from a Proprietor or Overlooker) shall for every offence, forfeit Five Shillings.

8th.

EACH Person shall clean the Necessary belonging to the room in which he or she is employed, when thereunto required by the Overlooker; and any one neglecting or refusing so to do, or wilfully dirtying the same, or any part of the Factory, Yard, or adjoining Grounds, shall forfeit 2s. 6d.

9th.

ANY Person taking cotton or waste into the Necessaries, shall forfeit Two Shillings and Sixpence; and any one knowing of the same, and not giving information thereof, shall forfeit Five Shillings.

10th.

ANY Person smoking Tobacco, or having a pipe for that purpose, in any part of the Factory or Yard, shall forfeit Five Shillings.

11th.

ANY Person (excepting those specially appointed for that purpose) lighting the Gas, shall, for each offence, forfeit One Shilling.

12th.

ANY Person introducing a Stranger into the Factory without leave of one of the Proprietors, shall forfeit Two Shillings and Sixpence; and any Overlooker neglecting immediately to order such Stranger out, shall forfeit Five Shillings.

13th.

ANY Person or Persons neglecting thoroughly to clean the machinery under their care, when required by an Overlooker so to do, shall forfeit Two Shillings and Sixpence.

14th.

ANY Person temporarily leaving the frame at which he or she ought to be employed, or in any way neglecting his or her employment, shall forfeit One Shilling.

15th.

ANY Person taking tools out of the Mechanics' or Overlookers' Rooms, except the Mechanics or Overlookers themselves, shall forfeit Two Shillings and Sixpence.

16th.

WHEN any window or windows shall be broken, the party breaking the same shall pay the damage; but if the said party cannot be identified, the charges of repairing the the same shall be borne equally amongst all the Persons working in the room in which the said window or windows shall be so broken.

17th.

ANY Workman coming into the Factory, or any other part of these Premises, drunk, shall pay Five Shillings.

18th.

EACH Person employed in this Factory, engages not to be a member of, or directly or indirectly a subscriber to, or a supporter of, any Trades Union, or other Association whatsoever (the regular and legal Sick Clubs alone excepted.)

19th.

ANY Person destroying or damaging this Paper, shall pay Five Shillings.

20th.

TO avoid any misunderstanding or disputes, it is hereby determined, that when a breach has been made in any of the foregoing Rules, and the Person committing the same cannot be identified, double the penalty hereby inflicted shall be taken from the People employed in the department where the fault has been committed, whether it may extend only to one room, one Overlooker's department, or the whole Factory. And that all the above Payments, Fines, and Penalties shall be deducted out of the offenders' wages.

PRITT, PRINTER, 29, FISHERGATE, PRESTON.

Fig. 33
Preston Lock-Out
1853

ILLUSTRATED
E AN EXCHANGE
OTHER DELEGATES
OD WORK-
OPLE
WELL MANAGER THOSE KNOBSTICKS WILL NEAVER DO I MUST SEND THEM BACK-A-GAIN WHERE THEY COME FROM
I AM COMMING FOR THE MR LARGE FIRM THY TIME IS UP THOU GRINDER OF THE POOR
FULL
EW KNOBSTICKS
T FIVE SHILLINGS
CARRAGE
MR LARGE FIRM

It is no surprise that time became known as 'the enemy', as in 'how's the enemy?' – 'what time is it?' The item most often saved up for by miners was a pocket watch. By the same token, victories over time were hard won and energetically celebrated; this 1890 Amalgamated Engineers' Union banner from Newcastle celebrates a reduction by one hour of the working week. The progressive shortening of the working week is one of the key ways that organised labour could demonstrate its effectiveness.

The phrase opposite is the content of a text message sent to a zero-hours worker, informing him that his labour would not be required on the day in question. It is thought that as many as one million people in the UK are currently working on zero-hours contracts: employment agreements that give the worker no guarantee of shifts or of regular work patterns in any given week. The worker is effectively on call and there is no obligation for the employer to provide sick or holiday pay. While this kind of contract offers a certain amount of flexibility, the advantage is largely on the side of the employer, making it very difficult for the employee to plan and control their finances, creating a new form of day labouring in the service and digital economies.

Fig. 34
Amalgamated Engineers Union Banner
1890

Hello,
Today you
have
day off

Fig. 35
Text Message
to Worker on
a Zero-Hours
Contract
2013

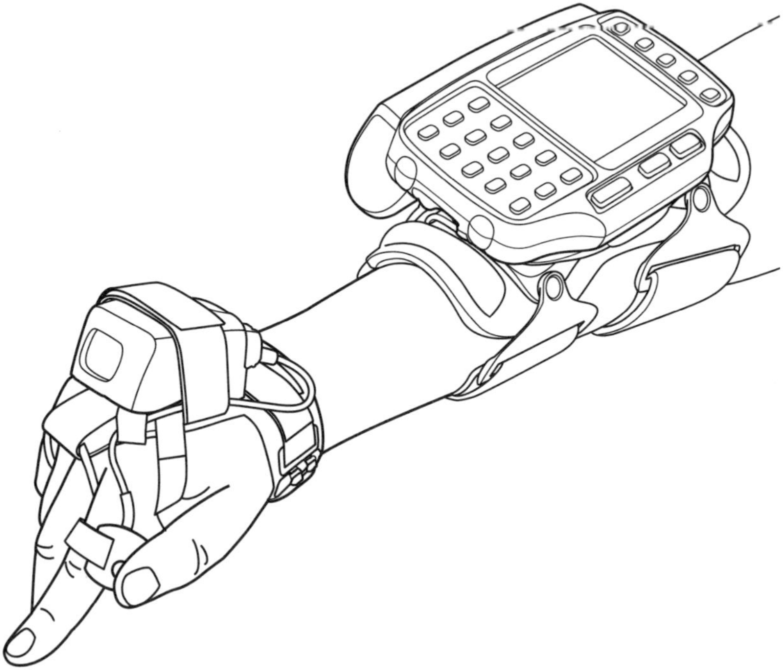

Many zero-hours contracts are for low-wage work in warehouses, where a further time discipline is enforced by productivity devices, like the Motorola WT4000: a tracking device designed to increase productivity and reduce errors. Worn on the wrist, the device informs the worker where to go and what to do and will also track how fast tasks are completed, sending the worker messages to speed up as the system considers necessary. The sheer scale of the Amazon warehouse in Rugeley, Staffordshire, where similar devices are used, would no doubt have impressed John Martin.

'The rooms are all crowded with dangerous machinery; so close that you can hardly pass… Not any of this machinery is boxed off, or guarded in any way. It is a frightful place, turn which way you will. There is a constant hammering roar of wheels, so that you could not possibly hear any warning voice…' — Richard Hengist Home, *Report of the Royal Commission on Children's Employment in Mines and Factories*, 1842

Fig. 36
Motorola WT4000 Wearable Terminal
2013

Fig. 37
Ben Roberts
Amazon Fulfilment Centre, Towers Business Park, Rugeley
2013

In the working environment discipline was imposed as much by the ever-present threat of injury as by any positive actions of employers, and these dangers were not insignificant. The miner John Evans was trapped underground for 12 days after a mine collapse at Wrexham in Wales, in 1819; he survived by eating candles and drinking mine water and was pulled out in a delirious state. A coffin was made for him in anticipation of his death, which he used as a wardrobe. The print above was possibly used as a fundraiser tool for him.

Fig. 38
A. R. Burt
John Evans
1819

Fig. 39
Dean Shaw
Toni Iommi, Black Sabbath, Donnington
2012

In 1965, the 17-year-old Anthony Frank – a budding guitarist – lost the tip of his middle finger and part of the ring finger of his right hand in an accident at a sheet metal factory in Birmingham. This injury affected his playing style and, as it turned out, popular music history. To ease the string tension on his injured hand he detuned his guitar – his bassist followed suit and they developed a foreboding minor-key sound that became a mainstay of heavy metal music. Anthony Frank is now known as Tony Iommi – lead guitarist and songwriter in Black Sabbath – his sacrificed fingers an offering to the machines, creating a new type of twentieth-century industrial music. His injury is not so different from those occurring 100 years before:

'Little boys and girls are here seen at work at the tip-punching machines (all acting by steam power) with their fingers in constant danger of being punched off once in every second, while at the same time they have their heads between whirling wheels a few inches distant from each ear. "They seldom lose the hand", said one of the proprietors to me, in explanation; "it only takes a finger at the first or second joint. Sheer carelessness – looking about them – sheer carelessness!' — Mr. Horne's Report, *Parliamentary Papers*, 1843, quoted in E. Royston Pike, *Human Documents of the Industrial Revolution in Britain*, 1970

It was not unusual for factory accidents, or even the mundane incidents and experiences of nineteenth-century industrial life, to be recorded and memorialised in a type of popular song known as the 'broadside' – a musical form that gave a voice to the new working-class experience. Sold in the street, often in the absence of newspapers, the broadside was a truly reactive form of urban music.

The broadside offered up similar themes to the American blues music so beloved of Iommi and his peers: migration, exploitation, sex and the tough new world of work. 'The New Bury Loom' is a masterpiece of workplace erotica and innuendo, using the technical language of weaving to tell a story of love amongst the machines. It also speaks of the new relationship between worker and technology. There is love of a different kind in 'Utick's Trip to Manchester', a classic cautionary tale in which the protagonist travels from the countryside to the corrupt city, where he is taken in by a woman, only to later discover that she is a prostitute.

Though often comical, they also articulated the social and human stresses that the rapid rate of change in the industrial era had brought about. 'Jone O' Grinfield' a misery protest song about the plight of an impoverished cotton weaver, carries suggestions of insurrection if the workers' situation does not improve. The popularity of broadsides waned with the advent of the music hall, a more organised form of mass entertainment, in which songs became associated with specific performers, setting the trend for popular music as we know it.

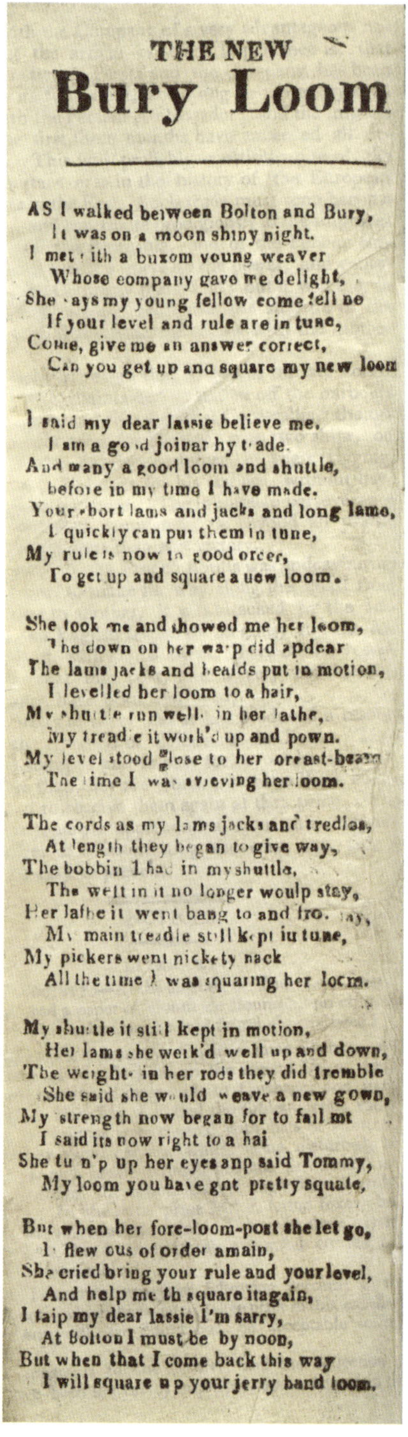
THE NEW
Bury Loom

AS I walked between Bolton and Bury,
It was on a moon shiny night.
I met with a buxom young weaver
Whose company gave me delight,
She says my young fellow come tell me
If your level and rule are in tune,
Come, give me an answer correct,
Can you get up and square my new loom

I said my dear lassie believe me,
I am a good joinar by trade.
And many a good loom and shuttle,
before in my time I have made.
Your short lams and jacks and long lams,
I quickly can put them in tune,
My rule is now in good order,
To get up and square a new loom.

She took me and showed me her loom,
The down on her warp did apdear
The lams jacks and healds put in motion,
I levelled her loom to a hair,
My shuttle run well in her lathe,
My tread e it work'd up and powu.
My level stood close to her breast-beam
The time I was squeving her loom.

The cords as my lams jacks and tredles,
At length they began to give way,
The bobbin I had in my shuttle,
The weft in it no longer woulp stay,
Her lathe it went bang to and fro.
My main treadle still kept iu tune,
My pickers went nickety nack
All the time I was squaring her loom.

My shuttle it still kept in motion,
Her lams she work'd well up and down,
The weight in her rods they did tremble
She said she would weave a new gown,
My strength now began for to fail me
I said its now right to a hai
She tu n'p up her eyes anp said Tommy,
My loom you have got pretty squate,

But when her fore-loom-post she let go,
It flew ous of order amain,
She cried bring your rule and your level,
And help me th square it again,
I saip my dear lassie I'm sarry,
At Bolton I must be by noon,
But when that I come back this way
I will square up your jerry band loom.

Fig. 40
'The New
Bury Loom'
Early nineteenth
century

Fig. 41
'Utick's Trip
to Manchester'
Early nineteenth
century

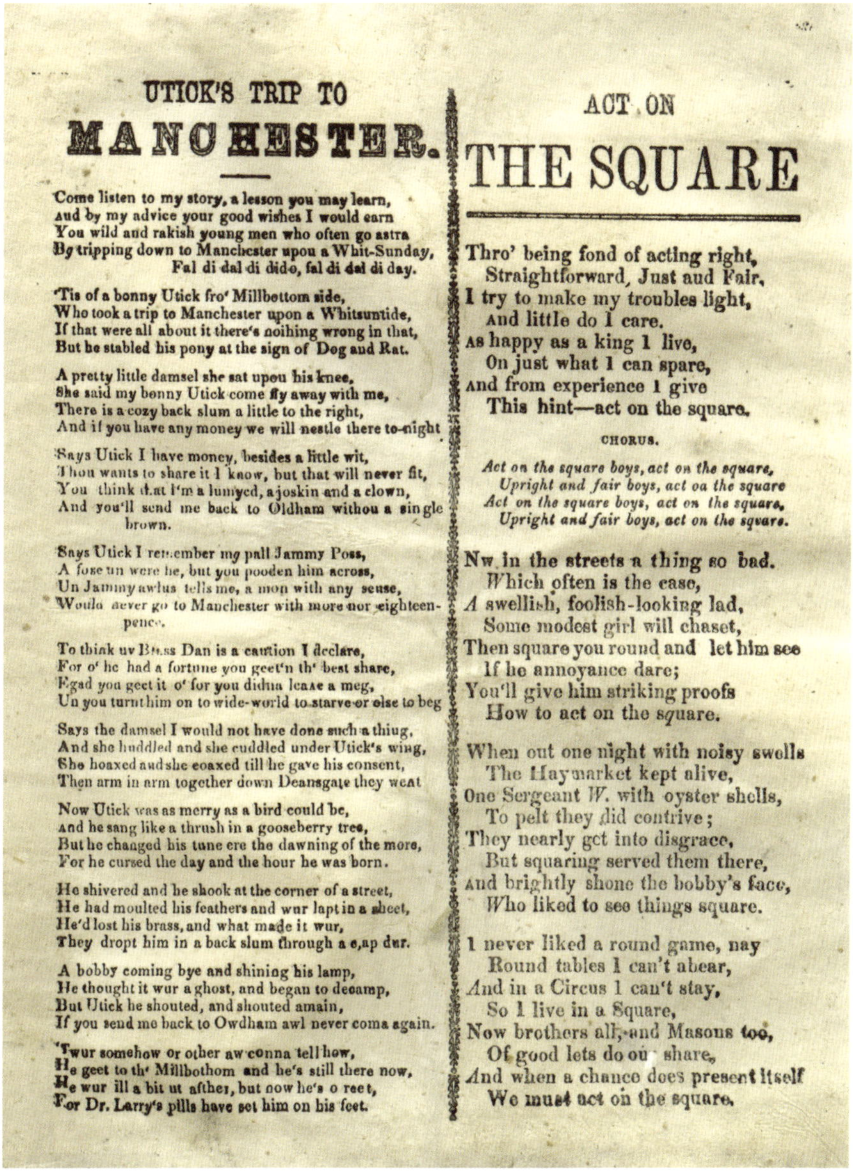

UTICK'S TRIP TO

MANCHESTER.

Come listen to my story, a lesson you may learn,
And by my advice your good wishes I would earn
You wild and rakish young men who often go astra
By tripping down to Manchester upon a Whit-Sunday,
Fal di dal di dido, fal di dal di day.

'Tis of a bonny Utick fro' Millbottom side,
Who took a trip to Manchester upon a Whitsuntide,
If that were all about it there's noihing wrong in that,
But he stabled his pony at the sign of Dog and Rat.

A pretty little damsel she sat upon his knee,
She said my bonny Utick come fly away with me,
There is a cozy back slum a little to the right,
And if you have any money we will nestle there to-night

Says Utick I have money, besides a little wit,
Thou wants to share it I know, but that will never fit,
You think that I'm a lumyed, a joskin and a clown,
And you'll send me back to Oldham withou a single
brown.

Says Utick I remember my pall Jammy Poss,
A fose un were he, but you pooden him across,
Un Jammy awlus tells me, a mon with any sense,
Would never go to Manchester with more nor eighteen-
pence.

To think uv Brass Dan is a caution I declare,
For o' he had a fortune you geet'n th' best share,
Egad you geet it o' for you didna leave a meg,
Un you turnt him on to wide-world to starve or else to beg

Says the damsel I would not have done such a thiug,
And she huddled and she cuddled under Utick's wing,
She hoaxed and she coaxed till he gave his consent,
Then arm in arm together down Deansgate they went

Now Utick was as merry as a bird could be,
And he sang like a thrush in a gooseberry tree,
But he changed his tune ere the dawning of the more,
For he cursed the day and the hour he was born.

He shivered and he shook at the corner of a street,
He had moulted his feathers and wur lapt in a sheet,
He'd lost his brass, and what made it wur,
They dropt him in a back slum through a c,ap dur.

A bobby coming bye and shining his lamp,
He thought it wur a ghost, and began to decamp,
But Utick he shouted, and shouted amain,
If you send me back to Owdham awl never coma again.

'Twur somehow or other aw conna tell how,
He geet to th' Millbothom and he's still there now,
He wur ill a bit ut afther, but now he's o reet,
For Dr. Larry's pills have set him on his feet.

ACT ON

THE SQUARE

Thro' being fond of acting right,
Straightforward, Just and Fair,
I try to make my troubles light,
And little do I care.
As happy as a king I live,
On just what I can spare,
And from experience I give
This hint—act on the square.

CHORUS.

Act on the square boys, act on the square,
Upright and fair boys, act on the square
Act on the square boys, act on the square,
Upright and fair boys, act on the square.

Nw in the streets a thing so bad,
Which often is the case,
A swellish, foolish-looking lad,
Some modest girl will chaset,
Then square you round and let him see
If he annoyance dare;
You'll give him striking proofs
How to act on the *square.*

When out one night with noisy swells
The Haymarket kept alive,
One Sergeant *W.* with oyster shells,
To pelt they did contrive;
They nearly get into disgrace,
But squaring served them there,
And brightly shone the bobby's face,
Who liked to see things square.

I never liked a round game, nay
Round tables I can't abear,
And in a Circus I can't stay,
So I live in a Square,
Now brothers all, and Masons too,
Of good lets do ou share,
And when a chance does present itself
We must act on the square.

Migration to cities, as touched upon in 'Utick's Trip to Manchester', was only enhanced by a dramatic population increase in the UK – from 8.9 million in 1801 to 13.9 million in just 30 years. Urbanisation separated the worker from traditional poor-relief arrangements, structured around the country parish. Cotton workers were at the sharp end of this change, entering into an industry of the new factory owners' invention, where poor pay meant that whole families were forced to work in cotton mills. Handloom-weaver pay decreased from 23s per week in 1805 to 6s 3d in 1833, as mechanisation took away the need for skilled labour. Income suppression was used, in turn, as a form of social control: subsistence wages ensured worker obedience and willingness to work. These days, high rent has a similar effect, whilst depressing domestic demand and taking an increasing percentage of income. All the while the new middle classes were creating an increasingly unequal society, as this description of Manchester illustrates:

Fig. 42
'Jone O'Grinfield'
c. 1860

'There is no town in the world where the distance between the rich and the poor is so great or the barrier between them so difficult to be crossed... There is far less personal communication between the master cotton spinner and his workmen, between the calico printer and his blue-handed boys, between the master tailor and his apprentices, than there is between the Duke of Wellington and the humblest labourer on his estate.' — Canon Parkinson, *On the Present Condition of the Labouring Poor in Manchester*, 1841

These class divisions in the workplace persisted beyond the Industrial Revolution and became a feature of the steady post-war decline of UK industry. Labour was becoming an abstracted element in the economic process, at the very time when unprecedented pressure was being placed upon the mass of people working in cities. The belief in the importance of a supportive society was losing currency among the emerging managing class. Thomas Carlyle identified this obsession with a mechanistic interpretation of human relationships:

'Not the external and physical alone is now managed by machinery but the internal and spiritual also... The same habit regulates not our modes of action alone, but our modes of thought and feeling. Men are grown mechanical in head and heart, as well as in hand. They have lost faith in individual endeavours, and in natural force, or any kind. Not for internal perfection, but for external combinations and arrangements for institutions, constitutions, for mechanism of one sort or another, do they hope and struggle.' — Thomas Carlyle, *Signs of the Times*, 1829

JONE O'GRINFIELD.

I'm a poor cotton weaver as many one knows,
I've nowt to eat i'th house an I've worn out my cloas,
You'd hardly give sixpence for all I have on,
My clugs they are brossen and stockings I've none,
You'd think it wur hard to be sent into th' world,
To clem and do th' best ot you con.

Our church parson kept telling us long,
We should have better times if we'd hold our tongues,
I've houden my tongue till I can hardly draw breath,
I think i' my heart he means to clem me to death;
I know he lives weel by backbiting the de'il,,
But he he never pickced o'er in his life.

I tarried six week an thought every day wur t' last,
I tarried and shifted till now I'm quite fast;
I lived on nettles while nettles were good,
An Waterloo porridge were best of my food;
I'm telling you true I can find folks enew,
That are living no better than me.

Old Bill o' Dan's sent bailiffs one day,
For a shop score I owed him that I could not pay,
But he wur too le[illegible] for [illegible]d Bill o' Bent,
Had sent tit and cart and taen goods for rent,
We had nou bur a stoo, that wur a seat for two,
And on it cowered Margit and me.

The bailiffs looked round assly as a mouse,
When they saw aw things were taen out ot house,
Says one to the other all's gone thou may see,
Aw sed lads never fret you're welcome to me;
They made no more ado, but nipp'd up th' owd stoo,
And we both went wack upoth flags.

I geet howd of Margit for hoo wur strucken sick,
Hoo sed hoo ne'er had such a bang sin hoo wur wick
The bailiffs scoured off with owd stoo on their backs,
They would not have cared had they brook our necks,
They're mad at owd Bent cos he's taen goods for rent,
And wur ready to flee us alive.

I sed to our Margit as we lay upoth floor,
We shall never be lower in this world I'm sure,
But if we alter I'm sure we mun mend ,
For I think in my heart we are both at far end,
For meat we have none nor looms to weave on,
Egad they're as weel lost as found.

Then I geet up my piece and I took it em back
I scarcely dare speak mester looked so black,
He said you wur o'erpaid last time you coom,
I said if I wur 'twas for weaving bout loom;
In a mind as I'm in I'll ne'er pick o'er again,
For I've woven mysel toth' fur end.

Then aw coom out and left him to chew that,
When aw thought again aw wur vext till aw sweat,
To think that we mun work to keep them and awth set,
All the day o' my life and still be in their debt;
So I'll give o'er trade an work with a spade,
Or go and break stones upoth road,

Our Margit declared if hoo'd cloas to put on,
Hoo'd go up to Lundun an see the big mon
An if things didn't alter when hoo had been,
Hoo swears hoo'll feight blood up toth e'en,
Hoo's nought again th' Queen but likes a fair thing,
An hoo says hoo can tell when hoo's hurt.

SALLY SLY.

Printed and Sold Wholesale and Retail, by
[illegible] ıgton [illegible] ieu-street, Oldham
Road, Manchester.

At six in the morning awaking,
Coals taking,
Love making,
With barrow, I cry;
I knock and sing at the areas,
My care is
The fairies,
With coals to supply.

I'm in love! I'm in love! Oh my eye!
I'm going for to meet her to-morrow—
Sally Sly! Sally Sly! Sally Sly!
I'm going for to meet her to-morrow—
Sally Sly! Sally Sly! Sally Sly!

We meet where the walls they've been
While walking (chalking,
And talking;
We're both tall and straight,
With apples and cherries I treat her
Sweet creature,
I meet her
To-morrow, at eight.
I'm in love, &c.

One day, Jemmy Raspell, the baker,
To take her
And make her
His tool, he did try;
He told her to kick Jemmy Snivel
To the devil—
How civil;
Then she blacken'd his eye.
I'm in love, &c.

32.

Fig. 43
Thomas Alm
Swainson Birley Cotton Mill, Near Preston, Lancashire
1834

Fig. 44
John Petherick
Ironworks Manager Dozing
c. 1830

Fig. 45
Robert Havell
Factory Children
1814

This inevitably led to abuses, especially of the young – the lowest of the low in the production process.

'Alexander Dean, overlooker in a flax-mill at Dundee… having no parents to take care of him, he obtained his first job at the age of 12 in a flax mill in Dundee, where they worked no less than 17 hours a day, exclusive of meals, and for wages "sometimes we got the clothes which were taken from others who deserted the service". Was beaten very often. His story continued: "One time I was struck by the master on the head with his clenched fist, and kicked, when I was down. I saw one girl trailed by the hair of her head, and kicked by him, when she was down, till she roared 'Murder!' several times. The girl told me that the master had wished to use familiarities with her, and she had refused the night before; and he found a small deficiency in her work, and he took the opportunity of abusing her."' — 'The Girl Who Got Away', cited in E. Royston Pike, *Human Documents of the Industrial Revolution in Britain*, 1970

This account is taken from the 1832 parliamentary report into the employment of children in factories. Even those in the middle classes who believed in the self-regulating nature of the factory system realised that their livelihoods were threatened if social meltdown did occur. There was an increasing awareness that this fast-moving social and technological change was unsustainable, as people took stock of what had been happening underground and in factory buildings in the preceding 40 years. It's not too far fetched to compare this situation to today, as we begin to fully understand how the digital revolution has changed the world and our relationship to the world.

In the new industrial cities, the unprecedented concentration of people and, more importantly, ideas could and did lead to unrest to the point that whole towns were occupied by workers. By the middle of the decade known as the 'hungry forties', Friedrich Engels noted that, 'in this country social war is under full headway' (*The Condition of the Working Class in England*, 1845). The Merthyr Rising of 1831, in South Wales, is thought to have been the first occasion that the red flag was raised in protest. The anger and imagery used in descriptions of the event are primal – at odds with portraits of local workers only a few years later. And it's easy to see how the events scared the life out of the authorities.

'At Hirwaun, up on Aberdare Mountain, the rebels ritually sacrificed a calf, washed a flag in its blood and impaled a loaf of bread on the staff. His arms drenched to the elbows, the bearer set off with his bloody talisman of the people's martial law to summon the 'Sons of Vulcan' to insurrection.'
— Gwyn A. Williams, introduction to John Gorman, *Banner Bright*, 1973

The portraits of the workers from Hirwaun and Treforest are distinctly at odds with the revolutionary temper of the times in South Wales. The paintings were produced when Francis Crawshay was running the factories. Crawshay ran an unorthodox business, living with one of the workers and siring children with a number of others. The fact that we still know all the names of those painted is notable, when compared to the anonymity of the women steelworkers.

Fig. 46
Merthyr Rising
1831

Fig. 47
W. J. Chapman
Francis Crawshay Workers Portraits
1835
(and overleaf)

Strikes and protests were often incorrectly defined by their criminality rather than the political or social grievances they were trying to address. A contemporary concern about street crime confused the issue, with fears around gangs almost quaint in comparison to the impending threat of social meltdown.

The street gang is a uniquely urban phenomenon – concerned with defence of an area, street, or corner even – of which the 'scuttlers' were a late-Victorian example. These young men were identified by their elaborate hairstyles and colourful scarves – a precursor to and influence on the 'teddy boys' of the next century, unlikely embodiments of Hobsbawm's description of the city dweller, who 'no longer need[s] tradition, they [are] their own reward' (Eric Hobsbawm, *Labouring Men*, 1964).

Fig. 48
William Bramian,
'The Captain',
Labourer, 20 Years
c. 1884

Fig. 49
(top left)
John Wallace,
Labourer, 18 Years
c. 1884

Fig. 50
(top right)
Patrick Hefferon,
Labourer, 20 Years
c. 1884

Fig. 51
(bottom left)
James Kerrighan,
Labourer, 19 Years
c. 1884

Fig. 52
(bottom right)
William Brooks,
Labourer, 20 Years
c. 1884

Not all gangs are united by criminality, most share common interests in sport or culture, and so the concept of the 'group' shares a direct lineage with the street gang. Furthermore, the cultivation of the blank stare to camera is more of a mug shot than a portrait – the uniform group identity and camaraderie are very similar. To be in a group is to be in an arrested state of adolescence, with licence to behave like a 16-year-old for the rest of your life.

Occasionally, though, echoes of the Industrial Revolution return through bands. In 1987, Ian Tilton and the Happy Mondays went on a tour of pre-Media City, Salford, to make some publicity shots. Though not quite as dramatic as the image of Adrian street and his father, these still show a group in a former industrial town that is trying to work out out what to do next. Shaun Ryder, the band's singer and songwriter, has a family tree that is a history lesson in itself.

Fig. 53
Ian Tilton
Happy Mondays, Salford
1987

Fig. 54
Ian Tilton
Happy Mondays, Salford
1987

Fig. 55
Ian Tilton
Happy Mondays, Salford
1987

Richard Ryder
Born: 1830, Farnworth
Occupation: Millwright

Mary
Born: 1834, Wrightington

Joesph Greenhalgh
Born: 1835, Little Lever
Occupation: Coal miner

Elizabeth
Born: 1840, Prescott

John Fletcher

William Fletcher
Born: 1858, Derbyshire
Occupation: Labourer

James Baxendale
Born: 1823, Sapden
Occupation: Paper hanger

Helena
Born: 1822, Sapden

Jane Baxendale
Born: 1853, Salford

Fig. 56
Jeremy Deller
Hallelujah!
Shaun Ryder's
Family Tree
2008

Fig. 57
John Davies
Stockport Viaduct
1986

The photographs of John Davies are family trees too, with buildings instead of people indicating change. These epic views of towns owe much to Davies' interest in how cities work, showing how we live with the Industrial Revolution every day.

This broadside, written in 1873, imagines a world 100 years hence; it is a sci-fi nursery rhyme of nonsense and freedom, including sexual emancipation. The line about 'Brigham Young' refers to the Mormon leader. American Mormons escaped persecution in their homeland and cannily settled in the expanding industrial centres of the UK, where new religions could offer some form of order amongst the confusion of the city life. The photograph of Adrian Street and his father was taken in 1973 (page 28), and perhaps he even exceeded the broadside writer's expectations of life in the future. The reality was a little more mundane – the images on the following pages are stills from Super-8 home movies all filmed in 1973.

Fig. 58
John Davies
Mersey Square, Stockport
1986

Fig. 59
'A Prophecy for 1973'
1873

A PROPHECY FOR 1973.

Written by THOMAS YATES, *of Blackburn.*

TUNE:—"The Henpecked Club."

(*Copyright.*)

NOW they tell us this world's ne'er at an end,
But to prove its contray, is what I intend,
In a song what I've wrote, if you live you will see
In One thousand Nine hundred and Seventy three,
I was dreaming last night, and I prophesied plain,
That the world has turned over and over again,
And everything changed, that I plainly could see,
In One thousand Nine hundred and Seventy three.

Chorus :

Oh, Dear! Oh, dear! what things you will see,
In One thousand Nine hundred and Seventy three

No governmet laws we shall have, it is true,
There will be no Magistrates, no Bobbys in blue
To charge "*Ten Bob and Costs,*" when a man's been on the spree,
You can drink like a fish, far down in the sea:
You can act *Brigham Young*, all the days of your [lives,
And if *one's not enough*, you can get forty wives,
If you are tired of *one*, or she turns out *a bore*,
Get another and *send her* to the chap next door.

Everyone will be rich, there will be no need to beg
Nor stump up and down, with an old wooden leg
If your limbs are blown off, with a bullet or breeze
The Doctors will replace you new one's with ease
And children, then they will hatch them by steam
And feed them with nutmegs, blacklead or cream
And they will grow to such a size, you can tell,
They can peep o'er the moon, and look down into *H—l.*

Young lovers, you'll see them in dozs. and crowds
Courting by moonlight, on the top of the clouds,
And if a wet evening, around them should creep,
They can drop through the skylight *to bed* and [asleep
And pigs will commence flying up in the air,
And men flying after them everywhere,
So then, if Pork stakes you should want for to fry
Live pigs will drop down ready cook'd from the sky

Then Bullocks you'll see, wearing ladies kid gloves
And Billy-goats turned into young Turtle Doves,
And Jack-asses, walking about all the day,
In Parsons' black gowns, with the Shakers to pray
And Elephants, working the Sewing Machine.
And making wheel-barrows to travel by steam,
Red Herrings will starch Paper collars and Cuffs
And Mangles *be turned* into young ladies Muffs.

760.

DOWN BY THE VILLAGE WELL.

Ladies' Version, (Copyright.)

By L. M. THORNTON.

'TWAS in the spring not long ago,
I lived in Lincolnshire;
And often to the well did go,
For water sweet and clear.
One morning I the handle turned,
To let the bucket down,
When such a fine young man I saw,
Dressed in a suit of Brown.

Chorus.

Down by the village well,
Down by the village well,
'Twas there that Harry charm'd me quite,
Down by the village well.

A twelvemonth from that very time,
He came a courting me;
And no one more affectionate,
I'm sure than him could be.
With joy I leant upon his arm,
As far we used to stray,
And sighed when at the hour of ten,
Adieu I had to say.

The ring is on, the bells have rung,
A little cot I share,
And whosoever enters it,
Will find that peace is there.
It was a lucky day for me,
(I'm proud the truth to tell,)
When charming Harry I beheld,
Down by the villiage well.

:oXo:

Boot-jacks will be *turned* into Gooseberry Pies,
And Cod-fish will be turned into Crickets & Fies
All other Fishes will turn into Beef in each brook
You can draw out a 40lb. lump, with a hook;
And Bobbies will turn into Lobsters and Crabs,
And Churches be turned into Coaches and Cabs,
Then Bishops and Parsons will turn it is clear,
To sweep Chimneys and live on the soot all the year.
There will be no Old People, they'll always be young,
Men will not be plagued with a cross woman's [tongue,
Bum-bailiffs will swallow the County Court then.
Old Nick will be loose, upon earth once again;
The Sun and the Moon, will be changed never fear
Into large Suet Dumplings, and Barrels of Beer,
Teetotallers will turn into Water Butts free,
If you doubt it, just go to *Old Davy* and see.

Fig. 60
(top left)
Rachael's Christening
1973

Fig. 61
(top right)
Traffic in Central Lancashire
1973

Fig. 62
(bottom)
7 Days in Butlinland
1973

Fig. 63
7 Days in Butlinland
1973

Afterword and Thanks

Roger Malbert
Senior Curator, Hayward Touring

All that Is Solid Melts into Air is a quotation from Marx and Engels.[1] It was translated from the original German into English via Prospero's speech in *The Tempest*, which ends, 'We are such stuff/As dreams are made on; and our little life/Is rounded with a sleep' – a distinctly anti-materialist thought. *All that Is Solid Melts into Air* was also the title of an influential work of Marxist sociology in the 1980s by Marshall Berman, subtitled *The Experience of Modernity*. This trail of references is worth mentioning in the context of a project concerned with lineage. The society we have inherited, the towns and cities of England, the social formations, cultural traditions, class divisions, inequalities of wealth and opportunity, derive to an overwhelming extent from the nineteenth century, the age of the Industrial Revolution and the British Empire. If, to quote Marx again, 'the tradition of all the dead generations weighs like a nightmare on the brain of the living',[2] there may be more reasons for reflecting on this period in English history than we might immediately realise.

As an artist who rejoices in people, as both the subject and often the medium of his work, Jeremy Deller is naturally less interested in utilitarian assessments of the economic benefits of the Industrial Revolution than in imagining the lived experience of the young men and women, adolescents and children, who toiled in the factories and mines that produced Britain's wealth. Deller's breadth of sympathies and his engagement with popular culture, especially music, give a particular emphasis to his perspective on this history. Deller has been described by Hayward Gallery Director, Ralph Rugoff, as 'a social cartographer revealing neglected ley lines of cultural history'; here he is also a social archaeologist, uncovering affinities and connections across historical epochs and finding new meanings in familiar images and stories. The dead are – in our imaginations – coexistent with the living. Their songs, complaints and protests, represented here in quotations, broadsides and song-sheets, resonate with those of our own time.

All that Is Solid Melts into Air has been curated by Jeremy Deller for Hayward Touring. We are indebted to him for his extraordinary generosity and commitment to both the book and the exhibition, which exemplify his highly personal, free-ranging and egalitarian approach to art and politics. The idea for the exhibition was first explored in a project at Palais de Tokyo, Paris in 2008. Many of the images of the Industrial Revolution here – prints, photographs and drawings – have rarely been seen, others may be familiar as documents of social history, while a certain number are accredited works of high art. Deller's lateral interpretation of this diverse material offers a fresh context in which hierarchies are dissolved; printed ephemera and historical artefacts and texts are shown alongside and on equal terms with major paintings; and analogies are drawn between the (brutal) past and the (indifferent) present. Importantly, the exhibition, although containing a wealth of historical material, is in essence a contemporary project – and a work of art in its own right.

Artist-curators James N. Hutchinson and Lesley Young have provided essential curatorial and logistical support, initiating and researching many aspects of the exhibition. Jeremy Deller's artistic collaborators, banner-maker Ed Hall and muralist Stuart Sam Hughes, are producing new works for the show, and a selection of industrial sounds and music has been assembled for a jukebox. The folk music historian Roy Palmer has given us invaluable guidance and Scott King lent his expertise to the design of the Shaun Ryder family tree.

We would like to thank all of our lenders, both institutions and individuals: Anson Engine Museum; Blackburn Museum and Art Gallery and the Sharples Family; Bradford Museum and Galleries; British Film Institute; Chetham's Library, Manchester; John Davies; Harris Museum and Art Gallery, Preston; Laing Art Gallery, Newcastle; Manchester Art Gallery; Manchester Libraries, Information and Archives; Museum of Science and Industry, Manchester; National Museum of Wales; Motorola Solutions; North West Film Archive at Manchester Metropolitan University; North West Sound Archives, Clitheroe; People's History Museum, Manchester; Ben Roberts; Science Museum; Adrian Street; Peter Kennedy Collection at the British Library Sound Archive; and Gavin Watson.

Many individuals have shared their knowledge and enthusiasm, and without them the exhibition would not have been possible: Keith Badder, Jukebox Selection Co.; Sue Bannister, genealogist; Kevin Bolton, Manchester Libraries, Information and Archives; Duncan Broady, Greater Manchester Police Museum; Sallyann Browning, Museum of Science and Industry (MoSI); Geoff Challinor, MBE; Anson Engine Museum; Neil Child-Dyer, The Work Foundation; Andrew Davies, University of Liverpool; Tony Dykes, British Film Institute; Phil Dunn, People's History Museum, Manchester; Mark Etheridge, National Museum Wales (NMW); Oliver Fairclough, NMW; Mark Furness, John Rylands Library, University of Manchester (JRL); Clare Grundy, Manchester Art Gallery; Stella Halkyard, JRL; David Hendy; Emma Heslewood, Harris Museum, Preston; Marion Hewitt, North West Film Archive (NWFA); Rebecca Hill, Blackburn Museum and Art Gallery; Gail Hunter, Paisley Museum; Boris Jardine, Science Museum; Susan Jeffrey, Paisley Museum; Kevin Johnson, Science Museum; Jack Kirby, MoSI; Meg McHugh, MoSI; Beth McIntyre, NMW; Will McTaggart, NWFA; Roy Palmer; Maggie Pedley, Bradford Museums and Galleries; Michael Powell, Chetham's Library, Manchester; all at Quarry Bank Mill, National Trust; Nic Rayner, Greater Manchester County Record Office; Jennifer Reid, researcher and performer; Steve Roud, author; Andrew Schofield, North West Sound Archive, Clitheroe; Janet Small, Black Country Living Museum; Philippa Smith, London Metropolitan Archives; Laura Smyth, The Vaughan Williams Memorial Library, English Folk Dance and Song Society (EFDSS); Malcolm Taylor, EFDSS; Dr. Matt Thompson, Ironbridge Gorge Museum; Nicholas Thornton, NMW; Vanessa Toulmin, National Fairground Archive, The University of Sheffield (NFA);

I. M. Trowell, NFA; Shane and Aaron at Vinyl Carvers, London; Sandra Underwood, Ances-Tree Family History Research; Pauline Webb, MoSI; Kathy Whalen, Chetham's Library, Manchester; Katherine White, Trowbridge Museum; Emily Yates, Science Museum.

Thanks to colleagues at our partner galleries on the tour: Manchester Art Gallery, Maria Balshaw, Director, and Tim Wilcox, Curator; Nottingham Castle Museum & Art Gallery, Deborah Dean, Visual Arts and Collections Manager, and Tristram Aver, Exhibitions Officer; Mead Gallery, University of Warwick, Sarah Shalgosky, Curator, and Fiona Venables, Assistant Curator; Laing Art Gallery, Newcastle, Julie Milne, Chief of Art Galleries and Lesley Richardson, Assistant Keeper.

Hayward Touring Assistant Curators Vanessa North and – following Vanessa's departure – Gillian Fox have organised the exhibition with unparalleled dedication, energy and resourcefulness. This publication has been produced by Hayward Art Publisher, Ben Fergusson, and Editor, Faye Robson, and we owe them immense thanks for their skilful editing, patience and flexibility, whilst Hettie Judah has provided crucial support in the creation of the text in this book. The graphic designers, A Practice for Everyday Life, have been instrumental in helping us to conceptualise both the book and the exhibition and their contribution to the project cannot be overstated.

At Southbank Centre we thank Ralph Rugoff, Director, Hayward Gallery, Alan Bishop, Chief Executive, Jude Kelly, Artistic Director, and Sarah O'Reilly, General Manager, Hayward Gallery, for their ongoing support, and the following colleagues in the Hayward Gallery and Touring team for their essential contributions: Dave Bell, Steve Bullas, Mark King and Dave Palmer, Senior Technicians; Peter Brown and Ben Hudson, Transport Technicians; Ruth Pelopida, Hayward Operations Manager; Marcia Ceppo, Hayward Operations Coordinator; Vicky Skelding-Bloor, Registrar; Alison Maun, Bookings and Transport Administrator; Oliver Krug, Visual Arts Press Manager; Nadine Monem, Hayward Publisher; Steve Burridge and Sarah Cashman, Picture Researchers.

[1] The full quotation reads: 'All that is solid melts into air, all that is holy is profaned, and man is at last compelled to face with sober senses his real conditions of life, and his relations with his kind.' Karl Marx/Friedrich Engels, *The Communist Manifesto*, 1848
[2] Karl Marx, *The Eighteenth Brumaire of Louis Napoleon*, 1852

List of Works

All measurements are given in centimetres, height x width x depth. Numbers by works denote plates in catalogue.

List of Exhibited Works

Anonymous/Unknown

Employ Only Best British Workmen, date unknown
Enamel on metal
40 x 79
Bradford Museums & Galleries

64 *We Are the Lions of the Industry*, c. 1910
Enamel on metal
46 x 114
Bradford Museums & Galleries

James Sharples as a Smith, date unknown
Albumen print photograph
45.5 x 31.5
People's History Museum, Manchester

14 *Photograph of James Sharples (Oval Cameo)*, date unknown
Carte de visite albumen print photograph
16.5 x 10.7
People's History Museum, Manchester

A Kiln for Burning Coke, near Maidstone, Kent, 1799
Aquatint print, with hand colouring
54 x 45.5
Science Museum, London

Effects of Alston Brewery, c. 1805
Pencil drawing with red ink
20 x 26
Science Museum, London

23 *Miner with Candle, Climbing Ladder*, c. 1805
Pen and sepia wash on paper
23 x 19
Science Museum, London

30 *Double-dial Longcase Clock from Park Green Silk Mill, Macclesfield*, c. 1810
Wood and metal
147 x 62 x 28
Museum of Science and Industry, Manchester

Pully System to Connect Double-dial Longcase Clock to Park Green Silk Mill, Macclesfield, c. 1810
Wood, rope and metal
Dimensions variable
Museum of Science and Industry, Manchester

Smoke Consuming at Ancoats, Manchester, 1820
Etching
38 x 27
Science Museum, London

'Owdham Town at Dinnertime', early nineteenth century
Black-and-white printed, single-sheet letterpress
10 x 25.3
Manchester Libraries, Information and Archives, Manchester City Council

'Salford Bastille', early nineteenth century
Printed black-and-white, single-sheet letterpress
17 x 21.1
Manchester Libraries, Information and Archives, Manchester City Council

40 'The New Bury Loom',
early nineteenth century
From a book of
collected broadsides
6.6 x 23.2, in book 37 x 26 x 3.5
Manchester Libraries,
Information and Archives,
Manchester City Council

41 'Utick's Trip to Manchester',
early nineteenth century
Printed black-and-white,
single-sheet letterpress
18.3 x 24.8
Manchester Libraries,
Information and Archives,
Manchester City Council

32 *Rules to Be Observed in this Factory from Thomas Ainsworth & Sons., Church Street Mills, Preston*, c. 1830
55.7 x 44.2
Printed poster on paper
(printed by Pritt, Preston)
Harris Museum & Art Gallery,
Preston

Towers Yard Factory Bell, 1835
Metal, rope
Cast by Thomas Mears of London
in the Whitechapel Bell Foundry
Dimensions variable
Anson Engine Museum, Poynton

'Things that Ought Not to Be',
from a book of Manchester
songs and ballads compiled by
Robert Holt, c. 1843–73
Album comprising 424 broadsides
6 x 24 x 31
Chetham's Library, Manchester

'Victoria Bridge on a Saturday
Night', from a book of Manchester
songs and ballads compiled by
Robert Holt, c. 1843–73
Album comprising 424 broadsides
6 x 24 x 31
Chetham's Library, Manchester

59 'A Prophecy for 1973', c. 1860
Printed black-and-white,
single-sheet letterpress
19.5 x 25
Chetham's Library, Manchester

'Five in the Morning', c. 1860
Printed black-and-white,
single-sheet letterpress
19.5 x 25
Chetham's Library, Manchester

42 'Jone O' Grinfield', c. 1860
Printed black-and-white,
single-sheet letterpress
19.5 x 25
Chetham's Library, Manchester

'Just What We'd All Like to See',
c. 1860
Printed black-and-white,
single-sheet letterpress
19.5 x 25
Chetham's Library, Manchester

'Lines upon the Explosion
at Witton', c. 1860
Printed black-and-white,
single-sheet letterpress
19.5 x 25
Chetham's Library, Manchester

Shaft Cage of the Hester Pit, New Hartley, Showing its Construction and Damage Following the Breakage of the Beam in January, 1862
Lithographic print
21.6 x 27.9
Discovery Museum, Newcastle
upon Tyne

34 *Amalgamated Engineers' Union Banner*, 1890
Painted cotton sateen
237 x 237
Laing Art Gallery, Newcastle
upon Tyne

17 *Steel*, 1945
Colour film; dir.: Ronald Riley;
cinematographer: Jack Cardiff
35 minutes
British Film Institute

36 *Motorola WT4000*
Wearable Terminal, 2013
Plastic and electronics
2.6 x 9.3 x 14.2
Courtesy Motorola Solutions

Thomas Allom
Swainson Birley Cotton Mill near
Preston, Lancashire, 1834
Pencil drawing with pen,
sepia and wash
12 x 19
Science Museum, London

J. Bluck (after R. H. Marten)
13 *Salt Mine, Cheshire*, 1814
Coloured aquatint engraving
15 x 25
Science Museum, London

G. F. Bragg
10 *Treforest Tin Works, Glamorganshire*,
c.1840
Hand-coloured lithograph
50.8 x 68.5
National Museum Wales, Cardiff

A. R. Burt
38 *John Evans*, 1819
Engraving with wash on paper
28.6 x 20.6
National Museum Wales, Cardiff

W. J. Chapman
47 Selection from *Francis Crawshay*
Workers Portraits, 1835
16 paintings, oil on linen
Each 36.3 x 25.6
National Museum Wales, Cardiff

George Childs
Dowlais Ironworks, c.1840
Watercolour over pencil on paper
23.8 x 34.8
National Museum Wales, Cardiff

William Clayton
1–5 *Iron Workers, Tredegar, Wales*, 1865
28 cartes de visite albumen
photographic prints
Dimensions variable
Manchester City Galleries

John Davies
58 *Mersey Square, Stockport*, 1986
Silver gelatin photograph
71.3 x 104
Courtesy of Michael Hoppen
Contemporary

57 *Stockport Viaduct*, 1986
Silver gelatin photograph
71.3 x 104
Courtesy of Michael
Hoppen Contemporary

Jeremy Deller
Hallelujah! Shaun Ryder's
Family Tree, 2008
Vinyl lettering on wall
Dimensions variable
Courtesy the artist
Design: Scott King

28 *So Many Ways to Hurt You*
(The Life and Times of
Adrian Street), 2010
Digitised film as part of
mixed-media installation,
with wrestling costumes
Dimensions variable
Courtesy the artist

There's a New Sensation:
Bryan Ferry's Family Tree, 2013
Vinyl lettering on wall
Dimensions variable
Courtesy the artist

Jukebox, 2013
Jukebox with sound and music
recordings, with mural backdrop
by Stuart Sam Hughes
Dimensions variable
Courtesy the artist

Audio Recording of the Weaving Shed at Queen Street Mill at High Volume, 2013
Sound piece
Continuous on a loop
Courtesy the artist and North West Sound Archive

60–63 *Promotional Film for All that Is Solid Melts into Air*, 2013
Projected video
Approx 16 mins
Courtesy the artist

Take Me Back Home: Noddy Holder's Family Tree, 2013
Vinyl lettering on wall
Dimensions variable
Courtesy the artist

Hello, Today you have day off, 2013
Fabric banner made by Ed Hall
Dimensions variable
Courtesy the artist

35 *Zero-Hour Contract*, 2013
Printed paper
Dimensions variable
Courtesy the artist

G. Greatbach (after H. Warren)
9 *'The Black Country' near Bilston*, 1869
Engraving
23 x 29
Science Museum, London

Robert Havell (after George Walker)
Factory Children, 1814
Hand-coloured aquatint
26 x 36
Science Museum, London

The Collier, 1814
Hand-coloured aquatint
25.5 x 34.5
Science Museum, London

Thomas Hornor
18 *Rolling Mills, Merthyr Tydfil*, 1819
Watercolour on paper
41.4 x 54.2
National Museum Wales, Cardiff

Attributed to G. Jameson
A Keelman Getting his Orders, c.1811
Watercolour on paper
16.4 x 12.8
Laing Art Gallery, Newcastle

21 *A Pitman Going to Work*, c.1811
Watercolour on paper
16.2 x 12.9
Laing Art Gallery, Newcastle

Judas Priest
19 *Unleashed in the East*, 1979
12-inch album in sleeve
Private collection

Dennis Hutchinson
26 *Adrian Street with his Father at the Pithead of Brynmawr Colliery, Wales*, 1973
Black-and-white photographic reproduction
Dimensions variable
Courtesy Jeremy Deller

S. Lacey (after H. Gastineau)
Nant y Glo, Monmouthshire, c.1835
Engraving
12.3 x 17.9
Science Museum, London

J. W. Lowry (after James Nasmyth)
31 *Thomas Robinson's Power Loom Factory, Stockport*, 1849–50
Engraving
17.5 x 32
Science Museum, London

John Martin
6–8 *The Destruction of Sodom and Gomorrah*, 1852
Oil on canvas
136.3 x 212.3
Laing Art Gallery, Newcastle upon Tyne

Newman & Co.

12 *Penrhyn Slate Quarries, near Bangor, Wales*, 1842
Lithograph
28 x 39
Science Museum, London

William Pickett

'Iron Works, Colebrook Dale', from *The Romantic and Picturesque Scenery of England and Wales*, 1805
Hand-coloured aquatint engraving
45 x 33
Science Museum, London

Ben Roberts

65 *Adam Hoccom, Facilities and Engineering, Amazon Fulfilment Centre, Rugeley*, 2013
C-type photographic print
190 x 127
Courtesy the artist

37 *Amazon Fulfilment Centre, Towers Business Park, Rugeley*, 2013
C-type photographic print
190 x 127
Courtesy the artist

Bev Horton, Outbound Despatch, Amazon Fulfilment Centre, Rugeley, 2013
C-type photographic print
190 x 127
Courtesy the artist

James Sharples

Sheet of Anatomical Details, Blackburn School of Art, Aged 18 (Muscle Study), 1843
Lithograph
53.4 x 74.5
People's History Museum, Manchester

15 *Sketch of Forearm (detail from The Forge)*, date unknown
Pencil on paper
14.3 x 18.5
People's History Museum, Manchester

The Forge, c. 1848
Oil on canvas
129 x 169
Blackburn Museum and Art Gallery and the Sharples family

16 *The Smithy*, (published by the executive estate of the late James Sharples), 1894
Goupil gravure
43 x 62
People's History Museum, Manchester

Dean Shaw

39 *Tony Iommi, Black Sabbath, Donnington*, 2012
Digital C-type photographic print
42 x 29.7
Courtesy the artist

Adrian Street

Union Jack Cape, 1969
Majestic metallic lamé, reversible
Length: 150
Courtesy Adrian Street

Purple Gown, 1971
Yellow satin brocade and velvet, decorated with lace and rhinestones
Length: 150
Courtesy Adrian Street

Ian Tilton

55 *Happy Mondays – Bridge*, 1987
Black-and-white photographic print
42 x 29.7
Courtesy the artist

53 *Happy Mondays – Cinema*, 1987
Black-and-white photographic print
42 x 29.7
Courtesy the artist

Happy Mondays – Marina, 1987
Black-and-white photographic print
42 x 29.7
Courtesy the artist

54 *Happy Mondays – Mural*, 1987
Black-and-white
photographic print
42 x 29.7
Courtesy the artist

Gavin Watson
11 *Slough Centre, End of the Night*, 1989
42 x 29.7
Courtesy the artist

Images in Publication Only

Anonymous / Unknown

46 *Merthyr Rising*, 1831
Etching

22 *Girl with Belt and Chain Dragging Coal Tubs Underground*
Published in *Parliamentary Papers*, 1842
Etching

33 *Preston Lock-Out*, 1853
Ink and watercolour on paper
Lancashire Archives

48–52 *Police Book Containing Images of 'Scuttlers'*, c. 1884
Record book and photographs
Greater Manchester Police Museum

25 *Adrian Street as Teddy Boy* (second from right), *Wales*, c. 1957
Black-and-white photograph
Courtesy Adrian Street Archive

24 *Adrian Street Bodybuilding*, 1975
C-type photograph
Courtesy Adrian Street Archive

27 *Adrian Street at an Airport in the US with his Valet, Miss Linda*, Mid-1980s
C-type photograph
Courtesy Adrian Street Archive

John Martin
8 *Plan for Preventing the Pollution of the Water of the Thames*, 1834
Etching
City of London, London Metropolitan Archives

REX/Andre Csillag
20 *Judas Priest – K K Downing, Dave Holland, Rob Halford, Ian Hill and Glenn Tipton, London*, 1981
Black-and-white photograph

Copyright credits

Photographic credits

Published on the occasion of the exhibition
Jeremy Deller: All that Is Solid Melts into Air

Manchester Art Gallery
11 October 2013 – 19 January 2014

Nottingham Castle Museum
and Art Gallery
31 January – 22 April 2014

Mead Gallery
University of Warwick, Coventry
3 May – 21 June 2014

Laing Art Gallery, Newcastle
12 July – 26 October 2014

Exhibition curated by Jeremy Deller, with James Hutchinson and Lesley Young. Exhibition organised by Vanessa North and Gillian Fox.

This exhibition has been made possible by the provision of insurance through the Government Indemnity Scheme. Hayward Touring, London, would like to thank HM Government for providing Government Indemnity and the Department for Culture, Media and Sport and Arts Council England for arranging the indemnity.

Published by Hayward Publishing
Southbank Centre, Belvedere Road
London, SE1 8XX, UK
www.southbankcentre.co.uk

Art Publisher: Ben Fergusson / Nadine Monem
Staff Editor: Faye Robson
Sales Officer: Alex Glen
Press & Marketing Coordinator: Diana Adell
Catalogue Design: A Practice for Everyday Life
Colour Management: Dexter Pre-Media
Printing: Henry Ling, Dorset

A catalogue record for this book is available from the British Library.

ISBN 978 1 85332 319 5

Distributed in North America, Central America and South America by
D.A.P. / Distributed Art Publishers, Inc.,
155 Sixth Avenue, 2nd Floor, New York, NY 10013
Tel. +212 627 1999
Fax. +212 627 9484
www.artbook.com

Distributed in the UK and Europe by Cornerhouse Publications
70 Oxford Street, Manchester, M1 5NH
Tel. +44 (0)161 200 1503
Fax. +44 (0)161 200 1504
www.cornerhouse.org/books

HAYWARD TOURING
SOUTHBANK CENTRE

LOTTERY FUNDED
Supported using public funding by
ARTS COUNCIL ENGLAND

In the Greater World

Chico Xavier

In the Greater World

Dictated by the Spirit
André Luiz

Translated by: Darrel W. Kimble and Ily Reis

FEB

Second Edition – 9/2020

Original title in Portuguese:
NO MUNDO MAIOR
(Brazil, 1947)

ISBN 978-65-5570-142-5

Published by
BRAZILIAN SPIRITIST FEDERATION
Av. L2 Norte – Q. 603 – Conjunto F (SGAN)
70830-106 – Brasília (DF) – Brazil
www.febeditora.com.br
editorial@febnet.org.br
+55 61 2101 6198

INTERNATIONAL DATA FOR CATALOGING IN PUBLICATION

L953m Luiz, Andre (Spirit)

In the Greater World / dictated by the spirit Andre Luiz ; [received by] Francisco Cândido Xavier ; [translated by Darrel W. Kimble and Ily Reis]. – 2st edition – Brasília, DF (Brazil) : FEB, 2020.

260 p.; 21 cm – (Life in the spirit world; 5)

Original title: No mundo maior

ISBN 978-65-5570-142-5

1. Spiritist Novel. 2. Spiritism. 3. Psychographic works. I. Xavier, Francisco Candido, 1910-2002. II. Brazilian Spiritist Federation. III. Title. IV. Series.

CDD 133.93
CDU 133. 7
CDE 00.06.02

Contents

On the Evolutionary Journey

Every day, human voyagers depart by the thousands from the four corners of the earth, heading for the realm of death. They leave from illustrious European cultural centers, bustling New World cities, old Asian circles and harsh African climes. They leave from metropolises, villages, fields …

Very few lived on the mounts of sublimation, engaged in ennobling duties. The majority are made up of the lesser in spirit, those who struggled to earn titles that would glorify their personality. They did not reach their wholeness as men and women. They traveled the *mare magnum*[1] of humanity in continuous experimentation. Many a time, they succumbed to all sorts of vices, willfully holding themselves back on the path of folly. In spite of this, however, they often attributed to themselves the undeserving designation of "the elect of Divine Providence"; and fixated in such a presumption, they judged their neighbor without focusing on their own wrongs, expecting a heaven full

[1] Lat. "The great ocean." – Tr.

of grace for themselves and a hell of endless torment for others. When lost in the intricate meanderings of blind materialism, they unjustifiably believed that their memories would be buried in their graves, and save for a few, those affiliated with the various religious sects and denominations counted thoughtlessly and inconsequentially on privileges they never earned.

Where should this strange and endless caravan be lodged? How could the same destination be awaiting travelers of such diverse cultures, positions and baggage?

The Malgache[2] and the Briton enjoy the same rights before Supreme Justice. Nevertheless, on account of their individual conduct, they will not be one and the same before the Divine Law, which invariably distinguishes between virtue and vice, work and idleness, truth and pretense, goodwill and indifference. All, however, saints and villains, the diligent and the lazy, are part of the continuous pilgrimage to the grave.

How can one measure so many different vessels by using one single standard? Considering our common origin, aren't we all children of the same Father? Why judge guilty wrongdoers with unappealable condemnation if the words "regeneration," "love" and "mercy" are inscribed with letters of fire in the divine dictionary? Would the Lord order the compulsory nurturing of hope in individuals, while he himself despaired? Would he glorify goodwill among humans and remain in the dark dungeon of negation? Could the primitive who slays his fellow tribesmen with arrows have had the same learning opportunities as the super-civilized European who kills his neighbor with a machinegun? Would either one be ready for permanent entry into the heaven of endless bliss merely because of his symbolic baptism, or a belayed repentance on their deathbed?

---

[2] Madagascar. – Tr.

Logic and common sense do not always square with immutable theological arguments. Life never stops its natural course in response to the imposition of artificially contrived dogmas. And if a mere work of human art, whose final destination is the moldy placidity of museums, requires years of patience before it is finished, what can be said of the sublime work of perfecting the soul, destined for imperishable glories?

Some have found Andre Luiz's collaboration strange as he provides us with information on some sectors of the realms closest to the most common of mortals.

Deceived by the theory of the least effort – non-existent in the higher realms – they looked forward to personal preeminence in a heaven of contemplative delight and lavish with pleasing comfort, but having given no testimony of service or dignified work. They would prefer the ease of theaters in a state of permanent bliss, where the divine greatness would be limited to prodigious shows, whose amazing performances would be the responsibility of high order spirits dressed as brightly clad jesters.

Andre Luiz's mission, however, is that of revealing the treasures that we will happily inherit in eternity, the indestructible riches whose possession we will attain only by means of the indispensable acquisition of Love and Wisdom.

To do so, we do not labor in miraculous laboratories of improvised happiness, where inexpensive dowries and coarse wings of wax might be obtained. We are God's children in the process of growing. Be it in arenas of condensed matter, such as those of the physical struggle, or in the spheres of subtle energies, such as those of the higher realms, the ascendants that preside over our destinies are of an evolutionary order, pure and simple, with an infallible justice following us closely on the way to the glorious and compassionate light of Divine Love.

Death will not provide anyone with a free passport to celestial bliss. It will never compulsorily promote humans to angelhood. Everyone will go through eternity's customs inspection solely with the bags that they themselves have packed, and they will learn that order, hierarchy and the peace of constructive labor are unchangeable features of the Law everywhere.

After the grave, no one will enjoy a rest they have not earned, for the "Kingdom of God does not come through outward appearances."

Those living the human experience understanding the sublime ladder whose rungs must be climbed at the price of their sweat, taking advantage of the heavenly blessings by means of tirelessly practicing the good, will not be surprised by the stories of this messenger interested in serving out of love. Preoccupied as they are with carrying out the Divine Purposes, they know they would not have received the gift of life to simply kill time, or the gift of faith to confound their fellow-being. Our fraternal messenger's statements, however, will provoke discontentment and perplexity in the believers of favoritism, still caught in the web of old illusions even while holding the most honorable credentials.

This is natural, however: each cultivator breathes the air of the field he or she has chosen.

Even so, we invoke the blessings of the Eternal: for them and for us.

Emmanuel

Pedro Leopoldo (MG), March 25th, 1947.

1
Between Two Planes

The moon was shining, draping every corner of the landscape in resplendent light. To the west, the wonderful cumulus clouds spread out on the horizon resembled castles of milky froth lost in the vast blueness. Confined within this immensity, the earthly scenario, a vast plain covered in a forest of deep dark-green, contrasted with the sweet enchantment of the firmament. To the south, whimsical clouds curled down from the sky toward the earth like decorations of fluttering gauze. I thought of incarnate humankind and asked myself if those white strips in the firmament might not be heavenly bands watching over the earth as it rested.

The full moon's imposing solitude filled me with awe because of the melancholy of its majestic and unspeakable beauty.

The idea of God enveloped my thoughts, drawing respect and gratitude that I couldn't utter. In the middle of the night, I rendered loving worship to the Eternal One, who had laid the

sublime foundations of silence and peace for the respite of the souls incarnated on the earth.

The luminous lunar disc radiated wonderful suggestions. Earth's evolution had begun beneath it reflective rays and countless civilizations had modified the course of the human experience. That same suspended lamp had lit the way for primitive humans, had directed the steps of the conquistadors, and had guided the journeys of the saints. An impassive witness, it had watched the founding of magnificent cities and had followed their prosperity and decadence; it had contemplated the never-ending renewals of the world's political landscape; it had shone down on the crowned brows of monarchs and the staffs of the poorest shepherds. For long millennia, it had witnessed the daily birth and death of millions of beings. Its stately serenity reflected divine peace. Down below, whether discarnate or incarnate possessors of relative intelligence, we proceeded with our experiments, repaired our roads, contracted moral debts or fostered virtues amidst hopes and troubles, always learning and recapitulating. The moon, however, lonely and glistening, conveyed to us the idea of the unshakeable serenity of the Divine Law.

"The meeting place is nearby."

Assistant Calderaro's voice interrupted my thoughts.

The warning alerted me of our work, our responsibility; above all, it reminded me I was not by myself.

Neither of us had made the trip bereft of purpose.

In a few minutes, we would share in the endeavors of Instructor Eusebio, a selfless champion of Christian love in the service of those in need.

Eusebio had long devoted himself to administering spiritual assistance and had earned considerable credit on our plane. He had declined distinguished positions and had postponed his ascent to higher spheres to dedicate himself entirely to those

hungering for the light. He was in charge of a prestigious support organization in an intermediate zone, tending to relatively spiritualized learners who were still attached to the corporeal realm, as well as disciples recently delivered from it.

The huge institution to which he dedicated his brilliant guidance was populated with souls situated between the lower and the higher planes. They harbored countless problems and questions of all sorts and required his utmost patience and wisdom. However, in spite of the complex services that continued to accumulate, the tireless missionary still found time to descend weekly to the planet's surface. There he would tend to the immediate interests of candidates for discipleship, since they still lacked the spiritual growth needed to come to him and his enlightening instruction in the higher realms.

I didn't know him personally. Calderaro, however, received guidance from him in conformity with the hierarchic system, and would speak of him with the enthusiasm of a subordinate who is linked to his superior by bonds of love more than obedience.

Calderaro, too, rendered active service down on the earth, directly attending to his incarnate brothers and sisters. He had specialized in the science of spiritual help, the kind which, among the world's scholarly types, we might call "enlightened psychiatry," a field that had long held a strong attraction for me.

With a week at my disposal without any set obligations regarding my normal duties, I applied for admission to the training team for which Calderaro had become the eminent director. He accepted me with the kindness typical of true missionaries of the good and offered to guide me. He was in a favorable position to assist me with my learning goals because his regular training team had gone to a different region to carry out spiritually constructive activities. In light of this, he would be able to give me his full attention and assist me as I desired.

He kindly explained that the cases for which he was responsible didn't present substantial continuity: they unfolded; they were impromptu, subject to unexpected demands or situations. In other areas of action, planning was required, conditions and circumstances were determined beforehand. However, regarding his own set of responsibilities, the norm didn't apply. Problems had to be monitored just like the unforeseen manifestations of life itself. In light of such fluctuations, he didn't strictly plan things out in detail. He carried out his responsibilities wherever, whenever and however the higher purposes might determine. The essential scope of his duties was limited to providing immediate help to unfortunates, preventing insanity, suicide and severe moral downfalls as best he could. To accomplish this, the industrious missionary had to posses a deep understanding of the psychic forces at play, with special dedication to the good of his fellow brothers and sisters. In this particular, Calderaro left no doubt. His spontaneous goodness was a sign of his virtue, and his unshakable serenity revealed his wisdom.

I had just joined him; we had met for the first time the previous day. Nevertheless, it had taken no more than a minute of mutual affinity for there to be a sound rapport between us. Although I recognized his verbal temperance, from the moment we met we spoke like old friends.

Thus, following him with a soul edified by fraternity and trust, I found myself a short distance from a large park right in the middle of nature.

All around, sturdy trees with rustling branches were lined up like sentinels purposefully positioned to watch over our work.

The wind blew, singing in a whisper. Illuminated by light imperceptible to the human eye, the place held a few hundred fellow spirits temporarily disengaged from their physical bodies by the liberating power of sleep.

Friends from our realm were diligently assisting them, showing devoted interest, pleasure in serving, and saintly patience. I noticed that many of them were standing; others, however, had sat on mounds of earth covered with soft grass to engage in serious and respectful conversation.

To accustom me to that moment of extreme spiritual beauty, Calderaro advised me:

"In today's meeting, Instructor Eusebio will receive students from various branches of spiritualism, and who are candidates for front line work."

"Oh!" I exclaimed, inquisitively. "So, this meeting isn't a gathering of individuals affiliated indiscriminately with various schools of faith?"

The Assistant immediately explained:

"That wouldn't be advisable within the scope of our area of specialization. The Instructor has a particular fondness for assisting incarnates and individuals who have been freed recently from the physical plane, and he needs to make use of his time delivering lectures for maximum benefit. The diversity of principles found in hundreds of individuals, each with his or her own opinion, would lead to too many digressions and would cause a regrettable waste of opportunity."

He gazed at the crowd at length and added:

"There are approximately twelve hundred people here. Out of that figure, eighty percent are learners from spiritualist churches of various branches, but they are incapable of great flights of knowledge, despite their aspirations to take part in the Divine Plan. They have an excellent potential for virtue. They exemplify goodwill and are working on their inner enlightenment through praiseworthy efforts. However, they still haven't developed a core of trust. They quake before the common storms they meet on the pathway and they hesitate in the area of the trials they need for the enrichment of

their souls; thus, they require our special care. Through their diligent efforts in spiritualizing work, they are the future instruments for the endeavors that lie ahead. In spite of the clarity of the rules they live by, they still suffer disharmony and afflictions that threaten their incipient stability. Even so, they aren't left without the assistance they need. In our spheres of action, institutions for restoring their energies open their welcoming doors to them. Freedom from the body during sleep is the direct resource of our manifestations of fraternal support. At first, they receive our influence unconsciously; then their minds are slowly strengthened and they begin recording our concourse in their memory as we give them ideas, suggestions and opinions along with beneficial and redeeming inspirations by means of imprecise recollections.

He paused briefly and concluded:

"The rest are coworkers from our plane who are here to carry out tasks of assistance."

The organization of the meeting was truly worthy of admiration. We were in an area that was substantially terrestrial. Impregnated with aromas spread all around by the breeze, the atmosphere reminded me of a warm night back at my garden-surrounded home on earth.

What might I have accomplished in the physical world if I had received this blessed opportunity for enlightenment back then? That handful of mortals under the rays of the moon seemed like a gathering of privileged beings favored by heavenly deities. The millions of men and women sleeping in nearby cities, shackled to their immediate interests and eager to exchange the vilest sensations, wouldn't have the least suspicion of that unprecedented gathering of candidates seeking the inner light, who had been summoned to work hard at preparing for more lasting and effective incursions into higher spirituality. Did they have any idea of the sublime opportunity that was welcoming them? Would

they take advantage of that gift with enough understanding of eternal values? Would they march fearlessly onward, or would they draw to a halt upon contact with the first obstacles of their illuminative endeavor?

Calderaro perceived my silent questioning and added:

"Our group is essentially dedicated to the maintenance of balance. You are of course aware of the fact that changing an individual's mental plane is never forced: it is the fruit of time, effort and evolution. In today's world the edifice of human society has been shaken to its very foundations, compelling a huge number of people to unexpectedly seek self-renewal. You surely wouldn't be surprised if I told you that, with the rise of the modern mind and its paralyzing collision with the sentiments, reason is at risk. Material progress has numbed the souls of heedless men and women. For centuries, masses and masses of individuals have been far removed from the spiritual light. A purely scientific civilization is like a devouring Saturn, and humankind nowadays is faced with implacable demands for accelerated mental growth; hence the urgency for our assistance. The need to prepare the spirit has intensified at an appalling pace."

At that moment, we reached the peaceful crowd.

My companion smiled, emphasizing:

"Chance doesn't perform miracles. Any undertaking requires planning, execution and completion. The miracle of changing a physical person into a spiritual one requires a lot of collaboration on our part."

He gave me a meaningful look and concluded:

"The sublime wings of the eternal soul cannot spread out within the narrow confines of a hatchery. One must work, improve, endure."

At that moment, someone approached us. It was a thoughtful coworker informing us that Eusebio had arrived. In

fact, the missionary appeared prominently nearby, flanked by six assistants surrounded by auras of intense light.

The selfless instructor didn't show any traces of the venerable old age we generally associate with apostles of divine revelation. He had the appearance of a robust man in full spiritual adulthood. His dark, peaceful eyes resembled founts of great magnetic power. Smiling, he looked at us as a colleague.

His presence imposed a respectful silence. All conversation stopped, and amidst the threads of light the workers from our plane were weaving all around to isolate us from any possible assault from low order energies, only the calm breeze lifted its voice, whispering beautifully and mysteriously to the foliage.

We all sat down to listen, while the Instructor remained standing. Observing him almost face-to-face, I admired his majestic appearance, emanating security and comeliness. His serene face radiated unsurpassed goodness, understanding, tolerance and gentleness. His loose, light-green tunic emitted emerald sparkles. His vigorous personality instilled us with veneration, tenderness, trust and peace.

Once quiet had settled in, he lifted his right hand to heaven and prayed with a moving tone of voice:

Lord of Life,
Bless our purpose here
of entering upon the path of Light! . . .

We are your children,
Still enslaved to limited spheres,
But our yearning for the Infinite
Rends the veil of our existence.

Heirs of immortality,
We seek your eternal founts,
Faithfully awaiting your mercy.

Lord, of ourselves we can do nothing.
Without you, we are like broken branches
That the fire of experience
Tortures or transforms ...
However, united in your love,
We are glorious workers
Of your endless creation.

We are a few thousand
On this terrestrial plane;
But above all,
We praise your greatness
Which does not oppress our smallness ...

Broaden our perception of life,
Open our eyes
Clouded by the sleep of illusion
So that we may behold your endless glory!
Softly awaken our hearing
So we may perceive the canticle
Of your sublime eternity.
Bless the seeds of knowledge
That your messengers have scattered
On the field of our souls;
Fertilize our inner soil
So that the divine seeds do not perish.
We know, Father,
That the sweat of labor

And the tears of redemption
Constitute abundant fertilizer
For the germination of what we have sown;
But without Your blessing,
Our sweat languishes
And we weep in despair …
Without your compassionate hand,
The infestations of the passions
And the storms of our vices
Would ruin our incipient harvest …

Awaken us, O Lord of Life,
To the light of current opportunities;
So that the difficulties of our struggle may not be futile,
Guide our steps toward the supreme good;
Clothe our hearts
With your paternal serenity,
Strengthening our endurance!
O Powerful Lord,
Sustain us in our weakness,
Correct our errors,
Enlighten our ignorance,
Shelter us in your loving bosom.

Beloved Father, may your sovereign will
Be done
Now and forever.
So be it.

Concluding his moving plea, the Instructor lowered his teary eyes. Overwhelmed with joy, I saw crystalline streams of a singular light beginning to pour down on us from on high.

Particles similar to etherized silver rained down on the premises, penetrating the roots of the nearby trees.

An unknown enchantment filled my soul. Upon contact with those divine emanations, I noticed that my energies were gradually settling down into wonderful receptivity. The same notes of happiness and beauty floated all around us as calmness and bliss transpired on all faces ecstatically turned to the Instructor, around whom one could see intense waves of heavenly light.

Sublime happiness flooded my whole being, immersing me in an indescribable bath of renewing energies.

My eyes were powerless to restrain the happy tears that the beautiful sparkles drew out from the hidden recesses of my soul. And before the noble mentor began to speak again, I silently gave thanks for the response from heaven, once again realizing that prayer was not only a manifestation of religious reverence, but also the means to access the inexhaustible sources of Divine Power.

2
Eusebio's Lecture

Standing erect, his upper body lit with soft illumination, the Instructor spoke movingly:

"We address you, brothers and sisters, who, for the time being, have the opportunity to learn in the blessed school of the flesh.

"Spurred on by necessity, whether in your thirst for knowledge or in the anguish of the love that bridges abysses, you have overcome heavy vibratory boundaries and now find yourselves at ground zero on the unique path that lies before you. While your physiological organism is reposing far away, getting itself ready for death, your nearly-free soul shares in fraternity and hope with us, training your faculties and sentiments for the true life.

"Of course, because the deficiencies of the brain render it incapable of supporting the burden of two lives at the same time, you will not retain a full recollection of this hour upon reentering the corporeal envelope. Nevertheless, the memory of

our meeting here will linger in the depths of your being, guiding your higher inclinations toward lofty purposes and opening your intuitive portal so that our fraternal thoughts may assist you."

The speaker paused briefly, fixing his calm and lucid gaze on us. Under the incessant light rain of silvery rays, he continued:

"Weary of the repeated sensations of the dense plane of existence, you intend to step into other realms. You are searching for something new, some unknown comfort, the solution to tormenting enigmas; however, do not forget that the flame in one's heart, which has become a sanctuary of divine light, is the only lamp capable of illuminating the spiritual mystery on our progress up the path of redemption and evolution. At the side of each man and woman in the world, God's will is alive regarding the duties they must fulfill. Each one faces the work for which he or she is responsible, just as each day brings with it special opportunities for accomplishing the good. The universe conforms to an absolute order. As free birds in limited skies, we interfere in the divine plan as we create either prisons and shackles, or liberation and advancement for ourselves. Therefore, we must adapt to the divine balance, attending to the individual role that has fallen to us within the swarming beehive of life.

"How long have we done and undone, finished and started over on the reparative journey, only to return, perplexed, once more to the beginning? On the terrestrial stage, we are the same actors of the evolutionary drama. Each millennium is a short act; each century, a brief scene. Even though we inhabit sacred bodies, we act like carefree children who are entertained only by child's play and we lose the sanctifying opportunities of our existences. Thus, we become reprobates of the sovereign laws, ensnared in the ruins of death like shipwrecked pirates, who, for a long time, are unworthy of sailing the seas once again. While millions of souls enjoy good opportunities of correction

and readjustment, once more involved in regenerative efforts in earth's cities, millions of others mourn their defeat, lost in dismal disillusionment and suffering.

"We are not referring to the heroic missionaries, who, out of self-denial and love, solidarity and sacrifice, endure the bloody wounds of bitter testimony. They are lights temporarily separated from the Divine Light, and they return to their heavenly abode like loyal workers coming home at the end of their daily tasks.

"We are referring to the vast multitudes of indecisive souls, imprisoned by ingratitude and doubt, by weakness and waste; souls formed under the light of reason, but enslaved to the tyranny of instinct."

And with Christian humility, Eusebio continued:

"We are speaking of all of us, travelers wandering about in the desert of our own denial; of us, birds with broken wings, trying to reach the nest of freedom and peace, while continuing to flail around in the wasteland of pleasures of the lowest order. Why not restrain the course of the corrosive passions that afflict our spirit? Why not bridle the impulses of animality we have taken pleasure in ever since the first sparks of reasoning? The awful dualism of light and darkness, of compassion and perversity, of intelligence and bestial impulse continues. We have studied the science of consoling spirituality ever since we learned how to reason; however, since the remotest times, we have devoted ourselves to degradation and destruction.

"We sang hymns of praise with Krishna as we learned the concept of the soul's immortality in the shade of the majestic trees that aspired to the peaks of the Himalayas, only to descend immediately afterward into the valley of the Ganges, killing and destroying in order to enjoy and possess. We perceived universal love with Siddhartha Gautama, but then pursued our fellow beings in an alliance with Sinhalese and Hindu warriors. We

were heirs of wisdom in the far-distant past of the Sphinx, but from reverence for the mysteries of initiation, we switched to blood-thirsty hostility on the banks of the Nile. Accompanying the symbolic ark of the Hebrews, over and over we read Yahweh's commandments contained in the sacred scrolls, but we disregarded them at the first clangor of war against the Philistines. We wept in religious rapture in Athens, but murdered our brothers in Sparta. We admired Pythagoras, the philosopher, but followed Alexander, the conqueror. In Rome, we exalted virtue and offered generous gifts to the gods in marvelous sanctuaries, only to draw arms a few minutes later in the courtyard of the temples, spreading death and enthroning crime. We wrote beautiful sentences of respect for life with Marcus Aurelius, but ordered the killing of people who were blameless and useful to society. With Jesus, the Divine Crucified, our attitude has not been any different. In cruel vindication, we poured out rivers of blood over the remains of martyrs sacrificed in the arenas, igniting pyres of religious sectarianism. We supported arbitrary and ignominious rulers from Nero to Diocletian because we were hungry for power, and when Constantine opened to us the doors of political domination, we changed from being apparently faithful servants of the Gospel into criminal arbiters of the world. Little by little, we forgot the blind of Jericho, the paralytics of Jerusalem, the children of Lake Tiberias and the fishermen of Capernaum to stroke the crowned brows of victors, even though we knew that the earth's conquerors cannot escape the journey to the tomb. The idea of the Kingdom of God became naive fantasy because we could not leave our place at the right side of kings thirsting for worldly prominence. Still today, after almost twenty centuries have passed since the Savior's cross, we continue to bless bayonets and cannons, machine guns and tanks in the name of the Magnanimous Father, who makes the sun of mercy shine equally on the just and the unjust.

"That is why our storehouses of light have remained empty. The gale of fulminating human and national passion howls from one pole to the other, sowing evil omens.

"How long will we be masterminds of destruction and wickedness? Instead of loyal servants of the Lord of Life, we have been soldiers of the armies of illusion, leaving behind millions of tombs opened under a torrent of ash and smoke. In vain, Christ has exhorted us to seek the manifestations of the Father within us. We nurture and expand only selfishness and ambition, vanity and fantasy. We continue to incur onerous moral debts and enslave ourselves to the sad outcomes of our deeds, lingering indefinitely in a crop of thorns.

"In such a state we have reached the modern era, in which madness is widespread and men and women's mental stability is on the verge of disaster. With an evolved brain and an immature heart, we hone our art of wrecking our spiritual progress."

The eminent Instructor made a lengthy pause, during which I observed the audience around me. Men and women, some firmly holding each others' hands, displayed extreme paleness on their dread-stricken faces. Some of them, like myself, were obviously there for the first time, judging from the stunned astonishment stamped on their faces.

Fixing a penetrating gaze on the assembly, the Instructor continued:

"In centuries past, flourishing cities disappeared under massacres or battles of cruel conquerors, or were paralyzed by deadly waves of unknown and untreated plagues. Today, human communities still suffer the siege of murderous swords, and rains of bombs are dropped on defenseless populations. Nonetheless, yellow fever, cholera and smallpox have been conquered; leprosy, tuberculosis and cancer are tirelessly fought. There is a new threat to the planet, however: the profound

imbalance, the generalized disharmony and the infirmities of the soul that subtly undermine your stability.

"Your pathways do not seem to be traveled by conscious beings; instead, they are like strange roads, along which hallucinated goblins dance for joy. As the product of dark times characterized by oppression and reciprocal cruelty and hatred, we have watched the earth become an arena of endless hostilities. Humans and nations pursue the myth of easy gold. Susceptible individuals abandon themselves to the disturbances of the passions. Vigorous minds lose their inner vision, blinded by their concept of individualism and authoritarianism. Engaged in endless disputes, in dreadful duels of opinions and driven by demented inferior ambitions, the children of earth have drawn near to a new abyss, which their disturbed gaze does not let them perceive. This open-mouthed vortex, my brothers and sisters, is that of mental alienation, which not only disaggregates the cellular structures of physical life, but also touches the subtle tissue of the soul, invading the core of the perispiritual[3] body. Almost all the areas of modern civilization have been compromised in their fundamental structure. Hence, we must mobilize all the efforts at our disposal to serve the human cause – which is also our own.

"The effort of salvation does not belong exclusively to religion: it is a ministry common to all, for the day will come when people will realize that the Divine Presence is everywhere. Our responsibility is not geared toward a particular interest: it is generic work for the entire community, the effort of honest and sincere servants interested in the wellbeing of all.

[3] "The spirit is surrounded by a substance that might look vaporous to you but which is still quite dense to us … As a fruit seed is enveloped by the perisperm, the spirit per se is surrounded by an envelope, which, by comparison, may be called the perispirit." (Question nº 93, *The Spirits' Book*, Allan Kardec). The physical body has the very same form as the perispirit – Tr.

"Even though you may have sought out our company for guidance in the sublime work of the spirit, do not forget your own light. Do not count on someone else's torch for the journey. On the misery-filled planes of regenerative suffering in the flesh, millions of men and women weep bitterly. Having abused the help of good people, they fell into the darkness after losing in the grave the ephemeral eyes with which they admired the landscape of life in the sunlight. Careless and recalcitrant, they neglected every opportunity to light their own lamp. They loathed the difficulties of earthly struggles and chose physical pleasure as the supreme objective of their purpose on earth. And when death closed their satiated eyelids, they came to know a longer and denser night filled with anguish and terror."

Eusebio paused for more than a minute; his gaze became pensive, as if he were recalling touching scenes evoked by his words.

I noticed the restlessness of the group as they waited for him to start speaking again. Women displayed strong emotions on their transfigured faces, and all of us listening to that dedicated and moving lecture kept still, unable to move.

Long seconds elapsed before the speaker continued with energetic and patriarchal inflection:

"You have come to us for the guidance you need to face your tasks. Seduced by the light of the higher realms and captivated by the first notions of universal love, you desire the grace to take part in the sowing work of the future. You are asking for wings for the sublime endeavor, and you aim to cooperate in the effort of spiritual growth.

"Of course, such intention could not be nobler. It is, however, essential that you consider the need to fulfill your daily duties. It is impossible to progress in a century without attending to the obligations of an hour. For now, it is crucial to restore your energies, readjust your aspirations and sanctify your desires.

"It is not enough to believe in the immortality of the soul. We can no longer postpone our self-enlightenment in order to become a sublime light ourselves. The simple recognition of the survival of the soul after death and the interaction between the two worlds is not enough for the bold commitment to redemption. The frivolous and the evil, the ignorant and the foolish, can also correspond with each other from afar, from country to country. First of all, it is of the utmost importance to uplift the soul, to break down the walls that enclose us in darkness, to forget the illusions of ownership, to rend the thick veils of vanity, and to abstain from the deadly liquor of shameful self-centeredness so that the radiance on the peaks may glow in the depths of the valleys in order for the eternal sun of God to dissipate the transitory human darkness.

"If you wish to be pioneers of the living faith in the world, from now on, in spite of the difficulties, a complete demonstration of your conviction of divine spirituality will be required of you.

"The Higher Plane is not interested in incorporating devotees eager for a beatific paradise. Would you perchance accept your stay on the earth without a specific purpose? If the tender herb must produce in consonance with higher objectives, what can be said of the magnificent intelligence of incarnate humans? What would then be expected from reason illuminated by faith! Would we receive such a sacred trust of constructive knowledge for nothing? Would we have the solace of such blessings to strengthen the selfish purpose of reaching heaven without preparatory steps, without purifying activities?

"Our goal, my friends, is not compatible with egotistical exclusivism. The divine door does not open for spirits who have not divinized themselves through incessant work in cooperation with the Almighty Father. And the soil of the planet, to which

you have bound yourselves temporarily, represents the blessed arena of cooperation the Lord has entrusted to you. Gather the heavenly dew in the heart eager for peace; contemplate the stars that wave to us from afar like sublime peaks of the Divinity; however, do not neglect the field of present struggle.

"Modern spiritualism cannot confine God within the walls of an earthly temple, for our essential mission is to change the whole earth into the majestic temple of God.

"For our vanguard of determined and brave workers, the phase of futile experimentation, disorderly investigation and peripheral reasoning has passed. We are experiencing the structuring of new sentiments, cementing the pillars of the world-to-come with the light that has been lit in our inner being. It is natural for newly-arrived learners to experiment, examine, probe and evoke brilliant theories in which hypotheses compete alongside showy personalities: this is understandable and reasonable. Every school is characterized by the various subjects that make up its courses and areas of discipline. However, we are not addressing those who still dream within the confinement of the 'self', entangled in the thousand obstacles of the illusion that crystallizes their beliefs. We are speaking to those who are eager for universality, nameless friends of the humankind that is making an effort to emerge from the darkness into the light. How can you accept stagnation as a principle and exclusivist happiness as an end?

"Let us nourish renewing hope. Do not call on Jesus to justify longings for undeserved repose. Jesus did not reach the culmination of resurrection without climbing Calvary, and his lessons refer to the faith that moves mountains.

"Therefore, let us not expect admission to happier worlds before improving our own. Forget the old error that the death of the body represents the miraculous immersion of the soul in the river of enchantment. Let us pay homage to everlasting life and

perfect justice, and let us adapt to the Law that always evaluates merit according to our own deeds.

"Our ministry is one of enlightenment and eternity.

"The Universal Government has not limited our activities to guarding perishable altars. We have not been summoned to keep watch in the private circle of an exclusivist interpretation, but to cooperate in setting the incarnate spirit free, opening brighter horizons to the human mind and rebuilding the edifice of redeeming faith forgotten by literalist religions.

"The powerful winds of the evolutionary wave are sweeping the earth. Every day we see the collapse of conventional principles held inviolable for centuries. The perplexed human mind is forced to make distressful changes. The subversion of values, the social experiment and the accelerated process of selection through collective suffering perturb the timid and inattentive, who represent the overwhelming majority everywhere ... How to assist these millions of spiritually needy if you do not accept the responsibility of offering fraternal help? How to cure the incipient madness if you do not transform yourselves into magnets that maintain stability? We know that inner harmony is not an article for sale found in earthly markets, but a spiritual acquisition accessible only in the temple of the spirit. Hence, we must light our hearts in fraternal love in serving. A faith that hopes will not be enough for our accomplishments. What is crucial is the love that trusts and assists, transforms and uplifts as a true vessel of Divine Wisdom.

"Let us be instruments of the good rather than expectants of grace. The task demands courage and supreme devotion to God. If we do not make ourselves a light within our own circle, it is in vain that we will try to overcome the darkness outside. And in pursuing the work for which we are responsible, let us not forget

that evangelizing the relations between the visible and invisible realms is a duty as natural and pressing as evangelizing individuals.

"Do not go looking for miracles: yearning for them can become addictive and lead to your loss.

"Link yourselves to the higher planes through prayer and constructive work, and these will provide you contact with the divine storehouse that supplies each of us according to our just necessity.

"Your burdens on the earthly landscape, however rough or displeasing, represent the Supreme Will.

"Do not jump over obstacles or try to go around them in a deliberate attempt to escape: conquer them using will and perseverance, providing an opportunity to develop your growth.

"Make sure to journey through the physical world with due caution, for you are often like the careless moth. Attend to the demands of each day, rejoicing in the satisfaction of your smallest tasks.

"Do not attempt to fly without having learned to walk.

"Above all, do not inquire about your apparent right to the divine banquet before completing your human commitments.

"It is impossible to be an angel without first having been a judicious human.

"Sovereign and infallible laws preside over our destinies. We are known and examined everywhere.

"The gifts granted to sanctified spirits – gifts that we admire so much – are lavished on us by God everywhere. It is our job, however, to take advantage of them. Earthly machines can lift your physical body to considerable heights, but spiritual flight, which will free you from animality, will have to be accomplished with your own wings.

"The consolation and friendship of incarnate and discarnate benefactors will enrich you with comfort like gentle and blessed flowers of the soul; however, they will die like

one-day roses if you do not prepare your heart with faith and understanding as well as unshakable hope and immortal love, the sublime nourishment that propitiates their development through your tireless effort.

"Do not covet the repose of your hands and feet; before harboring such an objective, seek inner peace in the serenity of the conscience.

"Forsake illusion, before illusion forsakes you.

"Take charge of your own existence and plant the good on the pathway of your steps.

"Only the servants who actively work imprint landmarks of advancement in their journey. Only those drenched in the sweat of personal effort are able to coin new forms of life and renovating ideals. The others, stagnant in their idleness, whether monarchs or princes, ministers or legislators, clergy or generals, are classified among the ranks of earth's exploiters. They do not stand out in their temporary stay on the planet, but rather flutter around like multicolored insects, returning to the dust they had left for a few moments.

"Thus, as you return to the body of flesh, take advantage of the light for the spiritual growth you need.

"Let us participate in the glorious Spirit of Christ.

"Let us convert ourselves in redemptive light.

"Widespread and growing instability has taken over the human mind. Nations and ideologies, systems and principles fight desperately with each other. Once a truce is signed ending international conflict, deplorable civil war breaks out at home, arming brother against brother. Unrest fosters strikes; yearning for freedom shakes people's dwellings. The spheres of action battle each other; incarnates and discarnates with ignoble tendencies collide brutally by the millions. Countless homes become environs of rebelliousness and discord. Humankind struggles with itself in the current accelerated process of transition.

"Therefore, steady yourselves in the spiritual growth required of you, knowing full well that it is impossible to fool the Law or betray the universal decrees!"

In closing, Eusebio uttered a beautiful and moving prayer, invoking divine blessings for the assembly, while sublime manifestations of light descended on us.

With the lecture finished, participants still bound to the physical world began to leave in respectful silence.

Calderaro took me to the Instructor and introduced me. The director received me with friendliness and kindness, generous in his words of incentive. We must serve, he explained, emphasizing the need for spiritual assistance everywhere, and that requires self-sacrificing and loyal coworkers.

When Calderaro told him of my plans, Eusebio smiled paternally, and offering advice regarding several different steps to take, he recommended we contact a group of spirit helpers with whom he was actively involved.

Upon departing soon afterwards in the company of the assistants who comprised his group, the noble mentor kindly encouraged me:

"Be happy!"

Directing an expressive look at Calderaro, he added:

"When suitable, get him involved in the assistance work in the caverns."

Taken with curiosity, I thanked him wholeheartedly and resigned myself to waiting.

3
The Mental Realm

Once again in Calderaro's company on a bright morning, I was focused on my plans of expanding my ideas regarding the manifestations of life close to the physical realm.

At the spirit colony, which had welcomed me with loving care, I had gotten to know a few instructors and faithful laborers of the good very well. Unquestionably, we were all engaged in intense work, with very few hours reserved for entertainment. We also enjoyed an environment of happiness and joy that truly benefited our evolutionary progress. Our houses of worship were blessed places of comfort and revitalization. In our cultural and artistic associations we found the continuity of our earthly existence, but it was now enriched with multiple educational elements. Social activities offered plenty of wonderful opportunities to develop priceless friendships. The homes in which we carried out our long-term work were built amid enchanting gardens resembling warm, cheerful nests in fragrant and peaceful branches.

We had ample directives, duties, order and discipline; nevertheless, serenity was our climate, and peace our daily gift.

Death had cast us into a sphere foreign to the physical struggle. The first sensation had been shock. We had been seized by the unexpected. We continued living, but without our physiological apparatus; however, these new conditions of existence didn't mean a reduction in the opportunities to evolve. The grounds for healthy competition and the potential for spiritual growth were infinitely profitable. We could seek the help of higher powers, foster edifying relationships, weave hopes and dreams of love, and plan more-constructive reincarnations by improving ourselves through our work and study and by expanding our capacity to serve.

In short, the passageway through the grave had led us to a better life. But ... what about the millions who had crossed over the narrow threshold of death, and who were still attached to the physical plane?

Countless multitudes of spirits of this order were still in the elementary stages of understanding. They possessed only rudimentary information about life. They called on high order spirits for help in the same way that primitive tribes ask for help from civilized human beings. They had to develop their faculties just as children have to grow. They did not remain attached to the physical world because they were evil, but because they lingered hesitantly on the soil of the earth like infants who snuggle in the maternal bosom. From their physical existence they retained only the memory of their sensations, and needed to reincarnate almost immediately because it was impossible for them to enroll in our schools of basic service and learning. On the other hand, it was also true that hordes of criminals and offenders continued living in turmoil not far from us after having crossed over the borders of the grave. At times, they spent countless years in rebellion and despair,

becoming horrid specters of darkness, much like what occurs on earth with obstinate criminals who are segregated from healthy society. But they always ended their insane wallowing in the dark recesses of remorse and suffering by finally repenting of their wicked deeds. Repentance, however, is a path to regeneration and never a direct passport to heaven, and for that reason these pitiable spirit wretches resembled living portraits of suffering and dread.

On many occasions, I saw them, troubled and afflicted, assuming forms difficult to look at.

In cases of obsession, they turned into mutual tormenters or cold-blooded torturers of incarnate victims. Whether roaming about or confined to areas of punishment, their display of endless pain and misery was always shocking.

The reality, however, was that, these unfortunates had passed through the exact same doors as we who continued working at our normal pace, and perhaps in many instances we had abandoned our material envelope under the siege of the same ills. Considering this possibility and wishing to acquaint myself with Divine Law – which neither grants a heaven of privilege nor establishes a hell for eternity – it grieved me to contemplate such long ranks of unfortunates.

Actually, I had come across many of them in the rectification chambers of several charitable institutions. These patients, however, housed in sectors of fraternal assistance, already showed signs of improvement because they had acknowledged their wrongs or had received spiritual credit, thanks to certain intercessory powers.

On the other hand, the unfortunate beings I am referring to had other origins. They comprised the ignorant, the rebellious, the troublemakers, the unrepentant, souls impermeable to any edifying advice, the infatuated and the vain of every sort, persisters in evil, wasters of vital energy in their wicked attitudes toward life.

On several occasions, my contact with them had been merely a fortuitous encounter, with no noteworthy learning on my part.

The questions remained: why did they linger for so long in the obscure sphere of incomprehension? Were they deliberately postponing receiving the light? Didn't their condition as self-condemned beings to long-term punishment grieve them? Weren't they ashamed of their intentional waste of time? I often stopped to look them over: the facial features of many of them looked monstrous, provoking irony and pity. What law governed the stereotyping of their forms? Had Mother Nature, who lavished her blessings on all planes, forsaken them? Or had they received such personal features as punishment imposed by higher designs?

These questions kept swirling in my mind, prompting me to try to find an opportunity to get them answered.

Eager to start, I approached Calderaro that morning. I explained my questions, describing my long-held expectations to his tolerant ears. I planned to find out more about those who kept themselves in evil, crime and inconformity.

He listened calmly. Smiling benevolently, he began to explain:

"Before anything else, Andre, let's look at the issue differently. In order to become true helpers for suffering spirits, whether discarnate or not, we must understand wickedness as insanity, rebelliousness as ignorance, and despair as infirmity."

In light of my perplexity, he added fraternally:

"Actually, these definitions aren't something I came up with myself. We learned them from Christ in his divine dealings with our lowly position on earth."

I thought the Instructor was about to go into a long verbal exposition on the subject, inserting priceless references and commenting on personal experiences. But none of that happened. Calderaro simply explained:

"Spiritual blindness is the result of dense ignorance in primary manifestations or the murkiness of reason in severe states of degradation. In assisting the unbalanced mind, we are interested in analyzing this latter aspect of the darkness that weighs upon the soul. Thus, it is crucial that, to some degree, you understand insanity within the ambit of civilization. To do so, we must study in more detail the disharmonious brains of incarnate and discarnate individuals, for the brain is the seat of manifestation for spiritual activity."

I wanted to continue listening to his clear and convincing explanations, but Calderaro went silent. After a few moments, he stated:

"I don't have much time to discuss matters outside my scope of service. Even so, let's approach this together, convinced that if we labor in good deeds, we will continue to learn the science of spiritual growth."

He smiled fraternally and added:

"Words used in the service of the good are the divine cement for immortal accomplishments. Hence, our conversation will serve our fellow beings in a substantial way, with increased benefit to ourselves."

I kept silent, feeling particularly uplifted.

I accompanied him and in a few minutes we entered a huge hospital on the physical plane, stopping in front of the bed of a particular patient the Assistant was going to help. Worn out and pale, the patient was connected to a pitiable spirit from our plane in a miserable situation of debasement and suffering. Although almost motionless, the patient's nerves were acutely tense, even though he couldn't see his sinister-looking companion. They seemed viscerally tied to each other – such was the abundance of extremely fine threads that kept them mutually entangled from chest to head, reminding me of two prisoners caught in a

fluidic net. Thoughts that belonged to one were obviously living in the mind of the other. Troubles and sentiments were being exchanged between them with mathematical precision. Spiritually, they continued to be perfectly identified with each other. I was astonished to watch the flow of their shared mental vibrations.

I was about to comment on the phenomenon, when, noting my intention, Calderaro suggested:

"Examine the brain of our incarnate brother."

I focused my attention on the delicate apparatus, concentrating my visual capacity to analyze it on the inside.

The skull didn't offer any resistance to my heightened visual abilities. Just as I had seen on other occasions, there lay the complicated area of mental production, resembling the most complex laboratory but the least accessible one as well. The separate circumvolutions were joined together in lobes that were equally distanced from one another by fissures, giving me the impression of an electric motor almost inaccessible to humans. As I compared the two hemispheres, I recalled designations of classical terminology and spent several minutes observing the special arrangements of the nerves as well as the characteristics of the grey matter.

My guide's voice broke the silence as he exclaimed unexpectedly:

"Notice the signaling process."

Astonished, I noticed for the first time that the radiations emanated by the brain contained essential differences. Each motor center was marked by diverse particularities through its radiant energies. I was surprised to discover that the entire cerebral region was divided into three distinctive areas delineated by luminous markings. The areas of association in the frontal lobes were sort of glistening. This effect decreased from the motor cortex down to the tip of the medulla oblongata, and got even weaker in the basal ganglia.

I had spent some minutes observing the nerve cells when my Assistant advised me:

"You have examined the brain of our friend who is still attached to his physical body. Now observe the same organ in the discarnate friend who has such a direct influence on him."

The spirit wasn't aware of our presence due to the circle of coarse vibrations in which he kept himself. All of his attention was fixed on the patient, reminding me of the sagacity of a feline watching its prey.

I saw that he had a strange wound in the thoracic area. I was about to investigate its cause by probing the lungs, when Calderaro unaffectedly corrected me:

"We'll deal with the wound during the assistance work. Focus your visual capacity on the brain."

After a few moments I concluded that, apart from the arrangement of the parts and vibrational rhythm, I was looking at two almost identical brains. The discarnate spirit's mental field was different, displaying some superiority in the area of the grey matter, which, in the perispiritual body, was lighter and less dark. I got the impression that if we were to wash the inside of the brain of the fellow lying on the bed, cleaning it of certain heavier particles, it would be essentially the same as the brain of the spirit I had been examining. The luminous divisions, however, were the same in all respects: more light in the frontal lobes, less in the motor cortex and almost none in the medulla, where the radiations were diffuse and opaque.

After an accurate examination, I stopped my comparative analysis to gaze at Calderaro in silent questioning.

My thoughtful mentor smilingly explained:

"After physical death, what is most surprising is the discovery that we are still alive. Here in the spirit world we learn that the perispiritual body, which gives us form in a lighter and

more malleable matter after the grave, is also the result of the evolutionary process. We are not miraculous creations destined as adornments of a cardboard paradise. We are God's children and heirs, acquiring qualities from experience to experience down through the millennia. There is no favoritism in the Universal Temple of the Eternal, and all the powers of the Creation are perfected throughout the Infinite: the embryonic consciousness existing in the rock that rolls along with the river current is involved in a process of emergence. The trees, often standing tall for hundreds of years, enduring the gales of winter and lulled by the breezes of spring, are developing memory. The tigress licking her newborn offspring is learning the rudiments of love. The ape, through its shrieks, is developing the faculty of speech.[4] Yes, God has created the world, but we are still far from the completed opus, as the beings that inhabit the Universe will toil in sweat for a long time improving it. The same goes for us individually. We are the Divine Author's creation and we must perfect ourselves completely. The Eternal Father has established as a universal law that perfection must be a work of cooperation between him and us, his children."

Calderaro was quiet for a few seconds, and I couldn't bring myself to make any comments on his lofty concepts.

He pointed to the medulla and continued:

"I don't think any reference to the primordial endeavors of our long drama of evolutionary life is really necessary. From the amoeba living in the lukewarm water of the ocean to human beings, we have invariably been struggling, learning and selecting.

---

[4] In Part One, Ch. IV, question nº 71 of *The Spirits Book*, Kardec explains: " ... first, inanimate beings, formed of matter alone, without vitality or intelligence – these are the solid bodies of minerals; second, animate, non-thinking beings, formed of matter and endowed with vitality but not intelligence; third, animate beings, formed of matter, endowed with vitality and possessed of an intelligent principle that gives them the ability to think." Read further, question nº 585 et seq., chap. XI, "The Three Kingdoms." – Tr.

To acquire motion and muscles, faculties and thoughts, we have experienced life and have been experienced by it for thousands of years. The pages of Hindu wisdom are writings of just yesterday and the Good News of Jesus Christ is the subject-matter of today, when compared to the millennia we have lived on our progressive journey."

After gesturing with his right hand, he went on:

"In the nervous system lies the primitive brain: the repository of instinctive movements and seat of the subconscious activities. We could picture it as the cellar of one's individuality, where we store all our experiences and register the minutest incidents of life. Then, in the region of the motor cortex, which is the intermediary area between the frontal lobes and the nerves, lies the developed brain, consolidating the motor powers our mind uses for the essential manifestations in the current evolutionary instant of our way of being. In the frontal lobe planes, still silent to the world's scientific investigation, lie substances of a sublime nature, which we will gradually access in our efforts at ascension. These lobes represent the noblest part of our evolving divine organism."

These simple, wonderful explanations thrilled me. Calderaro was an instructor of the highest ability. He taught without ever seeming tired, and he knew how to lead learners to a profound understanding without great difficulty.

As I appreciated his worthiness, he continued after a brief pause:

"We cannot say that we have three brains simultaneously. We have only one, which is nevertheless divided into three distinctive regions. We could picture it as a three-storey castle: on the first floor, we find the 'residence of our automatic impulses,' symbolizing the living summary of the work we have accomplished. On the second, we find the 'domicile of current

acquisitions,' where the noble qualities we are building are developed and consolidated. On the third, we have the 'home of superior concepts,' indicating the higher qualities we must yet attain. In the first dwell habit and automatism; in the next, effort and will; in the last, the ideals and higher goals to be reached. In this way we distribute the subconscious, the conscious and the superconscious among the three stories. As we can see, we possess within us the past, the present and the future."

During a longer pause I gave free reign to my ponderings, according to my old inquisitive habit.

His priceless explanations were straightforward and logical; nevertheless, I asked myself: could the brain of a discarnate be subject to illnesses too? I knew that in the corporeal world, the grey matter could be attacked by tumors, softening or hemorrhage. But in the new realm to which death had led me, what kind of illnesses could beset the mind?

Calderaro noticed my inquisitive look and explained:

"For now, we won't discuss physical illnesses per se. Those who, like us, have long followed the work of psychiatrists truly devoted to the good of their fellow humans, are fully aware that all expressions of human gratitude are still quite small when compared with the work of a Paul Broca[5], who identified impairments of the center of speech, or of a Wagner Jauregg[6],

---

[5] French anthropologist and pathologist, born June 28, 1824, died July 9, 1880; surgeon closely associated with the development of modern physical anthropology in France and whose study of brain lesions contributed significantly to understanding the origins of aphasia, the loss or impairment of the ability to form or articulate words. He founded the anthropology laboratory at the École des Hautes Études, Paris (1858), and the Société d'Anthropologie de Paris (1859). http://www.britannica.com. – Tr.

[6] Born March 7, 1857, died Sept. 27, 1940; Austrian psychiatrist and neurologist whose treatment of syphilitic meningoencephalitis, or general paresis [progressive dementia and generalized paralysis due to chronic inflammation of the covering and substance of the brain (meningoencephalitis)], by the artificial induction of malaria brought a previously incurable fatal disease under partial medical control. His discovery earned him the Nobel Prize for Physiology or Medicine in 1927. http://www.britannica.com. – Tr.

who dedicated himself to curing paralysis by pursuing the syphilis spirochete until he found it in the recesses of the grey matter, disturbing the motor areas. In light of such phenomena, it is understandable that cerebral harmony is broken as a result of the compulsory withdrawal of the principles of the perispiritual body from the cellular clusters of the physiological field. As a result, these clusters become disorganized in their structure and regular activities, much like a violin that is unsuitable for performing a musical piece perfectly because one or two strings are out of tune. We should not and cannot ignore the laws that govern the domains of the body ... Hence the impossibility of our wanting to have 'balanced psychology' without 'harmonious physiology' in the sphere of human science – this is a moot point. We shall refer only to spirit manifestations in their essence. You want to know if a discarnate mind can become ill ... What a question! Don't you believe that deliberate evil is a disease of the soul? That hatred does not constitute a terrible pathological state? Furthermore, don't you believe that sadness and non-resignation are 'mental worms'? Although we have the fortune of acting in a subtler and lighter body – thanks to the nature of our thoughts and aspirations, already far removed from the dense zones of the life we left behind – we still don't have the brains of angels. The preservation of our current body is an incessant endeavor on our way to more far-reaching achievements. We cannot rest during our process of enlightenment. We must continue to purify ourselves, select our inclinations and scrutinize our concepts so as not to halt our progress. Millions here live in the same conditions we are in, but millions of others remain in the flesh or on lower lines of evolution, under the iron hand of heartrending dementia. It is for these that we should consider the pathology of the spirit, assisting the most unfortunate ones

and interfering fraternally and indirectly in the solution of the difficult problems in whose black threads they are entangled. They are spirits in despair, victims of themselves in a terrible harvest of thorns and disillusionment. The human perispiritual body, the vessel of our manifestations, is for the time being our highest achievement on earth in the chapter of forms. For enlightened souls already illuminated by redemptive light, it represents a bridge to the higher realms of the life eternal that we have not yet reached. For coarse spirits, it is a crucial and just means of restriction. For guilty consciences it is an indefinable prison, for it registers the wrongs that have been committed, storing them with all the vivid details of the dark moments of failure. The type of life each person has led in the corporeal envelope determines the density of the perispiritual organism after the loss of the physical body. We know that the brain is the tool that bears the mind, the fountainhead of our thoughts; therefore, it is through the brain that we connect ourselves to either the light or the darkness, to good or evil."

Noticing my attention in following his invaluable explanations, Calderaro smiled meaningfully and asked:

"Understand?"

Pointing to the two suffering beings at our side, he went on:

"We are examining two sick beings here: one in the flesh and the other outside of it. The brains of both are compromised and completely attuned to each other. Spiritually, they have rolled down from the third floor (where superior concepts are located), and yielding to their unrestrained will, they missed the chance to take shelter on the second floor (the seat of personal effort), and have lost a valuable chance to pick themselves up again. Thus, they have fallen into the sphere of instinctive impulses, where all previous animalistic experiences are recorded. They both detest life; they hate each other; they despair; they harbor ideas of

torment, affliction and vengeance. In short, they're insane, even though the world can't perceive the extreme imbalance in their perispiritual organism."

I was ready to ask a long list of questions related to the two characters, but my companion had begun the work of direct assistance. Placing his right hand on the left frontal lobe of the incarnate patient, he said to me in an affable tone:

"Quiet your anxious questioning, my friend. Be patient. In the course of our work, I will give you the explanations within the reach of my understanding."

4
Studying the Brain

With his fraternal palm on the patient's forehead, as if transmitting energy-laden fluids of renewing life, Calderaro kindly explained:

"Approximately twenty years ago, our friend here put an end to the physical body of his current tormentor in a cruel, bloody episode. I began the work of assisting him just three days ago, but I've already become familiar with his dramatic story."

He gazed compassionately at the discarnate tormentor and proceeded:

"They used to work together in a big city and were involved in the trinket business. The murderer had been working for the victim since childhood, and when he reached legal age, he demanded that his boss – who had also been his mentor – pay him for his many years of work. His boss refused the demand outright, citing the many years he had dedicated to him during his childhood and youth. Instead, he would provide him with an advantageous position in the business and would

grant him a substantial stake in it, but he would not pay him a cent for the work he had done; that up until then, he had looked after him like a son in constant need of help. They started quarreling. Offensive words, exchanged amongst vibrations of rage, inflamed the young man's mind. At the peak of his wrath he murdered his boss, overwhelmed by wild fury. Before fleeing the scene, however, the criminal rushed to the safe, which contained several stacks of money. He took out the huge amount he thought he deserved, but left a large sum intact to mislead the police on the following day. As a matter of fact, the next morning he himself went to the store, where the victim had been staying while his small family spent the long season out in the country. Pretending to be worried by the locked doors, he asked a guard to accompany him so that together they could break one of the locks. In a few minutes, news of the crime was spreading. Confounded by the perpetrator's skill, however, human justice was unable to explain what had had happened. The murderer was very careful in safeguarding the interests of the deceased. He ordered the safes and books to be sealed. He made arrangements for laborious inventories. He requested the help of the legal authorities to conduct a detailed analysis of the situation. He acted as a real advocate for the widow and the two small children of his deceased mentor, and thanks to his loyalty, they received a substantial inheritance. He mourned what had happened as if the discarnate were his own father. With the case closed due to the justice system's inability to solve the mystery, he discreetly withdrew to a large industrial center, where he invested his financial resources in profitable activities."

With a different gleam in his eye, Calderaro paused briefly and then added:

"He managed to deceive others, but he couldn't deceive himself. The discarnate spirit focused his mind on the idea of

vengeance and began hounding him without mercy. The deceased clung to his victim's psychic organism like ivy on a porous wall. The murderer did everything possible to lessen his constant persecution. He doubled his business enterprises in hopes of relief, undertaking initiatives that resulted in huge sums flowing into his coffers, greatly increasing his bank accounts. Realizing that his large financial assets had not reduced his unconfessable suffering and feelings of dread, he rushed into marriage, eager to pacify his soul. He married a young woman with the highest moral qualities and they had five adorable children. Enveloped in the spiritual atmosphere of his wife, he managed to keep his balance somewhat, although his victim never let go of him. At times he became engulfed by the cruelest depression and was assailed by nightmares that were strange from his family's point of view. He continued to resist, however, supported to a certain extent by the assistance that his wife had long been guaranteed from our realm. Nonetheless, although human laws might reflect the fallibility of incarnate human beings, the divine laws never fail. Harboring the dark energies accumulated on his path since the night of the murder, our unfortunate friend had kept deep inside all the destructive impressions gathered in the instant of his downfall. A public confession of his crime repulsed him, although it could have mitigated his anguish to a certain extent by releasing disastrous, pent-up energies."

Calderaro paused again.

He touched the cortex area and then continued:

"The criminal's mind, besieged by the victim's constant presence disturbing his memory, became fixated in the mid region of the brain; the pain of remorse didn't allow him easy access to the upper region of the perispiritual body, where human beings' noblest principles build the sanctuary for the manifestations of Divine Consciousness. Terrorized by his

memories, he froze with relentless fear before the judgments of his conscience. On the other hand, ever more interested in ensuring his family's well-being – his sole oasis in the scalding desert of harsh reminiscences – the unhappy man, respected at the time by virtue of the social position money had conferred on him, plunged himself into frenzied and ceaseless activity. Living mentally almost exclusively in the mid area of the brain, he only felt a little peace by being constantly on the move and by working in any possible, albeit disorderly, way to keep his mind occupied as he tried to flee from himself through any means within reach. He would go to bed exhausted, and the following day he would wake up worn-out and drained from having dueled with his invisible persecutor during sleep. He ended up triggering the instability of his perispiritual body, which became reflected in the motor zone, giving rise to organic chaos."

Indicating with his index finger, he emphasized:

"Notice the cortical centers."

I looked in wonder at that marvelous microscopic world. The pyramidal cells – distinguishable by their size – displayed the importance of their functions in the laboratory of neural energies. On closer observation, it didn't seem like I was examining the living tissue of the gray-white matter at all: my impression was that the cortex was a robust dynamo at work. Could it be that we were looking at some complex electrical device? In spite of such impression, I noticed that the cerebral matter was beginning to soften.

I was puzzled, unable to utter anything worthwhile. The Assistant came to my aid and explained:

"We are looking at the perispiritual organ of the human being, which is fastened to its physical duplicate in the same way that certain parts of the physical body are in close contact with its outer cover. The entire neural organization of the individual represents the perispiritual powers that have been gradually

gained by the spirit over many millennia. Upon being reborn in perishable form, our subtle body[7] – characterized on our less-dense spirit plane by extreme lightness and extraordinary plasticity – is subjected on the physical plane to the laws of recapitulation[8], heredity and physiological development, according to the merit or demerit we bring with us on our mission or needed learning experience. The physical brain is a most complex device, in which our 'self' reflects its life. Through it, we sense external phenomena according to our receptive capacity, determined by experience. Therefore, it varies from individual to individual in light of the multiplicity of positions on the evolutionary scale. On their way toward the human species, neither apes nor anthropoids display brains completely equal to each another. Each individual presents a brain according to his or her progress. Primitives display a perispiritual brain with vibrations quite different from those of civilized humans. From this point of view, the brain of a saint emits waves that are different from those emitted by the mental source of a scientist. Earth's academic schools bind themselves to the conceptualization of the tangible form as it goes through the changes of infirmity, old age or death. Here, however, we examine the organism that models the manifestations of the physical realm, and we realize that the entire nervous system derives from a sublime order. The nerve cell is an entity of an electrical nature, nourished daily by the appropriate fuel. There are sensitive, motor, intermediary and reflex neurons. Some receive external sensations, whereas others collect impressions from the conscience. In the entire cellular cosmos, switches and conduits, elements of discharge and reception, are in motion. The mind is the director of this microscopic world, in which billions of cells and multiform energies are dedicated to serving

---

7 The perispirit. – Tr.

8 Repetition of experiences through reincarnation. – Tr.

it. Currents of willpower emanate from it, resulting in a vast network of stimuli reacting to the external milieu or catering to the suggestions of the inner self. Placed between the objective and the subjective, the mind is compelled by Divine Law to learn, verify, choose, reject, accept, collect, keep, enrich and illuminate itself, always progressing. From the objective plane, it experiences the difficulties and influences of the direct struggles of living; from the subjective sphere, it absorbs varying degrees of inspiration from the discarnate or incarnate minds that are attuned to it, as well as the results of its own mental creations. Although the mind seems stationary, it moves forward without retreat, under the unfailing actions of visible or invisible forces."

Following a natural pause in these explanations, countless related thoughts occurred to me.

How was I to interpret Calderaro revelations? Weren't the cells of the physiological body clothed in their own characteristics? Weren't they infinitesimal individualities, clustered together under the discipline of organic sectors, albeit almost free in their manifestations? Would they perhaps be duplicates of the spirit's cells? How did this theory reconcile with the liberation of micro-organisms following the death of the body? And if that were, in fact, the case, shouldn't the memory of incarnate humans be free of their temporary forgetfulness of the past?

The instructor perceived my unarticulated questions, calmly continuing as if to answer me:

"I understand your objections. I too voiced them once upon a time, when confronted with the newness of the subject. Today, however, I can tell you that if there is physiological chemistry, there is also spiritual chemistry, just as there is organic chemistry and inorganic chemistry, and it is extremely difficult to define the points where they act independently. It is nearly impossible to discern the dividing line between them,

and not even the most knowledgeable spirit would try to locate, with dogmatic precision, the point where matter ends and spirit begins. Cells are surprisingly differentiated within the physical body. They display a certain feature in the liver, another in the kidneys and yet another in the blood. They change endlessly, appearing and disappearing by the thousands in all the realms of organic chemistry per se. It is in the brain, however, that the domain of spiritual chemistry begins. There, the cellular elements are difficult to replace. The delicate landscape of a higher nature is always the same, for the work of the soul requires permanence, improvement and continuity. The stomach may be a distillery in which the microscopic world is revealed in all its animal-like tumultuousness. It is closer to the lower expressions of life because it doesn't have to remember which food was given to it to digest on the previous day. The organ of mental expression, on the other hand, requires chemical features of a sublimated nature because it is fed with experiences that must be registered, stored and remembered whenever appropriate or necessary. Hence, a higher form of chemistry takes place, endowing the brain with irreplaceable matter in the many departments of its inner laboratory."

The Assistant paused again for a few seconds, giving me time to digest it.

Then he continued attentively:

"Actually, there is no mystery in this at all. Let's look at our evolutionary ancestors. The spiritual principle dwelled in the tepid bosom of the seas through cellular organisms, which were preserved and multiplied through a process called fissiparity. Over thousands of years, it made a long journey in the sponge and began controlling autonomous cells, imposing on them the spirit of obedience and cooperation in the primeval formation of muscles. A long time passed before it rehearsed

the fundamentals of the nerve apparatus in the jelly-fish, then the worm, and then the amphibian as it dragged itself upward to emerge from the dark, murky depths of the waters to enjoy its first experiences in the meridian sun. How many centuries did it take, clothing itself in monstrous forms and improving itself here and there, aided by the indirect intervention of Higher Intelligences? That is impossible to answer for now. It nursed at the abundant breast of the earth, ceaselessly evolving through the millennia until it reached the highest region, where it managed to prepare its own food."

Calderaro gazed at me meaningfully and asked:

"Do you follow?"

The astonishment caused by the new ideas rousing my imagination kept me from any in-depth comment. My learned companion smiled and continued:

"As much as we try to simplify the explanation of this delicate topic, it always causes perplexity. What I mean, Andre, is that ever since the unknown moment of its creation, the spiritual principle has moved forward without stopping. It left the ocean floor, reached the surface of the protective waters, headed for the muddy banks, struggled in the mire, reached solid ground, experienced an abundant number of representative shapes in the forest, rose from the soil, contemplated the skies, and after long millennia, during which it learned to procreate, nourish itself, make choices, remember and feel, it gained intelligence … It has traveled from simple impulse to responsiveness, from responsiveness to sensation, from sensation to instinct, from instinct to reason. Throughout this laborious course, countless millennia have elapsed. In all epochs, we leave the lower realms in order to climb to higher ones. The brain is the sacred organ of the mind's manifestation on the journey from primitive animality to human spirituality."

My guide paused to pat my shoulder gently, like an experienced instructor encouraging his humble student, and added:

"In sum, humans of the last few dozens of centuries represent triumphant humanity emerging from primeval bestiality. We discarnates are still part of the many millions of still-unevolved spirits who participate in this condition, as we have not yet rid ourselves of all the inferior traits contained in our perispiritual body. After physical death, this circumstance compels us to live in equivalent forms in truly advanced societies, albeit similar to earthly communities. We oscillate between freedom and reincarnation, improving and perfecting ourselves, progressing until, through self-refinement, we gain access to the sublime expressions of the Superior Life, which we have not yet been given to comprehend. On both sides of existence, in which we move and within which we find the birth and death of the dense body as gateways of communication, constructive labor is a blessing that prepares us for our divine future. For all who remain observant of the Law, activities in the sphere we now occupy are richer in beauty and happiness because matter is more rarified and more compliant to our more lofty wishes. Nevertheless, in crossing over the river of rebirth, we are surprised at the hard work of recapitulation required for our learning. We sow there in order to reap here, improving, readjusting and upgrading ourselves until we harvest the perfect crop and fill our silos with sublime grain so that, capable and victorious, we may transfer to other 'heavenly worlds.' As for the work of redemption and expiation, however, we mustn't assume that the physical realm is the only one capable of offering the blessed opportunity of harsh, redemptive suffering. You are of course fully aware of the fact that in regions of darkness beyond the physical plane there are expiatory opportunities for the most unfortunate debtors, those who intentionally have contracted perilous debts before the Law."

I didn't interrupt the brief pause that followed, considering the inappropriateness of any questions on my part.

Calderaro continued kindly:

"You might ask why incarnates do not retain a full recollection of their extremely lengthy past, but it is quite natural, due to the perispiritual body's great ascendancy over the physiological mechanism. If the physical form has evolved and perfected itself, the same must be true of the perispiritual body down through the ages. Even we, in our relative spiritual condition, do not yet enjoy the process of full remembrance of the paths we have trod. We are not currently equipped with enough light to descend profitably into all the corners of the abyss of our origin; we will only acquire such an ability further on, when our soul is purified of all and any residue of darkness. However, in comparing our situation with the less lucid state of our incarnate brothers and sisters, it is important not to forget that the nerves, motor cortex and frontal lobes that we are now examining constitute regular points of contact between the perispiritual body and the physical apparatus, each being essential to the work of enlightenment and growth of the eternal being. More simply put, these points of contact are outlets for the impulses, experiences and higher concepts of the real personality, which is not extinguished in the grave, and which would not bear the burden of a dual life. In light of this, and because of the duties imposed on the waking consciousness for daily tasks, these outlets perform a buffer role: they are 'lampshades', acting beneficially for the incarnate soul so that it can work and evolve. Furthermore, for human beings in general, birth and death in the physical realm are biological jolts that are essential for renewal. In reality, there is no complete forgetfulness on earth, as there is no immediate restoration of memory in the spirit world in the periods that naturally follow the existences in the material

world. All humans preserve tendencies and faculties that are almost equivalent to an actual remembrance of the past, and after crossing over the grave, not everybody is able to suddenly recapture their memories. Those who are too materialized, lingering in low vibrational patterns in the realm of dense matter, cannot all of a sudden rekindle the light of their memory. They have to spend time ridding themselves of the heavy trappings to which they have inadvertently clung. Amid the human struggle, the neurons must be like more or less heavy 'resisters' so that the flow of memories does not diminish the edifying efforts of the incarnate soul engaged in the noble goals of evolution or redemption, progressive development or sublime ministry. It is important to realize that our mind acts on the perispiritual body here in the spirit world with much wider powers, thanks to the singular nature and elasticity of the matter that presently defines our form. Nonetheless, in our spheres of action, this does not prevent coarse manifestations, lamentable downfalls and complex illnesses, because, even here, the mind – the master of our body – is open to vice, negligence and ruinous passions."

I risked a question during a spontaneous break:

"How can we more simply interpret the three regions of the brain's life we are referring to?"

The Instructor didn't hesitate:

"In translating impulsiveness, experience and the higher concepts of the soul, the physical body's nerves, motor area and frontal lobes are areas of fixation for the incarnate or discarnate mind. Any excessive delay in one of those three areas, along with the actions to which they give rise, determines the destiny of the individual cosmos. Individuals who remain stationary in the realm of the impulses are lost in a maze of cause and effect, wasting both time and energy. Those who give themselves entirely to mechanical efforts, without consulting the past and

without organizing the bases for their future, mechanize their life, depriving it of edifying light. On the other hand, those who live exclusively in the temple of higher ideas expose themselves to the danger of contemplation without labor, of self-denial without benefit. In order for our mind to progress toward higher realms, it must be balanced, making use of past achievements to guide its current endeavors while simultaneously sustaining itself with the hope that flows crystal-clear from the lofty fount of higher idealism. By means of this fount, it can capture restorative energies from the divine plane and thus construct a sanctifying future. And since we are indissolubly linked to those who are attuned to us in accordance with infallible universal purposes, whenever we lose our balance due to an excessive mental fixation in one of the aforementioned areas, we contact other incarnate and discarnate minds whose conditions are comparable to our own."

With a fraternal air, my instructor asked:

"Do you understand?"

I nodded with sincere happiness because I had finally assimilated the lesson.

Calderaro made magnetic passes over the patient's head, enveloping him in beneficial fluids, and after a long pause, he said to me:

"Here are two individuals whose minds are fixated in the area of the primary instincts. The incarnate one, after pounding his thoughts with repeated vibrations fleeing from his memories and remorse, has ruined his motor centers. He has also disorganized the glandular system and has disturbed the vital organs. The discarnate one has converted all his energies to feed his ideas of vengeance, giving way to hatred, where he remains isolated from reason and altruism. Their situation would be different if both had forgotten the offense and had

picked themselves up through constructive labor and fraternal understanding in the sanctuary of true forgiveness."

The Assistant displayed a new twinkle to his penetrating eyes and added:

"This goes to show that Jesus Christ had plenty of reasons to recommend that we love our enemies and pray for those who persecute and slander us. This isn't mere virtue, but a scientific principle of liberation for the individual, of progress for the soul, of spiritual magnitude: it is in thought that causes reside. An age will come when love, fraternity and understanding – defining the states of the spirit – will be as important to the incarnate mind as bread, water and medicine. It's only a matter of time. It is right to always be divinely optimistic and expect the good. In general terms, the human mind ascends toward higher knowledge, even if it may sometimes seem to be doing the exact opposite."

For the next several minutes, Calderaro continued to apply vigorous magnetic radiations, which, enveloping the patient's head and spine, looked to me to be extremely restful, because the previously tormented patient soon fell into a peaceful sleep as if he had taken a very gentle anesthetic. Soon thereafter, he was on our plane, temporarily outside his dense vehicle and seized with dread before his merciless tormentor still sitting motionless at one of the corners of the bed.

I realized that the patient hadn't noticed our presence – unlike his tormentor, who sat in quiet expectation.

I thought that the Assistant would surely address them with long counseling. Calderaro, however, remained completely silent.

I couldn't contain myself:

"Why don't we help them with enlightening words?" The patient looked afflicted, while his persecutor was now assuming a more aggressive manner. "Why not restrain the cruel hand that threatens this wretched being? Wouldn't it be best to prevent a

quarrel that could lead to unpredictable consequences for the hospitalized patient?"

The instructor listened and answered calmly:

"We would speak in vain, Andre, because we still don't know how to love them as if they were our brothers or sons. To both of us – spirits of somewhat advanced reasoning but of less sublime sentiments – they are two unfortunates and nothing more. For the time being, we can give them what we have, that is, helpful intervention in their outward suffering, within the limits of our acquisitions in the area of knowledge."

He looked at the large door nearby and pointed out:

"Certain arrangements haven't been forgotten, though. Sister Cipriana, the supervisor for my fraternal assistance group, will be here shortly."

A few more minutes went by, during which both persecutor and victim exchanged bitter words. My helpful mentor continued:

"Do you remember De Puysegur[9]?"

Yes, I recalled him vaguely. A free association of ideas went through my mind, reminding me of studies that I had done on some of Charcot's[10] accomplishments. However, I couldn't specify details since psychiatry had not been my specialty.

Calderaro continued helpfully:

"De Puysegur was one of the first magnetizers to discover revelatory sleep, during which it was possible to talk to the

---

9 The Marquis de Puysegur (1751-1825), a pupil of Mesmer's, used 'animal magnetism' [to induce] a state of sleep ... to communicate [with the patient]. [Mesmer: (1734-1815), an Austrian physician, widely acknowledged as the 'Father of Hypnosis'.] http://www.northshorehypnosis.com. – Tr.

10 Jean-Martin Charcot: 1825-1893. French neurologist; physician of the Salpêtriére [at one time a place for the mentally disabled, criminally insane, epileptics, and the poor; under Dr. Charcot, it became world famous as a psychiatric centre; nowadays it is a general teaching hospital]. Dr. Charcot is known for work on hysteria and hypnotism, which influenced his pupil Sigmund Fred: (1856-1939), Austrian neurologist and founder of psychoanalysis. *Webster's New Biographical Dictionary*. – Tr.

patient in a state of consciousness apart from the common one. His discovery has impressed psychologists ever since then. With it, a new therapy for the treatment of nervous and mental disorders appeared. Nevertheless, to us 'on this side' of life, the phenomenon is normal: every day, millions of people sleep under the magnetic influence of spirit friends in order to be helped with pressing matters."

"Then why don't we try right now to give verbal enlightenment to our friends here?" I insisted, eager to add my own input as I observed the unfortunate antagonists exchanging insults and accusations.

"Because if knowledge helps on the outside, only love helps on the inside," added my instructor serenely. "With our knowledge, we correct the effects as much as possible, and only those who love manage to reach down into the deeper causes. Our unfortunate friends require an inner intervention in order to modify their mental attitudes once and for all … And both of us, for the time being, only have knowledge without knowing how to love …"

At that moment, someone appeared at the door.

It was a sublime woman, revealing the age of maturity. A soft, compassionate light shone in her eyes. Feeling touched, I bowed respectfully. Calderaro patted my shoulder gently and whispered in my ear:

"This is Sister Cipriana, bearer of the divine fraternal love that we still haven't acquired."

5
The Power of Love

The messenger greeted us and Calderaro kindly introduced me.

She gazed at the sad scene and said to the Assistant:

"I congratulate you on the help that you have been providing to our two unfortunate brothers over the past few days. Now we shall address the final part of our work, confident of our success."

"My efforts," added Calderaro humbly, "were almost nothing, merely preparatory."

Sister Cipriana smiled affably and remarked:

"How can we reach the end without having started with the beginning?"

"Ah, sister! Knowledge can do very little compared with the much that love can do."

Her face displayed a peculiar expression, as if the compliment had deeply wounded her natural modesty. Covering up how worthy she really was, she offered:

"The Divine Lord knows that I'm still far from having accomplished as much as you think I have. I'm fragile and imperfect, and I must progress infinitely more to acquire the love that strengthens and perfects."

Keeping her gaze firmly on my companion, she added:

"We are cooperating fraternally in the work that belongs to the Most High. I hope that you, my friends, continue to do most of the work. For my part, I will only be attending to the simple duties of a maternal heart."

Having said that, she approached both unfortunate men and assumed a posture of prayer.

What could this woman of such an extraordinary countenance be asking the Higher Powers? Captivated, I could sense her deep sincerity and faithful humility. Her short prayer must have been saturated with sublime power, because a gentle light soon descended from On High upon her venerable brow. Cipriana gradually became more beautiful. Divine rays flowed down from invisible sources to envelop and transfigure her completely. I had the impression that her perispiritual body was absorbing that wonderful light, retaining it within her being.

After a few moments, she was surrounded by a resplendent aura, whose sanctity I felt I had to deeply respect. Startled but not concerned, I saw radiations of faint and gentle light flow from her eyes, chest area and hands. She looked beautiful, radiant, as if she were the very materialization of Murillo's[11] *Madonna* in a miraculous apparition.

I almost prostrated myself before her transfigured person – such were my emotions during that unforgettable moment.

She didn't look at us, perhaps out of humility in her desire to conceal her lofty position.

---

[11] Bartolomé Esteban Murillo, Spanish Painter, 1617-1682. – Tr.

She stretched out her hands toward the two unfortunates and touched them with her loving magnetism. I was amazed as I saw the power of that sublime woman changing their vibratory field. They both felt weakened, overpowered by a force that compelled them to keep still. Experiencing both respect and fear, they looked at each other with unspeakable astonishment, overwhelmed by an irrepressible and unknown emotion ... They displayed an anguished questioning look, when Cipriana lightly touched the area around their eyes. I noticed that both registered a forceful, undisguised jolt.

Recognizing the emissary's endowment of divine power, I noticed that the patient – partially freed from his body – and his relentless persecutor could now see us. They were awestruck. Seized by surprise, they screamed loudly. Because we all judge what we see through the filter of our acquired knowledge, they thought they were being paid a visit by the eminent Mother of Jesus. They identified their surroundings in harmony with the religious notions the world had impressed upon them.

The patient suddenly fell to his knees and broke into copious tears, overwhelmed by irrepressible emotion. The other, however, albeit perplexed and shaken, remained standing as if the blessed privilege of that moment had not been granted to him.

"Mother of Heaven!" exclaimed our hospitalized friend, weeping convulsively. "How do you deign visit the criminal that I am? I'm ashamed of myself. I'm an unforgivable sinner, beaten down by my misery ...Your light has shown me the full extent of the darkness in which I struggle! Have mercy on me, Lady!"

There was immense sincerity combined with immense pain in those words of affliction and repentance. His sobbing choked him up and he couldn't finish his touching plea.

Cipriana regarded him with glistening, moist eyes. She tried to lift him up but was unable to make him leave his knees.

The pious missionary had obviously been informed of all the details required for the successful outcome of her mission in those moments, because, embracing him maternally, she called him by name, explaining:

"Pedro, my son, I am not who you think based on the living trust that has touched your soul. I am merely your sister in eternity. However, I was also a mother at one time and I know how much you are suffering."

Pedro raised his supplicant eyes and looked at her through a thick veil of tears. Although he was visibly moved by what she had said, he remained in his posture of reverence and humility.

"I killed a man!" he exclaimed, giving vent to his emotions.

Cipriana stroked his tear-soaked face and added:

"I know."

After a few moments, in which she divided her affectionate gaze between Pedro and his tormentor, who kept himself at a short distance out of respect, she addressed the patient intentionally so that she could be heard by his avenging companion:

"Pedro, why did you take your brother's life? Why did you think you had the power and right to violate the divine harmony?"

Showing that she perceived his innermost thoughts, she proceeded:

"You imagined you were serving justice with your own hands, when in fact you were only giving vent to destructive rage. How could you think you were balancing life by causing death? How could you reconcile justice with crime, when we know that a truly just person is one who labors and hopes in the Father, the Supreme Giver of Life? You committed murder long ago, supposing you were settling a heavy debt by spilling blood ...You destroyed the body of a friend who had become unappreciative and hard. However, ever since that tragic moment, you've heard your divine conscience repeating the age-

old question: 'Cain, what have you done to your brother?' You've been living a miserable and unhappy life. Your soul has been shackled to your victim, learning that evil will never harmonize with the good and that the Law charges double to those who oppose its wise and sovereign precepts. You destroyed a brother's peace and lost your own. You eliminated his physical vehicle but have been walking around shackled to your own, feeling it as a heavy burden … You believed you were applying the law to yourself, but ended up distorting destiny, putting a dangerous curve on your path, which could have been straight and bright otherwise. Fearing yourself for feeling like a reprobate in every way, you sought refuge in frenzied and mechanistic work. You gained wealth that never brought you peace. You achieved a high social position among men but felt increasingly sad and forsaken in its confines … Pedro, why haven't you ever considered sanctifying prayer? Why haven't you done penance, humbling yourself at the feet of your victim in a sincere and real desire for regeneration? Instead, you have preferred the mad chase after outward sensations, the flight into the realm of material gain, the transitory rise to positions of deceitful dominance … Terrified, you have tried to escape your inner tribunal, where the power of your spirit reproaches your condemnable behavior!

"But it is never too late to lift up your soul and heal your wounded conscience. Exhausted from suffering, you have given in to infirmity and have approached madness. With a wounded soul and a body in disarray, you appealed to Divine Mercy, and that is why we are here. However, my friend, we are not saying all of this to punish your spirit. It has already been punished and is unhappy enough! We have come to encourage you toward regeneration. Who could condemn anyone after partaking of the vicissitudes of the flesh? Who could feel sufficiently pure and sanctified enough to cast the

first stone, even after having crossed over the ashen borders of the grave? Who amongst us has gone through the waterways of the swamp without reproach? No, Pedro, the foundation of the divine work is immeasurable love. We are here to love you and our aim is to raise your consciousness to the infinite realms of the life eternal. You have prayed and called out to us. You have opened your mind to regenerative power, and we are your brothers and sisters. In the past, many of us too entered the dark valleys of murder, injustice and death. Nevertheless, we stopped along the way to renounce our crimes, and with tears we mended the links of the chain broken by our imprudence. And by cultivating forgiveness and humility, we learned that only love saves and edifies forevermore.

"Remember your own needs, cease your path of affliction, reconsider your attitude and make a new commitment before the Divine Justice."

After a long pause, Cipriana opened her maternal arms and added:

"Get up and come to me. I'm your spiritual mother in God's name."

With glistening, tearful eyes, the patient stood up like a child, which touched our hearts, and exclaimed:

"I deserve such grace?"

"Why not, my son? The Father doesn't answer our pleas with words of condemnation. We have come to you in the name of him who is our Supreme Lord."

As she said this, she held him to her heart. There was such gentleness in that unexpected embrace that, except for us, others might say that they were witnessing the reunion of a caring mother and her missing child after a long and excruciating separation.

Showing unbounded trust, the unfortunate fellow leaned his head on one of her shoulders and whispered like a child:

"Mother of Heaven, no one on earth has ever spoken to me like this."

One could see his relief, obvious by his happy countenance.

Cipriana kindly reassured him:

"You absolutely must quiet your excited mind and place your old anxieties in the hands of the Lord."

I was greatly touched. I looked at Calderaro and saw that tears weren't flowing from my eyes only. They were also streaming down his peaceful face.

Responding to my silent query, he spoke to me in a barely audible voice:

"God willing, Andre, we too may learn how to love and acquire the power to transform hearts."

Cipriana didn't seem to be concerned with our presence and moved toward the persecutor, supporting Pedro in her arms as if he were her ailing son. His persecutor waited for her, standing up straight and arrogant, unmoved by the words that had overwhelmed our hearts. Far from intimidated, the missionary approached and nearly touched him, addressing him humbly:

"What are you doing, Camilo, shutting yourself off to mercy?"

Displaying inconceivable indifference, the persecutor cruelly retorted:

"What can a victim like me do except hate without mercy?"

"Hate?" replied Cipriana, without being affected. "Do you know what that means? Victims impervious to forgiveness and understanding usually surpass the hardness and evil of the damned, causing horror and compassion. How many avail themselves of the title 'victim' just to manifest the monstrosities that fill their hearts! How many take advantage of someone's unfortunate moment of thoughtlessness to begin centuries of persecution in the hell of rage! Your status as a victim does not

confer holiness on you. You've availed yourself of this condition to sow ruin and misery, darkness and destruction along your pathway. Of course, Pedro hurt you in a moment of insanity, lost in the illusion of turbulent youth. However, even though you were the father of a family and supposedly a sensible and prudent man, you didn't find in your spirit the least trace of fraternal mercy to forgive him. For twenty years, you have emitted the poison of vipers like a starved jackal. Instead of winning the laurel of victors in Christ, you have preferred the dagger of vengeance, like the most hardened villains. Where will you end up, my son, with your despicable sentiments? To what wall of anguish will you be shackled by God's justice?"

Heavy tears flowed from Cipriana's eyes.

Camilo wavered between inflexibility and capitulation. His face was extremely pale, and when it seemed to us that he was about to reply, the missionary addressed my instructor and asked him humbly:

"Calderaro, my friend, please assist me. Let's go to Pedro's home, where Camilo will attend to our requests."

My companion didn't hesitate. He turned to me and replied:

"Out Sister will transport Pedro herself, but the other one is terribly enslaved to inferior thoughts and criminal intentions and is too heavy: you and I will have to carry him."

Offering him our arms, with Calderaro on his right and myself on his left, Camilo didn't react. Maybe he understood the uselessness of any rebelliousness and thus he let us take him without protest.

We set out on a quick journey.

In a few minutes we entered a comfortable home, where a woman was knitting in her living room with her two small children.

Their homey conversation was sweet and lofty.

"Mom," said the younger child, "where's Neneco?"

"He went back to work."

"What about Celita?"

"She's at school."

"And Marquinhos?"

"He's at school too."

"I wanted everyone to be here, at home …"

"How come?" asked the mother, smiling.

"Don't you know, Mom? So we can pray for Dad. Did you see how sad and gloomy he looked last night?"

The young mother displayed a certain affliction in her eyes, but objected firmly:

"We have to trust in God. The doctor told us not to worry, and I know that Providence will hear us."

She gave the child a knowing look and urged:

"Go have fun, Guilherme. Go play."

Little Guilherme, however, rested his right arm on a children's book, brooding as if he'd subtly detected our presence, while the woman, suddenly abandoning her knitting, went to weep in a remote bedroom.

We were touched by the scene, when Cipriana addressed Camilo, who was very displeased:

"Let's proceed. Yes, Pedro did take your physical life and contracted an awful debt. But doesn't the voice of this boy devoted to prayer touch your hardened spirit? This is the home that the criminal Pedro set up in order to form the renewed Pedro … He has been working exhaustively here to rectify himself before the Law. Acknowledging the terrible responsibility he assumed with the blow with which he thoughtlessly struck you, he plunged into disorganized and ceaseless activity, thereby destroying his physical centers' stability. Not yet fifty years old, his body shows obvious signs of decrepitude. Although he has committed a serious wrong, he has been doing his utmost to redeem himself

by leading a noble and useful life. He has provided support to a devoted wife and has given shelter to five little children, making an effort to guide them toward the good through honest work and edifying study. Pedro obviously has grown in the opinion of his friends and has climbed to a position of material wealth; however, from his own experience, he knows now that money doesn't solve the fundamental problems of destiny and that our lofty reputation before others doesn't always correspond to reality. Despite all the advantages gained in the material realm, he has been ill, unfortunate and miserable … But in spite of all that, he has to his credit the work he has carried out with good intentions, the acknowledgment of a wife who has ennobled him, and the prayers of five grateful children.

"As for you, what have you done? For exactly twenty years you haven't harbored any other purpose except to do away with him. Hateful vengeance has been the exclusive object of your destructive intentions. Your present suffering was born out of the pleasure of revenge. Is it worth being the victim, to receive the sanctifying crown of pain, only to sink so low on the ladder of life?"

The benefactress paused briefly, looked at him compassionately, and proceeded:

"Nevertheless, Camilo, our strong words aren't spoken in this sanctuary as an unappealable sentence. Above all, you are our brother, a creditor of our affection, of our loyal respect. The purpose of our visit is to help you. Maybe you will refuse our fraternal alliance, but we believe in your regeneration. In times past, we too lingered in the fatal abyss into which you have thrown yourself. We spent a long time in the role of a poisonous viper, focusing only on itself and waiting for a chance to kill or hurt. However, the All-Merciful Lord taught us that true freedom is that which is born out of perfect obedience to his sublime laws, and that only love has enough power to save, uplift

and redeem. We are all brothers and sisters, susceptible to the same downfalls, children of the same Father … Thus, we don't speak to you as angels, but as regenerated human beings on a pilgrimage to Higher Realms!"

There was such a caring inflection in those tender and wise considerations that the once cold and impassive persecutor suddenly burst into tears. In spite of such a change, he pointed at Pedro and exclaimed:

"I want to be good, but I'm suffering! I feel oppressed by atrocious suffering. If God is so compassionate, why has he forsaken me?!"

Those sobs bursting from his tortured soul struck me at the bottom of my heart. How could one not weep as well at that emotional scene? Didn't Camilo and Pedro, intertwined in crime and redemption, represent all of us fallible human beings? Didn't Cipriana, tolerant and maternal, personify Divine Compassion, always inclined to teach forgiveness and to correct through love?

Upon hearing the persecutor's words, the missionary remarked:

"Who among us, my friend, can understand the whole meaning of suffering? You have asked why the Lord has allowed you to undergo such a hard trial … Isn't that the same as asking a potter what compelled him to set the form of a delicate piece in scorching heat, or asking an artist what led to the hammering of a raw stone to turn it into a magnificent sculpture? Camilo, pain enlarges life and sacrifice sets it free. Afflictions are a problem of divine origin. In trying to solve them, the spirit can rise to a resplendent peak or plunge into a frightful abyss, for many draw from suffering the patience with which they kindle the light to defeat their own darkness, whereas others draw from it the rocks and thorns of rebelliousness, with which they fall into the darkness of the chasm."

Seeing that the wretched persecutor was weeping bitterly, Cipriana continued after a brief silence:

"Go ahead and weep! Let it out! Tears of remorse have a miraculous power for the wounded soul."

The emissary became quiet for a few minutes. Her very lucid eyes now seemed to roam a distant landscape ...

Almost automatically, she took Camilo into her arms, keeping the contenders snuggled to her bosom as if she were their mother.

After a while, she looked tenderly at Pedro's tormentor and proceeded:

"You talk about the misfortune that has harmed you; you invoke Providence with disrespectful expressions ... O my son, silence the gift of speech if you can't use it for the good. I too lived on the earth, but I didn't suffer as much as I should have, considering the treasure of spiritual enlightenment that I received from heaven through suffering. I lost my dreams, my home, my husband, my children! The Lord gave them to me; the Lord took them away. My two boys were murdered in a civil war waged in the name of legal principles. My two daughters, seduced by pleasure and gold, scoffed at my hopes and remain in the dark realms, entangled in dangerous illusions. My husband was the only friend left to me. However, when leprosy assailed my flesh, he too forsook me, seized by visible horror. All those whom I loved rejected me. All of the world's benefits vanished. Even so, as my limbs were falling off my wasting body, when I found myself delivered over to the extreme of abandonment by those dear to me, the song of hope grew strong within me. My soul glorified the Lord of Life Triumphant ... At one time he had granted me the blessings of health and youth; then, he took back those assets, which I had on loan. He deprived me of my loved ones, stripped me of my organic stability, and sent me hunger

and pain. Nevertheless, as my solitude turned bitterly complete, my faith arose clearer and stronger … What did a miserable woman like me need except to suffer in order to sanctify hope? And how much more will I still need in order to deserve access to higher sources? Who are we, if not vain worms whose minds are poorly used, to whom Endless Mercy has manifested itself in a thousand ways, but in vain?"

Then it was Camilo's turn to kneel.

A beam of light began radiating from Cipriana's chest and pierced his heart like a spear of crystalline moonlight.

Now on his knees, the poor wretch kissed her right hand in a moving gesture of gratitude, covering it with tears.

"No," he said, weeping, "you wouldn't have spoken to me like this if you didn't love me! It isn't your words that have convinced me … your sentiment has changed me!"

And as had happened with Pedro, he cried out:

"Mother of Heaven, deliver me from my passions! Unlock the shackles that I myself have forged … I want to flee my awful memories … I want to leave, to forget, to strive in the regenerative struggle to start over again!"

Cipriana entrusted to us the incarnate patient, whose body was resting in a nearby hospital. With a triumphant smile of maternal tenderness, she embraced the former persecutor and whispered:

"Blessed are you who have listened to the appeal of redeeming forgiveness. May the Father bless you forever! Let's go! Providence offers regenerative work to all of us."

She embraced the repulsive figure of the ex-persecutor, snuggled him to her heart and approached us, addressing us gently:

"My friends, I thank you for your fraternal cooperation. Our suffering brother will move on in my company. I hope to place him in restorative activity."

And before saying goodbye, she informed my guide:

"Brother Calderaro, I'll be waiting for your cooperation tonight on behalf of Candida, who must return to 'our side' tomorrow for good. We must save her little daughter from total insanity."

The messenger left, holding the deviant as if he were a precious burden, while a new light brightened my spirit.

The Assistant touched my shoulder and said:

"The heart that loves is filled with renewing power. Once upon a time, Jesus said that there are demons that respond to regeneration only 'through fasting and prayer.' Sometimes, Andre, as in this case, knowledge isn't enough. Human beings must be vitalized by the divine power that flows from the fasting derived from self-denial, and from the light of prayer born from universal love."

We were ready to take the patient back to the hospital, when the lady of the house appeared in the living room, dressed to go out, and told her children:

"Get ready, kids. We're going to visit your Dad in just a bit."

We took Pedro back to his bed, providing him with all the care possible.

He soon woke up smiling, feeling better – almost happy. He called the nurse, showing a new glimmer in his eyes. He no longer felt the persistent pain in his chest. Something – he thought – had eliminated the darkness in his head, like beneficent rain that cleanses and clears up a heavy sky.

After about an hour, his wife and children entered the room and shared in his well-being.

Weeping with joy, Pedro told them that he had had an enlightening dream. He assured them he'd been visited by the Holy Mother, who had reached out to him with her divine hands, overflowing with light.

As she listened to him, his wife broke out in abundant tears of joy and recognition. And Guilherme, his little son, filled with living faith, took his father's right hand and kissed it with filial affection and thankfulness to God.

Touched, I watched the intimate scene in which the family had found peace once again. Remembering Cipriana and her miraculously saving intercession, I understood that women, sanctified by sacrifice and suffering, are bearers of the Divine Maternal Love that intervenes in the world to ennoble human beings' sentiments.

6
Fraternal Help

In the darkness of the night, we were at the entrance to a modest room in a humble home.

A kind sister from our realm was waiting for us on the doorstep. She greeted us attentively.

Calderaro asked:

"And Candida? How is she?"

"She's doing fine. She should be with us for good tomorrow night. Sister Cipriana asked me to watch over her so that her disengagement would happen peacefully. I believe that our dear friend could have already passed to our side, but it seems that the young daughter she's leaving behind needs some care."

We went in.

A prematurely aged woman was lying in bed, awaiting death. The signs of the extinction of the vital tonus were obvious on her face.

Candida, the sister who deserved our attention so much, was still attached to her body by very fragile threads. Through

the soft light discharged by her mind and which haloed her brow, I could see the greatness of her soul and serene heroism.

A young woman with a pale face and weakened body was by her side stroking her gray hair. From time to time she would wipe the tears that streamed from her eyes.

The Assistant nodded to her and explained:

"That's her daughter who has come to say goodbye. Let's listen to them."

Candida, encouraging her with much difficulty, spoke movingly:

"Julieta, my daughter, take care of yourself. You know I probably won't be getting up again. I'm afraid of leaving you amid the conflicts of this world with no friendly hands ..."

The young woman was all choked up. Abundant tears bore witness to her utter anguish.

Her mom, however, tried hard to restrain her own emotions and continued selflessly:

"My sons have forsaken us. We're on our own and we must think things over. I've noticed that you've been more disturbed and afflicted these past few days. I get the feeling that the money we have isn't enough for our expenses. What's going on? I've been so much trouble for you in your young age! But I still trust in Jesus. Every day I ask the Lord not to forsake us. I'm afraid that your destiny might go awry because of me ... Other times, my dearest, I fear that you might end up going crazy."

And after a brief pause, during which she lovingly squeezed the right hand of the young woman, who looked no older than twenty, the ailing woman continued:

"Listen. You know that our expenses have been enormous over the past few months. My surgeries were extensive and difficult. The bills are huge. What about the money? Set my mind at ease, my dear!"

The young woman wiped her tears and replied:

"Don't worry, mom! We've got enough. I'm working."

"But there's so little money in sewing," emphasized the patient in dismay.

"Oh, don't worry so much! In addition to our normal income, I took out a small loan. In a few months everything will be back to normal."

"May God allow it."

After a longer pause, the ailing woman asked:

"Where's Paulino?"

Her daughter's face turned red and she answered, embarrassed:

"I don't know."

"You haven't seen each other for a while?"

"Nope," the young woman replied shyly.

"I'd like to see him. I'm afraid I might die at any moment ... and I can't think of anyone I could ask to help you. You're so young; what'll become of you, alone and at the whim of circumstances? The world is full of evil men waiting for a chance to disgrace ..."

A few tears escaped from Candida's lucid eyes, burning my heart.

"If I die, dear child," she said with touching emphasis, "don't give in to temptation. Seek your income in worthwhile work. Don't be taken in by the promises of an easy life. You know that my widowhood left us in dire straits, but your father left us in an honest poverty filled with blessings. It's true that your brothers were fascinated by material gain. They may have abandoned and forgot us, but I've never regretted humility and work ... I lost my health early on and my heart was soon struck by disenchantment; even so, in this small, poor bed of silence and grief, peace is the crown of my soul and I've come to realize

that there's no greater fortune than a peaceful conscience … The Lord knows the reasons for our suffering and privations, and there's every reason to praise him … From all that I've suffered, there's one treasure left to me: your dedication, my child. Your loving care has made me rich. I shall die happy, knowing that on earth a daughter's heart will remember me with prayers of everlasting love … But I don't want you to be good and gentle only for my sake; obey God too. Consecrate your love and trust to him. He is our Father of Infinite Goodness and he only asks us to have a simple heart and to live a pure life. Resign yourself, my daughter, to the divine purposes amidst the turmoil of human trials, and don't lose heart!"

"Oh mom, hush!" sobbed the young woman, letting her heart out. "Don't say such things! We'll always be together. You're not going to die. We'll live for each other. We'll never be apart … Don't worry! I don't want to see you suffering … Everything will pass. The doctor promised to start a more intensive treatment. Let's have faith!"

With a sad smile, Candida touched the young woman's hands and said:

"Thank you, dearest! I feel calm and happy."

She glanced at the hands of a nearby clock and added:

"Go in peace! Visiting hours are over."

They kissed each other emotionally, and after a tender farewell, Julieta left.

"Let's follow her," said Calderaro attentively. "We must assist her with magnetic resources. That's what Cipriana asked me to do."

On our way, my instructor shed some light on the dying woman's story:

"Candida became a widow when she was very young. She had three children: two boys and Julieta, and their education

imposed a bitter renouncement of life's riches on her. She struggled, worked and suffered with resignation and courage. Her sons hated the poverty of their mother's home, left her and traveled to distant places in answer to the unedifying impulses of youth. The widow persevered in her simple life and dedicated herself to preparing for her daughter's future. She got her into sewing, and the girl soon proved to be an excellent professional. However, after a few years of tough ordeals, the worthy mother collapsed from exhaustion. She was hospitalized and underwent several surgeries, with no appreciable results. Her condition worsened to the point that she's been hospitalized for the last ten months. At first, Julieta managed to take care of their financial demands by herself, but as time went by, the poor woman struggled amid necessity and exhaustion. Having depleted all her resources, she resorted to relatives, who cautiously declined. She appealed to friends, who showed indifference.

"Their expenses continued to grow relentlessly. Her sewing wasn't providing the income they needed. She visited her mom daily at end of the day, keeping abreast of her increasingly serious condition. Crazed with affliction, she knocked on every door but they all remained locked. Incapable of deeply analyzing the situation with her mother, who, of course, would not want her sacrifice, Julieta accepted an insidious invitation. She began working nights at a place of entertainment, with the sole purpose of earning more money. She would sing and dance, and consequently increase their income.

"From then on, she started playing the role of a lamb besieged by wild animals. For some time she resisted the appeals of the senses, but the time came when she could no longer avoid the power of physical sensations. Attracted by a man's proposals – the Paulino her mother referred to – she didn't have the strength to resist. She accepted his ill-timed protection. She forsook the

sewing machine and moved from the modest room where she had been living so meagerly. Thus, she settled in the midst of nighttime entertainment, and whenever she appeared in public, she was always accompanied by Paulino, who was interested in taking advantage of her youth and beauty like a vain gentleman showing off a jewel.

"Julieta hid the reality from her mother's eyes. She dressed modestly for her daily visits, and when Paulino accompanied her to the hospital for the first time, she introduced him to Candida as being a mere friend.

"The young woman's subsequent afflictions changed her health, however. She was exhausted and ill. Remembering her mother's example, her conscience bothered her atrociously. Easy pleasures didn't appease her sensitive and affectionate soul. Having a lot of money didn't succeed in lessening her dismay. At the same rate that she received from others the approval of her physical gifts, she seemed to lose her own peace of mind. Prey to irrepressible depression, she spent day and night afflicted by a highly troubled mind. Why hadn't she persisted in her modest life till the end? Why didn't she confess to her mom and receive the guidance she needed? On the other hand, she felt justified: she needed Paulino's financial help in order to help the one who had given her life. She had tapped all the sources that seemed clean and accessible to her, but every hand had remained closed to her pleas ... But was she doing the right thing? She didn't have the courage to return to the prayers of yester times. Her anguished mind struggled between the demands of the material world and the imperative claims of the spirit.

"Nonetheless," concluded Calderaro, attentively – her mother's prayers have accompanied her all along her rugged path. And Candida has not been suffering in vain. As a faithful collaborator of many areas of service, she is the creditor of many blessings."

After filling me in on that drama so common among young women of our times, I followed my guide to the room where Julieta would receive his assistance regarding her troubled state of mind.

Recalling what her mother had said, the young woman settled on a couch, where she burst into convulsive weeping. Torturous thoughts collided with one another in her diseased mind. Heavy, dark colored vibrations were filtering down from her head and settling in her respiratory system. They obstructed the pleura, invaded the alveoli and from there they moved on to the heart, impacting the exchange of blood, at which time the fluidic substance of these mental discharges vanished, absorbed by the arteries. I noticed, however, that this matter, originating from the disturbed mind and impressing itself upon the physiological mechanism, was assimilated by the blood, which in turn returned it to the physical brain where it accumulated in all the areas closest to the gray matter.

As a result, I noticed not only the young woman's red and swollen eyes, but also the harbingers of much more serious organic disturbances.

Having identified the disturbances manifesting in the brain and the medulla oblongata, I looked at my guide and asked:

"Isn't this the mysterious beginnings of lethargic encephalitis?"

"A lot worse than that," answered Calderaro. "The deranged mind emits destructive energies which, although they may strike others, first reach the organic cosmos of the sender. Having decided on a lifestyle that would cause her to suffer violent and continuous mental conflict, Julieta began discharging energies deadly to her. Her contact with her mother endowed her with a lofty education, which improved her principles and ennobled her sentiments, so much so that she can no longer

reconcile herself with a debased existence in the physical realm. As the spirit develops it invariably becomes enlightened. Thus, possessing a sublime inner light for the human journey, she would easily reap peace, joy and edification as a woman if the appropriate circumstances came her way, where she would feel the healthy manifestation of the abilities of her soul. Dignified marriage would be the field appropriate for her case as a woman ennobled by knowledge and virtue. But having surrendered to the temptations of which she was the target, she feels that she has "fallen down the ladder." Every day, she is constrained in silence to recall the examples of her mother, to reconsider her own attitude toward life and to realize that she is maladjusted. This incessant mental friction has been aggravated by the worst possible fluidic emissions from the environment she's frequenting now, and her mind has descended to the realm of the instinctive impulses. She is experiencing extreme difficulty trying to climb to the realm of loftier ideas, where the light of her conscience emits strong appeals for her to return to simplicity and harmony. This situation keeps her from fervent, sanctifying and regenerative prayer; hence the chaos the poor woman is fumbling around in. She's too well educated to reap any benefit from the milieu she's gotten herself involved in, and dominated by continuous anguish, she puts too much pressure on her grey matter, giving rise to lamentable organic imbalances."

Calderaro paused for a few moments, much like a teacher opening a pathway for his student's reflection, and added serenely:

"She isn't threatened merely by lethargic encephalitis: she's close to going mad, with various stages of disturbances brought on by cellular malfunction. But not only that. Under such circumstances, Julieta could be struck in other vital centers. She could catch pleurisy as an entryway for tuberculosis. Or she could easily fall prey to deplorable blood poisons, which would

be characterized by indefinable diseases of the veins or skin – or even fatal liver problems that would probably lead to the ruin and death of the body."

At this point my guide looked up and reflected:

"But ... divine justice never disregards compassion. Sometimes our headlong fall is a mere semi-disaster into which our despair has dragged us. Eternal Wisdom examines the motives of our actions, and whenever possible, it promptly lifts us up. Only when we completely eclipse ourselves from love and reason, deliberately fleeing the processes of divine assistance and keeping ourselves in the utter darkness of hatred and denial, do we face being fully unable to receive salvific influences; we must then await harsh trials over time under the compulsive forces of universal laws. Whereas the young woman cannot rise to a higher level – like a bird shot and wounded by a merciless hunter – her infirm mom remains in powerful, transforming prayer. Her daughter has fallen in order to aid her mother's body, but Candida has risen higher to save her daughter's soul. Consequently, Cipriana's loving power will take effect tonight."

Calderaro became silent, applying the weeping girl with magnetic assistance from our realm. With no problems worth mentioning, he removed a certain amount of dark matter emitted by her mind, and which had accumulated along the brain. However, I saw that he was leaving some of this substance in the cerebral chamber. I asked the reason why.

My friend took on a meaningful look and explained:

"I have instructions in this regard. Julieta mustn't receive our full assistance today. She must remain physically ill so that she misses her usual nighttime activities. In a few hours she and Paulino will be led in spirit to Candida's bedroom, where Sister Cipriana intends to use the few hours of partial disengagement through sleep in order to speak with Paulino."

I understood all this and once more I wondered at the order inherent to the spirit realm.

Next, Calderaro took me to assist a suffering brother – whose case we will examine in the next chapter so as not to break continuity in the process of assisting Julieta.

Around 2:00 a.m., my instructor and I returned to Candida's modest room. She was now outside of her withered material envelope and was resting in the arms of Cipriana, who was stroking her hair with the tenderness of a mother.

Enjoying extreme lucidity outside the physiological sphere, the patient was at peace and happy as she responded to our greetings. Other friends were beside her, reassuring her as her final hour approached.

We were conversing pleasantly, when two brothers from our plane entered the room leading Julieta and a gentleman whom I intuitively recognized.

Calderaro confirmed my intuition, and stated:

"This is Paulino. He has come to hear us out."

Both instinctively knelt before Cipriana, weeping emotionally as she held Candida in her loving arms. Aided by the magnetic assistance of the messengers who had brought them, they gazed at us in utter amazement; we could see, however, that they were more strongly attracted to Cipriana's light. They felt humiliated and vexed, recognizing the presence of some kind of heavenly power.

They were confused and tearful while Cipriana addressed the young man in particular:

"Paulino, I speak to you in the name of Divine Justice. May the Lord bless you so that you may listen to me with the ears of reason! Listen! Don't you think that Julieta is worthy of your strong, diligent support on her earthly journey? What are you making of your youth? A simple adventure of the senses?

Can't you see that human experience is a road that prepares us for eternity? What is life to you with its sublime gifts? Don't partake in the disgraceful conduct of our unenlightened brothers, who strive to turn women into unfortunate guinea-pigs for the game of the senses. Dignify your existence as a man by honoring the female mission. You were reborn on the earth and grew up in the care of your mother's devoted protection, and in a wife you will find the loving companion for your dreams of a rewarding fatherhood. So, why vainly persist in controlling a poor child out of a mere impulse of selfishness and ostentation? Doesn't it bother you to see Candida's prolonged affliction, tormented by cruel uncertainty regarding her daughter's future? Awaken to your commitments of a higher order. You haven't come into the world simply for pleasure. Earthly existence, my friend, is a blessed school of renewing enlightenment. What is driving you to such condemnable behavior? You are good and useful, intelligent and worthy. Why do you shun sanctifying responsibility?"

Weeping with unquenchable emotion, Paulino said nothing; but he did emit thoughts that were clear to us.

He shouldn't hesitate to get married, he thought, reflecting on the matter; however, he had met Julieta outside the sanctuary of her home in a circle of irresponsible persons and in surroundings not conducive to spiritual edification. Shouldn't he watch out? Shouldn't he plan marriage on more solid bases? After all, he had met the young woman in a nightclub. He had found her nearly homeless.

Sister Cipriana had grasped his ponderings, because she spoke again firmly after a brief pause:

"In response to your standard as a man of character, Julieta's afflictions render her a creditor of greater support. The poor girl didn't go looking for an objectionable nightclub because of ulterior motives. Aren't you aware of her consuming worries

as a dedicated daughter? Don't you realize that she went there looking for work and support, security and income? While you were interested in merely distracting your idle mind, Julieta was enduring humiliations while trying to obtain medicine for her sick mother ... How can you absolve yourself and condemn her? What gives you the right to stain the respectability of a young woman who has such sacred goals in mind? Are the sun's rays vile because they fall upon a swamp? Is the lily that adorns a corpse blameworthy? Paulino, awaken your conscience. It has been numbed by human indulgence! You haven't yet suffered sufficiently to bless and love life. Don't scorn the opportunity that is being offered to you! Help rescue this young woman; she didn't appear on your path by mere chance. Love and trust are not improvised endeavors: they are born under divine blessing, grow with one's struggles and consolidate down through the centuries. In most cases, affinity takes millennia to accomplish. You wouldn't have approached Julieta with such fondness if she hadn't been part of your spiritual past. Dedicate yourself to her; save her from madness and worthlessness. Offer her your support as a husband, and honor her life before death breaks your physical vessel to pieces with its invincible hands. It is nobler to give than to receive, more beautiful to love than to be loved, more divine to sacrifice oneself than to extort the sacrifice of others. Don't let the world's criticism affect you. At its basis human society is praiseworthy, but unjust when it exterminates the seeds of spiritual regeneration for a loftier life under the pretexts of self-preservation. Join us, Paulino! The Lord will bless your laudable gesture. Tomorrow, Candida will live the last hours of her current existence. Give her peace. Restore her well-being for all the grief she's gone through to preserve her daughter in a respectable position. Don't allow love to be corrupted in your soul. Sanctify it with responsibility

and fortify it with your inherent character, and Providence will be at your side forever."

The instructor became silent, but beams of sapphire light came from her heart to envelop the young man completely.

Paulino lifted his tear-filled eyes, gazed at her in gratitude and stated:

"I shall accept your words as if they were from my Mother in Heaven. Do with me as you please. I stand ready."

Cipriana affectionately returned Candida to her physical envelope and addressed the young couple:

"May the Father bless us all."

Julieta and Paulino were taken back to their room, while we stayed on in the patient's bedroom to assist with her discarnation process.

At 8:00 a.m. Cipriana suppressed the greater part of Candida's energies. Upon being called by the nurse on watch, the doctor stated that her death was imminent.

Her daughter was informed, arriving at midday in the company of Paulino, who looked visibly touched.

How beautiful is it to witness the indirect influence of the higher realm upon our incarnate fellow spirits!

Just as they had at the time of their corporeal sleep, upon realizing that the venerable woman was dying, they both knelt in tears, nearly in the same position of a few hours ago.

Candida gazed at the young man in a supplicant manner and spoke to him with difficulty, while Cipriana kept her right hand on her head so that her energies would not fade completely. The dying woman emotionally conveyed the anguish torturing her soul. She was afraid of leaving her inexperienced daughter in the world at the mercy of temptations. She appealed to Paulino's gentility, but he did not let her finish. With tearful eyes, he placed his index finger on the dying woman's lips and comforted her.

"Dona[12] Candida," he said respectfully, "don't mention this anymore. Today I awoke with my mind made up: Julieta and I will get married in just a few days. Tomorrow we'll start the paperwork for our commitment, before any circumstances interfere to jeopardize our wishes. So, you can rest assured. From now on, I too am your son."

Weeping copiously, the dying woman made a sign.

Julieta drew nearer her mother, while Paulino leaned his head on her prematurely gray hair. Supported by Cipriana, Candida united their hands in a symbolic gesture and kissed them affectionately.

That was the final gesture of her spent body. In a few minutes, her physical eyes closed forever, while her spirit eyes would open in our midst to contemplate the radiant trails of eternity.

[12] In Portuguese, a term indicative of respect. – Tr.

7
The Redemptive Process

As we were leaving the hospital the night before Candida's discarnation, Assistant Calderaro had remarked:

"There's no time to lose."

Our work of helping the dear patient had taken a few hours.

"The special aim of our effort," continued my esteemed friend, "is to impede the completion of the processes leading to insanity. The network of spiritual support to that end is almost infinite. A positive diagnosis of mental imbalance is always the end result of a long struggle. Of course, that does not include cases that are purely physiological, such as the invasion of syphilis into the cerebral matter. We are referring instead to the conflicts of personality imprisoned in introversion, instability, phenomena of involution, and tragedies involving crimes of passion – incidents that take place by the thousands each week all over the world. In the spheres closest to the daily struggles of ordinary individuals – where we are at present – there are many, many fraternal assistance organizations of such a nature.

This assistance is crucial for the human mind in its natural dislocations. The vast school of earth demands constant and complex spiritual collaboration. Of course, Divine Wisdom did not overlook a plan of service in this regard. If it has given Science the job of overseeing the harmonious unfolding of phenomena pertaining to the physical realm, and if it has given philosophy the task of accompanying Science to enrich its intellectual qualities, it has entrusted religion with the task of looking after the development of the soul, providing it with blessed enlightenment for the journey of ascension. Religious belief, however, especially during the past few years, has proven itself incapable of such an undertaking: it lacks suitable personnel. While scientific achievement has proven to be a gigantic tree harboring incarnate minds in its theory- and reason-filled branches, religion, subdivided into countless sectors, is more of a scrubby weed wasting away in the soil. Even so, Divine Love is aware of the obstacles that burden the circles of faith. Intellectual prowess may be sufficient for the investigation of knowledge, but the religious issue demands high sentiment-related capabilities. The former requires observation and persistence, whereas the latter entails an aptitude for self-denial. Consequently, in collaboration with resolute workers, countless legions of coworkers invisible to the human eye strive everywhere to aid those who are suffering and to encourage those who are serving the good as they continue to evolve. Thus, our efforts involving the incarnate mind are extensive and multiple. But we must agree that if this task is a cause for concern, it is also a source of satisfaction. We feel the contentment of older brothers and sisters in being able to help the younger ones. Undoubtedly, in humankind we are all one family."

Calderaro paused briefly so I asked out of curiosity:

"How is such help administered? Indiscriminately?"

"No," he explained, "the notion of order presides over our activity in all circumstances. It is nearly always the power of intercessory prayer that determines which help processes are to be used. Prayer, represented by an unmanifested desire, inner longings or spoken petitions, whether originating in the higher realms or emanating from the deep valley of disturbed human passions, is, strictly speaking, the starting point of all our activities."

I was about to pose a particular question arising from old concepts of religious separatism, when Calderaro, perceiving my thoughts, added calmly:

"We're not alluding to the prayers or longings of certain ideological currents: the label doesn't matter. We collaborate with the eternal spirit on its ascension to the divine realm, adding new strength to the good wherever it may be, regardless of any dogmatic formulas through which it manifests in human circles. Our rationale is not favoritism but higher spirituality, based on uniting substantial qualities on behalf of a better life."

At this point of his brief lecture as we were on our way to the task at hand, we finally arrived at a simple home that was surrounded by a well-tended garden.

"What we have here," he said, "is an embattled fellow spirit from a former time, who has reincarnated in a frightful condition. For a few weeks now, I've been assisting his mother with comforting passes. Because of the dreadful organic structure of her son, who has been linked to her for many centuries, the poor woman's mind is in peril. They are connected to each other through the shackles of serious commitments in the past. She is in the noble habit of praying at a set hour and we take advantage of these occasions to come to her aid."

The order in which our plane took care of matters was evident even in the smallest actions. Marveling at this fact, I silently followed Calderaro inside.

In a few moments we entered a small bedroom where a skinny, sick little boy was resting and whimpering. He was flanked by two spirits as miserable as he was, judging from their strange appearance. The boy inspired pity.

"This is the firstborn child of an apparently happy couple. He has been paralyzed since his rebirth eight years ago," stated Calderaro nodding toward him. He can't speak, walk or sit up; he sees very poorly and hears almost nothing on the human plane. On the mental plane, however, he is living as a convict aware of everything as he serves a harsh sentence of his own doing. About two centuries ago, he ordered the deaths of many of his compatriots during a civil insurrection. He took advantage of the political-administrative chaos in order to take revenge on personal adversaries, spreading hate and ruin. After his physical death, he experienced indescribable suffering in the Umbral. Many of his former victims have already forgiven him for his crimes, but many others have persistently followed him for years ... The once-numerous mob has thinned out little by little, and he is down to his last two enemies, who are now in the final process of transformation. After having endured dolorous struggles in darkness and Dantesque dens of suffering, the wretch finally readied himself for this conclusive phase of his redemption; consequently, he received his present incarnation to complete the effective healing process he has been going through for so many years."

It was a sad and heartrending scene. At his age, the patient, with his rachitic bones and nearly transparent skin, would otherwise have been a beautiful and happy child. But here he was, unable to move, emitting yelps and guttural sounds more typical of the subhuman realm.

With the respect owed to suffering and the observation demanded by science, I saw that the little paralytic looked more like a descendant of improved simians.

"No, the spirit doesn't regress at all," explained Calderaro. "But its forms of manifestation can suffer degeneration in order to facilitate the regenerative process. All the evil and all the good practiced during one's lifetime impose modifications on our appearance. For a long period of time, our unfortunate friend poisoned the active centers of his perispiritual organization. Surrounded by enemies and adversaries as a result of his criminal activities, he is almost completely unfeeling due to the darkness brought on by his enormous wrongs. Within the sphere of his conscience, he weeps and struggles under the yoke of the torturous memories that appear endless to him. His senses, however, even the physical ones, remain clouded, like imbalanced potentialities with no direction ... The thoughts of rebelliousness and vengeance emitted by those he deliberately harmed have been assailing his perispiritual body for more than a hundred years nonstop, pounding like blows disintegrating his personality. Far from the access to the higher realms of self, where we locate the 'castle of noble concepts,' the poor wretch has struggled hopelessly in the 'arena of present effort,' that is, at the point where we locate the motor energies. This is due to the fact that his unforgiving adversaries are attached to him through direct influence and are compelling his mind to focus on the automatic impulses in the area of the instincts. The Law has allowed this to happen, obviously because our unfortunate brother's behavior was like that of the jaguar that uses its power to overcome and kill. Abuses of reason and authority are grave wrongs before the Eternal Authority of our destinies."

The esteemed Assistant gazed at me with his lucid eyes and asked:

"Do you see?"

As if he wanted to see me sufficiently enlightened, he added:

"Spiritually speaking, this poor, sick child has not regressed. But the evolutionary process, the work of the divine spirit over

the millennia to arrive at a glorious destination, was trampled on, mocked and hindered by him. He sowed evil and now he is reaping it. He devised an audacious plan of extermination using the authority the Father had bestowed on him; he carried it out and now he suffers its natural consequences in order to correct himself. The worst is over. At present, most of his enemies are no longer persecuting him and he can count on his loving mother to help him with his transformation at the end of a long course of regeneration."

Observing the strange posture of the unfortunate discarnates shadowing him, I was about to ask something about them, when Calderaro read my mind:

"These unfortunate persecutors are goblins of hatred and revenge, just as our invalid is a remnant of crime. They are castaways in the final stage of being rescued after a huge shipwreck on the sea of life, where they have been lost for many years incapable of using the compass of forgiveness and goodness. Now, however, they are about to enter the harbor of assistance. They will return to the sun of earthly existence through the heart of a woman who, with Jesus, has understood the value of sacrifice. According to the redemptive plan already laid out, they will soon enter this very home as brothers of their old adversary. And when they join hands with the love of their selfless, tender and righteous mother in order to help him, they will kiss their old enemy with enormous affection. The dark shackles of hatred will be transmuted into shining bonds of light, in which eternal love will shine. When that time comes, the power of forgiveness will return our patient to freedom; like a happy bird, he will dispose of his wasted physical body, the suffocating prison for crime and its consequences, a struggle that has been going on for almost two centuries. Until then, it is important to carefully watch over this valorous woman, this pure lady of the house, in whom the

Divine Powers honor the call for sacrifice to illuminate life and enrich God's work."

Calderaro had barely finished, when one of the discarnate persecutors touched the boy's brain with his right hand. The Assistant suggested that I study the effects of this contact.

The paralytic's face blanched in a display of enormous anguish. I noticed that, through its hands, the unhappy spirit emitted black striae of a substance similar to tar, which reached the boy's brain to increase his feelings of dread.

I directed a questioning look at the Assistant and he replied:

"Love emits rays of light, whereas hatred casts daggers of darkness. On the frontal lobes we receive 'stimuli for the future'; on the cortex we harbor the 'suggestions for the present' and in the nervous system per se we archive the 'memories of the past.' Our poor friend is being bombarded by the destructive energies of hate located in the region of 'present service,' that is, in his current capacity for growth, accomplishment and work. Deriving from his guilt, this situation forces him to descend mentally to the region of the 'memories of the past,' where his behavior is of the lowest order, approaching the semi-consciousness of the early stages of evolution. A crushing majority of the phenomena of psychic alienation stem from mental instability. Observe his organic cosmos."

As a result of the affliction into which he had plunged, the little invalid went into contortions, displaying all of the characteristics of classic, severe mental impairment. His organs displayed strange displacements. The endocrine system displayed indefinable disturbances.

The instructor leaned over the patient compassionately and explained:

"The destructive rays have reached his motor zone, causing the paralysis of his centers of speech, movement, hearing,

vision, and the command of all of his glandular sectors. In fact, this grievous situation has become chronic by being repeated thousands of times for nearly two hundred years."

He made a significant pause and continued:

"Examine the boy's behavior. With his mind fixated in the extreme 'region of autonomic impulses,' his behavior pattern is effectively subhuman. He has returned to living the primitive stages from which the human individuality emerged many centuries ago. In other, less serious cases, modern medicine has been using electrical shock therapy, like an experimenter performing his studies in the darkness, examining the effects while ignoring the causes. However, we must realize that the wonderful endeavors of modern psychiatry have merited great care from our spiritual authorities, who support hardworking devoted physicians, guiding them simultaneously in many different cultural milieus for the common good. But for now, they cannot accept the truth as desired due to the need of safeguarding earthly medicine on conservative ground – there isn't much room for trailblazers. Later on, however, the 'priesthood' of human health will understand that electric shock, or hypoglycemia brought on by the invasion of insulin, are living appeals to the centers of the perispiritual organism, calling on them to readjust and compelling neurons to readapt themselves in order to serve the mind in a regenerative process. One must remember that this recourse of tapping the deep reserves of the psychic cosmos isn't new, however. In ancient times, victims of insanity were taken to snake pits so that their horrific terror would suddenly bring about the transformation of their imbalanced mind, the reason being that, since remote antiquity, humans have intuitively understood that most cases of mental alienation derive from the soul's voluntary or involuntary absence from reality. And from our more

enlightened point of view, we can add that every imbalance derives from departure from the Law."

Calderaro became silent for a few instants and then nodded toward the boy, emphasizing:

"But in this case, the shock applied by human science would not help at all. We are looking at the total eclipse of the mind, revealing the total absence of the Law in our patient's conduct. Rectification in this case takes a lot of time. The muddy waters of evil long dammed up in the soul are not flushed away easily. The mental realm of each one of us is not a vase of imaginary content: it is a repository of living energies, just as our physical vehicle is appropriate while we journey on the surface of this planet."

"But scientifically speaking, isn't this a typical case of Down Syndrome?" I asked.

The Assistant replied without hesitation:

"This is a case of complete imbalance of the spirit. On very rare occasions we encounter disturbances of this nature based on substantially physiological causes. It is impossible to disregard the psycho-physical parallel in the physical realm. Earth's inhabitants will always have to deal with the perishable form first. Thus, we cannot exclude the pathology of the soul from the dense corporeal envelope, nor disregard the collaboration of selfless physiologists, who attentively devote themselves to the study of microscopic fauna, the readjustment of physical conditions and the field of effects. But we mustn't forget that, in this case, we are analyzing the realm of causation."

My dedicated friend seemed ready to continue, expanding my knowledge on the issue, when we heard steps of someone approaching. The mother was coming to the child's room to seek help through prayer.

Calderaro hurriedly concluded:

"Our fellow spirits of human medicine label mental diseases as they please, dwelling on peripheral matters and distracted from the fundamental problems of the spirit. We'll talk tomorrow about scientific matters as we lend assistance to another young man."

Just then, the mother – not yet thirty years of age – approached the invalid without perceiving our presence as spirits. Looking downcast, she stopped and stood at the crib, stroking his sweat-beaded forehead as his final contortions ended. She removed the laced blanket, lifted him carefully and held him in her arms, soothing him with tender loving care.

The boy quieted down.

Immediately after, she began to pray bathed in tears, looking to me like a swan from the spirit realm singing a marvelous canticle.

While Calderaro worked to repair the boy's neural energies with a genuine transfusion of healthy fluids, which the devoted servant transferred from himself, I listened in true earnest to the mother's prayer.

The young woman blended human questions into her heartfelt prayer.

Why hadn't the Lord in Heaven heard her, allowing a miracle that would restore the boy to the balance he needed so much? She had married nine years ago with dreams of a home full of happy children. But the first offspring of her aspirations lay there, strangely displaying a dreadful look of monstrosity and suffering ... Why, she asked pleadingly, were children born on earth destined to such anguish? Why did little ones have to endure such torment? In vain, she had resorted to doctors and listened to specialists. Always the same disappointment, the same disillusionment. Her little one seemed inaccessible to any kind of treatment. She felt fragile

and exhausted ... She started to weep, imploring divine grace so that her strength would not fail her in the struggle.

When he had finished his task, Calderaro asked me:

"Would you like to answer her prayer in the name of Higher Inspiration?"

"Oh! No!" I declined the invitation, alleging that it would be completely impossible after having heard Sister Cipriana touching hearts through words set alight with love.

The counselor objected kindly:

"In this case we won't be speaking to hearts that hate, but to a tortured maternal spirit asking for fraternal encouragement. Knowledge and goodwill can do a lot."

He smiled benevolently and added:

"Also, we too must earn a degree in the science of love. So let's start being each other's brothers, with sincerity and a faithful willingness to serve."

Moved, I thanked him for his deference, but I still declined. Calderaro himself should speak. I was there as a learner. I was there to follow his sublime lessons.

My selfless friend placed his hands on the mother's frontal lobes as if he were directing her mind toward the most elevated region of the Self, and began to send her moving appeals like a loving father speaking to her heart. Deeply touched, I registered his words of encouragement and consolation, which the loving mother received in the form of lofty ideas and suggestions.

I noticed that the young woman's inner disposition gradually gathered renewed courage. I could see that a soft focus of radiant light had appeared in her pineal gland and that different tears had begun to flow from her eyes. The soft light flowing from her brain descended to her chest area, and from there fine strands of light radiated to connect her to her

unfortunate child. She gazed at the now calm boy through a thick veil of tears, and **I heard her sublime thoughts**.

No, God would not forsake her, she thought. He would give her strength to fulfill to the end the commitment she had taken upon her shoulders with the beauty of her first dream and with the courage of her first hour. She would uphold the unfortunate offspring of her flesh as if he were a treasure from heaven. Her love would expand with her beloved son's suffering; her maternal sacrifices would be sweeter every time pain came upon him with more intensity. Wasn't he worthier of her devotion and self-sacrifice because of the afflicted condition he was born with? The children of her old friends were beautiful and intelligent, like fragrant blossoms of life, promising infinite joy on the pathway of the future. Her little paralytic was also beautiful, even though he needed a greater amount of gentleness and support. God knew why he had come into the world without the faculty of speech and without manifestations of intelligence. Wasn't it enough to trust the Supreme Father? She would serve the Lord without question; she would love her son throughout all eternity; she would die if need be so that he could live.

In a flight of indefinable love, the young mother leaned over and kissed the boy with the joy of someone who was kissing an angel of heaven. I was surprised to see that countless sparks of light sprung from the loving contact between them and spilled over the two lower-order spirits, who, showing signs of some relief, also bowed before the worthy woman who would serve them as their mother later on.

Calderaro touched me slightly on the shoulder, concluding:

"Our work of assistance is over. Let's go."

Pointing to mother and child together, he concluded:

"Upon examining this suffering child as an unsolvable enigma, some unfeeling doctors would perhaps suggest

a 'painless death'; they would be unaware of the fact that, within the walls of this modest home, the Divine Doctor, using an incurable body and the sacrificing love of a mother's heart, is restoring the balance to eternal spirits so that, upon the ruins of the past, they may join with each other on their way toward a glorious destiny."

8
In the Sanctuary of the Soul

The night was dark. Calderaro and I entered a comfortable, elegant house, where, as he had promised, he would provide me with a few more explanations regarding the imbalances of the soul.

"This case isn't as serious as the paralytic we just visited," my helpful guide said in anticipation. "In fact, it involves a matter that has been almost completely taken care of. I've been assisting Marcelo with restorative fluids for quite some time now, and his situation is one of complete victory. Amenable to our influence, he found the supply of energy needed in prayer and spiritual activity. Yesterday, we witnessed a case in which the perispiritual elements were in complete disarray, resulting in the disaggregation of the nervous system in a heartbreaking scenario that only time will repair. Here, however, the picture is different. The underlying troubling problem has been resolved, readjustment to life has given him new hope, and peace has

returned to his organic tabernacle; however, certain memories still linger, with vestiges of past dramas rising to the surface as epileptoid phenomena – actions that are reflexes of the soul as it emerges from a vast and intricate tunnel of darkness into the realm of light. If it has taken evil a long time to establish itself, it is obvious that restoration to the good cannot happen over night. Such is the case with health and disease, and the loss and re-establishment of equilibrium."

After crossing the porch and being duly authorized to go inside, I was happily surprised by a charming scene of domestic piety: a gentleman, a lady and a young man were immersed in the divine vibrations of prayer, surrounded by a large number of friends from our realm.

We were warmly welcomed.

My guide invited me to take part in the task at hand since, through the precious help of the three incarnate fellow spirits, assistance was being given in several different ways to brothers and sisters newly-liberated from their bodies.

The sublime beauty of that small gathering devoted to the good and to the enlightenment of the spirit was well worth noting.

As he admired the harmony of those three souls interlaced by luminous threads of light as they partook of the same noble thoughts and purposes, the friendly Assistant commented:

"A family is a meeting of spirits in space and time, and as such the home is a sanctuary. Quite often – especially on the earth – many family members fall out of harmony with the higher aims of life; however, when two or three members finally understand the greatness of their evolutionary potential and intimately join each other for the accomplishments of the eternal spirit, wonderful spiritual growth can be expected."

I understood that my instructor would have liked to provide me with further explanations by delving deeper into the

sanctifying concept of the family, but the pressing work at hand cut our conversation short.

The task of assisting our suffering brothers and sisters was underway on "our side."

When the family trio's participation ended with an expressive and moving prayer, the spirits from our realm began leaving, while our incarnate friends continued in affectionate conversation.

With the happy smile typical of a worker who has done a good job, the gentleman said to the others:

"Thanks be to God, everything is fine now."

Gazing at the young man with immense paternal tenderness, he asked:

"How about you, Marcelo? Feeling better?"

"Oh! No doubt about it, Dad" Marcelo replied, cheerfully. "I'm amazed at the excellent results I've been reaping from our Thursday gatherings."

"Have the nighttime episodes recurred?"

"Nope. As long as I continue to try to understand the divine truths and use my will to practice the lessons I've learned, I think I continue to improve, get stronger on the inside and recover my lost health. But whenever I lose interest in my spiritual growth and get distracted from my need to evolve, the bouts return with a vengeance. During such dreadful times, I wake up in the middle of the night all tired and achy, worn out from convulsions that have left me senseless for several minutes."

The young man smiled upon making this sincere filial confession and continued:

"Fortunately, however, now that I'm dedicated to spiritual practice, I can tell that Mom's passes have become more effective. I've grown more receptive and I've noticed that goodwill is a decisive factor in my well-being."

They looked at each other happily, and the intimate understanding continued, edifying and replete with wonderful suggestions.

Assistant Calderaro, coaching my thoughts, stated:

"As you can see, Marcelo has a very good understanding with his parents. He has other siblings but they aren't in tune yet with the couple's sacred mission. Marcelo, however, is the bearer of lofty and generous sentiments. Like nearly all of us, his past is full of passions and abuses of authority: he held a lot of power in his hands, which he didn't know how to use constructively. He possessed a bright mind and soared to intellectual heights, from where he didn't always descend to comfort or help. He held several honorific titles but many a time forgot about them, plunging into the depths of criminal impulses. He imposed himself through despotism and thereby intensified the sowing of the thorns that would tear at him later. When the time came to harvest the nefarious crop, atrocious suffering came upon him. Countless victims were waiting beyond the grave to attack him. However, even though he had committed gross wrongs, he had also desired to do good on many occasions. Consequently, he had formed valuable allegiances, but they had to wait for an opportunity to assist him. Crying out furiously for due justice, his enemies kept him for a long time in the lower zones, satiating their old desires for revenge while battering his perispirit. With his conscience in darkness, he begged, wept and did penance for many, many years. Despite his own pleas and other intercessory appeals, his longed-for deliverance took time: remorse is always a bond between debtor and creditor, and his conscience was struck by cruel remorse. Thus, his perispiritual imbalances started to flog him the moment he crossed the portal of the grave, and they remained strong for years on end."

During a brief pause in his explanation, I added curiously:

"So, that means that the epileptoid phenomenon ..."

"... very rarely occurs due to mere alterations in the encephalon, like those caused by blows to the head," explained the Assistant, interrupting my reticent remark. "It's usually an illness of the soul, independent from the physical body, which, in such a case, simply displays reflex actions. It's been a long time since reason believed in heaven or purgatory as being realms 'out there' somewhere: heaven and hell are essentially states of our own conscience. Those who have acted against the Law find themselves involved in a correctional process for as long as it takes. This fact must lead us to conclude that, if there are many types of infirmities for the disharmonies of the body, there are countless others for the deviations of the soul."

My instructor made a short pause, nodded toward the young man and continued:

"Regarding Marcelo, I must tell you that he has gradually drained the heaviest substances from his cup of trials. Long years of imbalance, in which his victims-turned-tormenters afflicted him with dreadful convulsions through shocks and indescribable suffering, have cleared his inner horizons. Our brother finally managed to make contact with a thoughtful and wise spirit counselor, to whom he was connected in the remote past. He was helped and given support. He anxiously asked about souls that were particularly dear to him and was told that his strongest ties were back in the flesh again, dedicated to dignifying endeavors and testimonies. He begged to reincarnate and promised to accept commitments of spiritual service in order to redeem his huge debts, working for the good and for the evolution of former enemies. He received this gift at the recommendation of the noble mentor who had held him dear for many centuries. He returned to the corporeal realm and re-started his learning experience. He was reborn into the loving arms to which he has felt connected

over the course of many existences lived in common. At present, earnestly taking advantage of the blessings he has received from birth, he has concerned himself with readjusting precious moral qualities: ever since childhood he has been characterized by natural kindness and obedience, gentleness and tenderness. He spent his childhood in peace, albeit continuously watched by former invisible persecutors. This time, due to the regenerative work he had undertaken, he was not drawn to them; even so, whenever he encountered any of his opponents during times of the partial disengagement provided by physical sleep, his memories brought him bitter suffering. Life went on as usual. Under his parents' care, and with the help of his invisible benefactors, the boy prepared for future endeavors. However, as soon as he consolidated his physical heritage upon reaching the age of fourteen, and when his perispiritual body was fully melded with his physical envelope, Marcelo began recalling past events, and the so-called epileptic convulsions appeared with some intensity. The boy, however, immediately found the necessary antidote by taking refuge in the 'seat of noble principles,' that is, in the higher region of the personality, through the habit of prayer, fraternal understanding, the practice of the good, and higher spirituality. He thus limited his neuropsychic disharmony and reduced his cellular dysfunction, regaining his balance day by day by mobilizing the tools of his will. This endeavor gained him much sympathy, and he received considerable help from our realm. He availed himself of it fully by wisely sticking to his efforts of building himself up in the good. By accepting the struggle with serenity and patience, he instilled valuable receptive qualities in himself that made our cooperation easier. That is why hypnosis or shock therapy wasn't needed. By causing abnormal states in the perispiritual body, such treatment most often achieves nothing; it merely dislocates illnesses without combating them at their

origins. Hence, Marcelo's case offers valuable characteristics. By paying heed to the suggestions of those who are helping him and by adapting himself to reality, he has become his own doctor, the only formula in which patients can find their own cure.

At that moment, the boy gently bid good night to his parents and left for his room, where he went to bed after purifying his mind with thoughts of peace and gratitude to God.

In a few minutes, he left his dense vehicle and came to meet us, greeting Calderaro with special affection.

The Assistant kindly introduced him to me.

The young man displayed profound lucidity. Embracing us both in an unequivocal display of happiness, he commented on his hopes for the future. He displayed a burning desire to spread evangelical Spiritism, willing to participate in the edifying work that his parents were involved in. Much to my surprise, he referred to the activities of our spirit colony and asked me about my impressions of *Nosso Lar*, fascinating me with the appropriateness of his ideas and the beauty of his intelligent and spontaneous comments.[13]

In the middle of our conversation, two dark figures cautiously approached us. Who could they be except miserable, transient discarnates? I was completely distracted as I continued my humble comments, but Marcelo was obviously shaken. As if he had been touched by disturbing forces, he turned pale, placed his right hand to his chest and stared with wide-open eyes. I noticed that the thoughts in his perispiritual brain became confused and that he could not hear us very well; all of a sudden, he left and immediately returned to his body.

I was dismayed and tried to stop him because he was perfectly in tune with us. Something stronger than just a cordial

[13] Reference to the book by the same name. – Spirit Auth.

acquaintance connected me to my new friend – I recognized it the moment we met. However, I was unsuccessful in my attempt. Calderaro held me back firmly and stated:

"Let him go, Andre and we'll follow him. We mustn't forget that Marcelo isn't yet completely cured."

Indicating the provocative spirits not far from us, he continued explaining:

"All it takes is for his former enemies to appear and his mental condition changes. He becomes apprehensive and afflicted because he's afraid he'll have to return to the dolorous situation he experienced in the lower zones many years ago, so he rushes back to his physical body, much like someone who seeks help in the only refuge available in the face of an imminent storm."

The wandering spirits beat a retreat and we went back inside, where we found the young man seized with convulsions.

I embraced him as if he were a dear son.

The seizure abated but did not cease completely. I looked at my guide in silent questioning. Why such a disturbance? Marcelo's bedroom was insulated from direct exposure to the two low-order spirits. The three of us had been involved in an uplifting conversation and had kept ourselves in a healthful atmosphere of sanctifying thoughts. So what was the reason for the commotion?

The instructor gazed at me kindly and recommended:

"Observe the organic field, particularly the brain."

I noticed that the usual light of the endocrine centers had turned pale, and only the pineal gland continued emitting abnormal rays. In the encephalon the chaos was complete. The upper areas of the brain were emitting rays of mental light, which were, so to speak, bombarding the cellular beehive of the cortex. The various motor centers, including those of memory and speech, lay disorganized and lifeless. These abnormal rays

entered the deepest layers of the cerebellum, perturbing the channels of equilibrium and disrupting muscular tension. They caused strange changes in the neurons and penetrated the gray nervous system, annulling the activity of the fibers. The delicate encephalic system was totally inhibited. The motor areas, whipped by mental sparks, lost their order, discipline and self-control, and finally gave out, depleted of energy. Meanwhile, Marcelo-spirit writhed in anguish, juxtaposed on Marcelo-form, imprisoned in organic unconsciousness, dominated by convulsions that rent my soul.

After this detailed examination, I asked Calderaro:

"How can this be? After all, our friend is not under the despotic command of discarnate tormentors, but is in our company only."

The instructor was applying magnetic assistance to restore Marcelo's equilibrium, and suggested that I wait a few minutes. The disharmony was soon under control. Enveloping Marcelo's mental field in balsamic-fluidic emissions, the attack subsided. Marcelo settled down. His cerebral activity cleared up, like a town square that has become decongested. The nerve cells returned to their task; the traffic routes were normalized; the endocrine system returned to regularity, and the stimuli network was reestablished to its usual task.

Disappointed and drained, Marcelo fell into a deep sleep. Calderaro had thought it best to allow him to rest a bit more and didn't let him withdraw in his perispiritual body for the first few minutes of peace after the attack.

As he observed the young man in the comfort of his bed, my instructor asked me kindly:

"Do you remember Pavlov's work with conditioned reflexes?"

Of course I recalled Pavlov's famous experiments with dogs, applied to other phenomena.

"Well," Calderaro continued, "Marcelo's case has to do with the same principles. In past lives he erred in many ways, and remorse, that imperious force in the service of Divine Law, guarded his conscience like a watchful sentry, handing him over to his enemies in the lower zones, and leading him, right after the loss of his physical body, to harvest the thorns he had sown during one of his most intense periods of spiritual failure. As a consequence of such deviations, he wandered about in imbalance with his soul very ill and at the mercy of his former victims. He threw his perispiritual centers into disarray, harming them for a long time. Aided by an esteemed mentor who interceded on his behalf, he reincarnated, this time more serene, for the important work of redemption. However, the invaluable cooperation received on the outside was ultimately unable to transform the situation on the inside. He was free of his merciless enemies, whom he was to help from then on, but his perispiritual organism had archived the exact memory of the difficulties experienced while outside of the body. Consequently, Marcelo's motor areas, which symbolize the seat of the 'conscious forces' in their current manifestations, constitute a 'convalescing perispiritual region,' much like fresh scars on a physical body. Because his equilibrium has not yet solidified completely, whenever the young man is approached by former enemies, he is subject to violent psychic upheavals, during which his emotions run amok, keeping him from the harmony he needs so much. His mind in disarray loses control of the perispiritual organization and physiological elements, assumes eccentric conditions, and in disorganized movements, disperses the energies peculiar to it. These energies then clash with each other and emit low-frequency waves, much like the kind emitted by the hallucinated thoughts of his victims. These destructive emissions invade the delicate matter of the encephalic cortex, take possession of the cortical centers and

upset the centers of memory, speech, hearing, touch and sight, and countless other centers that govern various stimuli. We thus have the 'grand mal'[14] of dramatic symptomatology, causing convulsions in which the physical body, prostrate and overcome, is more like a boat suddenly left adrift."

Calderaro's explanation filled me with respect for the moral foundations of life. I now understood the uselessness of psychiatry devoid of the notions of the spirit. It reminded me of the secular struggle between physiologists and psychologists as they argued over the standards of treatment for the mentally alienated. Mesmer and Charcot, Pinel and Broca came to my mind, now enriched with new knowledge.

The pause in the Assistant's explanation didn't last very long. Actually, since the beginning of our conversations, such pauses had become customary. It seemed like Calderaro intentionally provided them so that I could assimilate his concepts.

In answer to my inner thoughts, he continued:

"One cannot hope for the cure of the mentally impaired through exclusively objective processes. One must penetrate the soul, examine the core of the personality, and treat the effects by addressing the causes. Consequently, we cannot restore sick bodies without the resources of the Divine Doctor of souls, Jesus Christ. Physiologists will always do a lot by trying to correct the malfunction of cells; however, it is necessary to intervene in the origins of the disturbances. Marcelo's case is only one of the multiple aspects of the 'epileptoid phenomenon,' – to use the terminology of incarnate doctors. This perispirit's imbalance, though, is marked by an extremely complex gradation. The confirmation of the theory of conditioned reflexes does not apply

[14] A form of epilepsy characterized by tonic-clonic seizures, involving two phases – the tonic phase, in which the body becomes rigid, and clonic phase, in which there is uncontrolled jerking. http://www.medterms.com. – Tr.

to it exclusively. There are millions of irascible individuals, who, due to their habit of easily giving in to anger, wreck fundamental nerve centers through the excesses of their undisciplined mind. They become bearers of the 'petit mal'[15], incipient psychotics, neurasthenics of all sorts, or patients on the epileptic fringes, dependent on insulin hypoglycemia or Metrazol therapy. Meanwhile, a mental education to correct their inner attitudes in the routine of life would be a more effective and appropriate treatment for them, because it would be regenerative and substantial. By stating such truths, we are not belittling the ministry of selfless psychiatrists who dedicate their lives to others, nor are we saying that all patients, without exception, can forego the aid of shock therapy, which is so necessary for many individuals as a shower for 'dust-covered nerves.'[16] We merely want to point out that, by their behavior, humans can either invigorate their soul or harm it. The altruistic character that has learned to sacrifice itself for the good of all is increasing its own storehouses for eternity. Murderers, by spreading death and despair all around them, establish the kingdom of suffering and darkness within themselves. Whenever we meet brothers and sisters who are under the dominance of perispiritual lesions – the living consequences of their actions as decreed by Universal Justice – it is crucial to go back to the source of the

---

15 A form of epilepsy with very brief, unannounced lapses in consciousness. A petit mal seizure involves a brief loss of awareness, which can be accompanied by blinking or mouth twitching ... Petit mal (little illness in French) seizures are also known as absence seizures. Petit mal seizures take the form of a staring spell: the person suddenly seems to be "absent." http://www.medterms.com. – Tr.

16 "Most people might be quicker to associate electroshock therapy with torture rather than healing. But since the 1980s, the practice has been quietly making a comeback. The number of patients undergoing electroconvulsive therapy, as it's formally called, has tripled to 100,000 a year, according to the National Mental Health Association. During an ECT treatment, doctors jolt the unconscious patient's brain with an electrical charge, which triggers a grand mal seizure. It's considered by many psychiatrists to be the most effective way to treat depression, especially in patients who haven't responded to antidepressants." http://www.msnbc.msn.com (August 2008). – Tr.

disturbances that assail them in order to assist them successfully. This cannot be accomplished through psychoanalytic discourse, but by assisting them through the power of fraternity and love so that they may acquire the understanding they need to modify themselves by readjusting their own forces."

Just then, noticing that Marcelo had disengaged again, the instructor interrupted his explanations and invited him to join us once more.

The young man embraced us, very touched.

"Well," he said, gazing humbly at Calderaro, "I was weak and I fell."

"Oh, no!" replied the instructor, comforting him. "You mustn't feel as though you have failed. You are still undergoing treatment – we cannot forget that. Your effort is admirable; nonetheless, you must await the input of time."

Calderaro smiled and emphasized:

"In times past you lost a valuable opportunity to follow the path of progress; you slipped and slid ... Now, you must cautiously resume your upward climb. A bird with weak wings cannot overdo its flight."

The young man regained his hope, and gazing gratefully at Calderaro, he asked:

"Do you think, dear mentor, that I should use hypnotics[17]?"

"No. Hypnotics are only useful during the harsh phase of complete mental unawareness, when it's necessary to neutralize the nerve cells due to the probable friction of the perispiritual organization. In your case, Marcelo, since your conscience has already awakened to higher spirituality, the most effective medicine consists of positive faith, self-confidence, worthwhile work and ennobling thoughts. Remaining in the highest region

[17] Also called soporifics and sedatives. – Tr.

of the personality, you will defeat the imbalances of the lower regions. So, you must pursue the renewing and sublime mission that was entrusted to you in the area of self-enlightenment and goodness toward others. Medical elements can exert despotic custody over the organic cosmos whenever the mind is unwilling to control it by resorting to educational factors."

The young man kissed his hands tenderly. Hiding his emotion, Calderaro spoke in good cheer:

"We've done nothing yet to deserve anyone's recognition. We are nothing more than imperfect workers in service, and service is the greatest power to keep our imperfections in check. We all have a divine creditor in Jesus, whose endless kindness we mustn't forget."

And patting Marcelo's head, he emphasized:

"You have already heeded Jesus' heavenly word and have forsaken evil, 'so that nothing worse may happen to you.' Thus, you are now fortunate. In fact, we are presently fortunate because our current goal is to achieve the Kingdom of God within us with Christ. Let us work with him, through him and for him, healing our injuries once and for all."

The young man embraced us as if he were a son close to our hearts, and we left together on a pleasant field trip while his physical body rested peacefully.

9
Mediumship

I was still very curious about Marcelo's interesting case, so the following day I asked Calderaro some questions that were bothering me.

Mightn't conditioned reflexes also be applied to various mediumistic phenomena? Mightn't they explain the unconscious mystifications that often interfere with sessions involving incarnate experimenters?

A number of devoted and honest students of Spiritism recognized the obstacles in the area of mediumship and created the theory of the medium's own animic manifestation, which would act in place of discarnate spirits. Mightn't this apply in this particular case? Upon evoking certain images, mightn't the medium's own thoughts be subject to certain associations, thereby automatically interfering with the communications between humans on earth and inhabitants of the Other Side? In many cases, such occurrences could cause serious imbalances. Mulling over what I had observed recently regarding this matter

in several Spiritist centers, I asked myself if the problem might not have something to do with Pavlov's principles.

My instructor patiently heard me out and then answered benevolently:

"The issue needs a more accurate examination. The animistic thesis is a respectable one. Originating from conscientious and sincere investigators, it was born to prevent the probable excesses of the imagination. However, it has been used cruelly by a lot of our incarnate coworkers as an inquisitorial tool, whereas they should use it as an educative element in a fraternal way. Thousands of incarnate fellow spirits avoid practicing mediumship. They have become frightened and have retreated from the hurdles of mediumistic initiation because animism has turned into a Cerberus[18]. What should have been serious and edifying instruction has turned into an oppressive system that obstructs candidates' pathway to mediumship through the natural progression of learning and application. Absolute precision is required of them, and elementary lessons from nature are disregarded. Positioned in their castles of theories, many of those who get together for the lofty work of communication with our realm habitually turn down workers who would otherwise grow and perfect themselves over time and with effort. They demand pure communication devices, as if spiritual light were transmitted in the same manner as electrical light by means of an ordinary light bulb. But just as trees do not sprout already producing fruit, any worthwhile faculty requires development. So, mediumship, too, has its evolution, field and course. Students can't enroll in an upper level course until they demonstrate efficiency in preparatory courses through years of struggle, effort and discipline; hence our rightful concern about the animistic

[18] In Greek mythology, the three-headed watchdog who guards the entrance to the nether world , Hades. www.pantheon.org. – Tr.

thesis, which purports to encapsulate all responsibility for spirit-related work in one single individuality: that of the mediumistic instrument[19]. We need higher appeals that motivate coworkers who are just starting out, providing them with ampler resources of knowledge on the path they are traveling so that sanctifying spirituality may be part of the phenomena as well as the studies pertinent to the spirit.

He paused and I didn't dare interrupt him, as I was fascinated by the loftiness of these concepts. He continued:

"Let's take a look at your suggestion. Actually, conditioned reflexes are, in fact, at the heart of the matter; however, we must investigate it more deeply. Pavlov's animals demonstrated mnemonic ability; they memorized facts through automatic mental associations. This means that they mobilized subtle matter, independently from their dense body and that they used mental energy in their body of primitive impulses. If the 'fragmentary consciences', that is, the animals in this experiment, were capable of using this energy, causing the repetition of certain phenomena in the cellular cosmos, what marvels could the mind of humans accomplish, yielding not to mere conditioned reflexes but to emissions from another mind in tune with their own? Within such principles it is imperative for the intermediary to grow in self-worth. Extraordinary and unknown occurrences take place in every aspect of life, but spiritual growth demands a fervent search. No one can receive the blessings of the harvest without the sweat of the sowing. Unfortunately, however, the majority seem unaware of such impositions of work and cooperation: they expect ready-made faculties. The mediumistic instrument is automatically nullified if it doesn't have the good fortune of exhibiting absolute harmony with discarnates in the three-fold

[19] Spirits refer to mediums quite often as "mediumistic instruments." – Tr

areas of mental, perispiritual and physiological capabilities. Do you understand the difficulty?"

Yes, I was starting to understand. His explanation was too enthralling for me to ask any more questions, however, so with the attitude of a humble learner, I waited for him to continue.

The Assistant perceived my inner attitude and continued:

"Take a simpler example. Let's look at the medium as being a bridge that connects two realms, between which there is an apparent discontinuity of contact due to differentiations in their vibratory fields. In order to be a relatively precise instrument, it is essential for the medium to have learned to yield, and not all beginners in mediumship can acquire such a quality in a short period of time. It requires devotion to the wellbeing of others, a high level of understanding of the collective good, an advanced spirit of fraternal cooperation, and serene control when facing conflicts involving someone else's opinions. To achieve such spiritual growth, it is crucial to take frequent shelter in the 'home of the higher principles.' Workers' minds must be focused on the highest realms of their being, where they learn the value of sublime concepts, renewing and perfecting themselves in order to become a model for those who will follow behind them. To help the present time, humans must live for the future of their race. This quite often imposes painful solitude and incomprehension on them. Such condition, however, represents an article of the Law that we must acquire in order to be able to give. No one can teach about pathways that they themselves haven't traveled: hence, in the case of constructive mediumship, the need to place instrumental energies in the highest sanctuary of the personality. We must realize that phenomena – no matter which kind – besiege creatures everywhere. True science entails the gradual conquest of Nature's forces and workings that used to be hidden from our limited comprehension. And since we are children of a Revealing

God, infinite in greatness, we can continue to expect to be faced with unlimited fields of observation, whose doors will open to our desire for knowledge according to our merits. Therefore, Andre, we believe that the most stable and comely mediumship begins at the level of pure intuition. Moses performed his task compelled by the occurrences of the phenomena surrounding him. Under incoercible force, he receives the sublime principles of the Decalogue, sensing the presence of materialized figures and voices from the spirit realm. However, at the same time that he transmits the 'You shall not kill', he himself does not seem very much inclined to unconditional respect for the lives of others. His doctrine, although praiseworthy, is based on exclusivity and fear. With Jesus, the mediumship aspect is different. The Master keeps himself in permanent contact with the Father through his own conscience and heart. He transmits the Divine Revelation to humans, living it within himself. He doesn't demand righteousness, nor does he ask for immediate understanding; instead, he loves and serves everyone by keeping himself at one with God. As a result, the Good News is a message of trust and universal love. Thus, we see two eminently different types of mediators from heaven itself, and we can see which one is the desirable standard. In common mediumship, therefore, workers serve with the mental matter proper to them, thus showing their natural imperfections for earthly investigations. Only after adapting to the noblest imperatives of personal renunciation will they build, not immediately but at the price of ceaseless work, the inner temple of service, where they recognize the superiority of the divine plan over their human whims. Once they come to this realization, they are prepared to connect with a greater number of discarnates and incarnates, offering to them as a beneficial bridge the opportunity of communicating with each other in their own evolutionary condition through constructive

understanding. I must tell you that we are not referring here to the incidental faculties that appear and disappear amongst mediumship candidates who lack the spirit of order and discipline – true test tubes for future flights. Rather, we mean the mediumship accepted by coworkers who are ready at any time for the common good. In commenting on activities and tasks, we must point out the standards that pertain to them, and this is the characteristic of the spiritual instrumentality in the higher realms. Logically, it is impossible to reach this level all at once; every endeavor requires a starting point."

My eyes revealed the emotion that had come over me in light of these concepts, so the Assistant changed his tone of voice to put me at ease:

"Referring once again to Christ, we have to realize that the Master lived insulated in the 'divine mount of consciousness', opening the way to the human valleys. Of course, none of us harbors the pretension of copying Jesus; however, we need to be inspired by his lessons. There are millions of human beings, both incarnate and discarnate, with their minds fixated on the less elevated region of the lower impulses. They are absorbed by instinctive passions and the remnants of their vile past, and are imprisoned by the conditioned reflexes of the perturbing emotions they defenselessly surrendered to. Many others, yoked to the flesh or out of it, keep themselves involved in disorderly activity or in aimless affective manifestations, in a feverish attachment to their past form or to a situation that is no longer justifiable. Still others are stuck in the pious state of exclusive religious mysticism, without personal achievements concerning experiences and merit that would integrate them into the field of true spiritual growth. Outside the physical body, the situation continues nearly always unaltered for the perispiritual organism, the result of patient work and a long period of evolution.

Although comprised of more pliable and subtle elements, this organism is still the material edifice that contains our conscience. Many people believe that heaven will clothe us in the tunic of an angel as soon as our body is lowered into the grave. But this is a serious mistake in the land of expectation. Of course, we are not referring to spirits like Francis of Assisi, nor to extremely perverse individuals: neither type is suitable for our picture. We are talking about neither the zenith nor the nadir of earthly evolution; we are referring to ordinary persons like ourselves, who are on a more or less normal, progressive journey. We must conclude that, depending on the mental state we nourish, we attract the incarnate or discarnate intelligences for which we become the natural instruments, albeit in an indirect way. The reality, my friend, is that all of us, who number in the hundreds of millions, cannot do without enlightened mediators who can put us in touch with the sources of Higher Supply. We need help from above and we require the concourse of benefactors who dwell above our realm. For this to occur, we must organize resources of receptivity. Our mind hungers for light, just as the earthly organism hungers for bread. Love and wisdom are divine substances that maintain our vitality."

The instructor paused briefly and added:

"Now do you understand the importance of mediumship, that is, the need to uplift our receptive qualities in order to achieve attunement with sources of a higher level?"

"Yes," I replied. I had understood his remarks and was pondering how remarkable they were.

"Mediumship isn't a service that we can organize from the periphery to the center," Calderaro proceeded. "It's the other way around. Incarnate humans are nearly always thrilled by the sleep of illusion; thus they may start out with the phenomenon. But as the more profound energies of their conscience are awakened,

they will feel the need to readjust, and will go back to the cause in order to hone the effects. It's an endeavor of construction, time and patience."

At this point, my instructor invited me to assist him with a dedicated woman, a medium in the process of development, who had been receiving his help so that she could proceed with her endeavor with the strength and serenity required.

In providing me with this fortunate opportunity, Calderaro concluded:

"This is an opportune case. You'll be able to observe the problems created by the animistic theory."

The clock read precisely 8:00 p.m. when we entered a comfortable room. Several spirits from our realm were with eleven incarnates in an intimate session devoted to prayer and psychic development. At the entrance, we were greeted by an attentive colleague, to whom I was introduced with sincere pleasure.

He began by giving me some brief information about himself, which I noted happily. He too had been a medical doctor. He had left the physical existence before he could fulfill old plans of fraternal assistance involving his many poor patients. He had the happiness of a peaceful conscience: he had cared for the general good as far as he could; however, foreseeing the potential of doing something on the Other Side, he had received permission to take part in this small group of friends, with the objective of carrying out a certain plan of assistance involving the infirm destitute. Communication with discarnates might not turn humans into angels overnight, but it can help them to become better people. It might not be possible to bring paradise to earth in just a few weeks; however, it was licit to take part in improving earthly society by encouraging the practice of the good and the devotion to fraternity. To this end, he remained there, interested in contributing to the watch-care of less affluent, ill persons.

I kept still as I admired what he was saying. Calderaro, however, asked courteously after being informed about the situation:

"And how are your worthy objectives coming along?"

"We've run into some problems," the other replied. "The communication resources available to me still do not inspire trust in most of the incarnates. In other words, I'm not interested in coming here to have my name glorified by classic terminology, nor would I offer new theories to compete with the medical world. I am guided only by the healthy desire to practice the good. Nevertheless ..."

"Haven't they heeded your appeals through Eulalia's mediation yet?" asked my instructor.

"No, not yet. Always the same suspicion of animism, of unconscious mystification."

The lecture was proceeding, when the Spiritist center's spirit director invited my colleague to give it a try. The time had come for him to approach the medium.

We approached the group of incarnates, who were immersed in profound concentration.

In preparation for transmitting the message that he desired to communicate to the physical realm, our new acquaintance approached a woman of distinguished appearance; meanwhile, Calderaro explained:

"Notice the group. I've already made my own observations. With the exception of three persons, there are eight others with a passive attitude that is amenable to mediumistic manifestation. Analyze sister Eulalia and you will see that she is in a highly receptive state. Of the eight potential workers, she is the one that best meets the type needed. However, our physician friend has not found the adequate psychophysical elements in her organization. She cannot connect with him through all of her perispiritual centers. She's incapable of raising herself to the

vibratory frequency of the communicating spirit. She doesn't have enough 'inner space' to share his ideas and knowledge. She cannot absorb all of his enthusiasm for science, since she did not bring it with her from other existences, nor has she constructed in her present existence the evolutionary elements she needs: only work that has been felt and experienced can give those to her. Nonetheless, she does have one, great ability – that of creative good will, without which it is impossible to begin the process of ascending to the highest realms of life. That is the most important door, through which she and the discarnate doctor will come to an understanding. For his part, in light of the circumstances he has to set aside official nomenclatures, scientific techniques, his own particular storehouse of words, new definitions and the renown that crowns his memory within the circles of his acquaintances and clients so that he can fulfill the worthy desire that animates him. He will be able to identify with Eulalia for a precise message, using his good will in turn. In adopting this form of communication, he will utilize mental communion more than anything else, thereby reducing to a minimum the influence on her neuro-psychic centers. In matters of mediumship there are identical types of faculties, but enormous inequalities in the degree of receptive capacity, which, like people, vary infinitely."

The instructor became silent for a few moments and then continued:

"Don't forget that we are now a team of workers involved in an experimental task. The hopeful communicator has not yet fully materialized the foundations for his plan, nor has the medium achieved sufficient clarity and permeability in order to cooperate with him. In a field of defined activities in this particular, we could act at will. But not here. Our stance must be one of mental neutrality, not of interference. Hence,

understanding that every resource available must be used for this praiseworthy effort to succeed, none of us will intervene by interfering or taking up time. We can exchange ideas and analyze the situation, but we cannot interfere in the least. The moment belongs to the communicator, and he has no better transmitting apparatus at his disposal for the time being."

He nodded toward to our colleague, who, standing beside Eulalia, was keeping his mind illuminated and vibrant in an admirable effort to overcome the natural wall between our realm and the realm of dense matter.

"Notice the particulars of the endeavor," Calderaro said in a significant tone of voice. "All the incarnates who are in a receptive state are absorbing the communicator's mental emissions in their own way. Just watch."

I went around the table and could see that the messenger's rays of positive energy were shining effectively on eight people. I realized that the central theme formulated by our friend regarding his plan of assistance to the infirm was reaching the brain of those who maintained a passive attitude. Each person was receiving the suggestive inflow on his or her mental screen filled with the concentration of mental energies which soon began causing the free associations discussed by psychoanalysts.

I concentrated my attention on the particulars.

Upon receiving the emission of energies from the worker of the good from the spirit realm, one gentleman remembered a moving scene in a hospital; another, a kind nurse of his acquaintance; another harbored thoughts of sympathy toward the destitute infirm; two women remembered the charitable mission of St. Vincent de Paul, and an elderly woman thought of visiting some of the bedridden people dear to her. A younger man recalled the noteworthy material he had read concerning fraternal piety toward all physically unwell people.

I also examined the three individuals who remained impervious to the commendable endeavor. Two of them were sorry they were missing a movie, while the other, an elderly woman, was thinking about her housework, which she felt was urgent and pressing, even there in that prayer circle, where she should have benefited from the peace enveloping the gathering.

Only Eulalia received the communicator's appeal with the most clarity. She felt him at her side; she was involved with his thoughts; she was not only receptive but was quite willing to serve him.

After a few minutes of expectation and silent preparation, the medium's hand, guided by the doctor and moving in cooperation with her psycho-physical stimuli, began writing in irregular characters, revealing the natural variation between "two different psychic fields," but dedicated to one common objective: the production of an uplifting message.

I followed the scene with interest.

A few minutes later, the brief message could be read.

The communication was simple in format, rendering a fraternal plea.

"My friends," the emissary had written, "may God bless us.

"Together in the building of the good, let us work to assist the infirm, who need our assistance in the long suffering of earthly trials. This service must include good will combined with living faith. The sowing requires selfless workers who can ignore fatigue, sadness and discouragement.

"Let us press on.

"Each tiny display of personal effort in the work of charity will receive the Lord's Divine Blessing.

"Let us therefore learn to aid the sick. Through the dark night of pain, they suffer and weep, often completely forsaken.

"Does this picture of suffering not move you? Let us remember the Divine Physician who walked the earth doing good. From him

we will receive the strength we need to continue. He will be with us on the long pathway of compassion for those who suffer.

"We put our trust in you, in your dedication to the cause of evangelical goodness.

"The road will perhaps be rugged and difficult; the Lord will be with us, nonetheless.

"Let us proceed fearlessly, and may he bless us now and forever."

The communicator signed his name and a few minutes later that evening's spiritual work was over.

The meeting's supervisor and other participants then began studying and discussing the message. Everyone agreed that it was edifying in essence, but it didn't provide conclusive proof of the individual's identity. Quite possibly, it hadn't originated from the well-known professional who signed it. It lacked special characteristics, since a real doctor would use suitable nomenclature and avoid common terminology.

At that point the animistic theory was posed as the acceptable solution for all. The conversation shifted to complex references related to the European world. The attendees talked extensively about Richet and international metapsychism; Pierre Janet, Charcot, De Rochas and Aksakof were all discussed in turn.

The communicator on our plane of action disappointedly turned to Calderaro, stating:

"Goodness gracious! I didn't mean to stir up such controversy. Our purpose was quite different. A little love for the sick; nothing more.

Calderaro smiled without uttering a word, and moving his attention to a more important concern, he approached the downcast Eulalia.

The medium had been listening to the particular comments with obvious dismay.

Her mind had become blurred, dimmed by a dense veil of doubt. The course of the discussion clouded her understanding. Her eyes filled with tears that did not fall.

Calderaro got close to her and said to me kindly:

"Our incarnate friends don't always examine situations through the prism of true justice. Eulalia is a dedicated and sincere worker. While she has not yet acquired an extensive scientific education, she is nonetheless sufficiently rich with love to contribute to the sowing of light. However, she finds herself unshielded among her inattentive companions. She remains alone, and besieged as she is, she is susceptible to becoming distraught. We need to help her right now."

The Assistant held his right hand open over our esteemed sister's head and emitted a bright light that went from her head down to her chest area like a renewing wave of energy.

The medium, who had seemed tormented, barely controlling her natural reaction to the opinions being voiced, returned to serenity. The look of disappointment fell from her face, and her destructive sadness dissipated. Her perispiritual centers returned to normalcy and her pineal gland radiated a soft light. The clouds of anguish vanished from her mind as if by magic. In other words, supported by the direct act of my instructor, Eulalia grasped the hurdles of this sort of service and gradually let a higher understanding take over.

With her peace of mind reestablished, Calderaro placed his hands on her frontal lobes, acting upon her inhibitory fibers. Next, I observed another change. As if withdrawing into itself, the medium's mind lost interest in the conversation around her and became more attentive to our field of action. Imperceptible to her, the Assistant's beneficial contact severed her interest in the pointless discussion, placing her in a more direct contact with us.

With paternal kindness, Calderaro kept his hand in place and spoke caringly into her ears:

"Don't be discouraged, Eulalia! Faith is the power that sustains the spirit in the front lines of the battle for the victory of the divine light and universal love. Our friends are not accusing you, nor are they hurting you: they're only dreaming in a sleep of illusion, disconnected from the truth. Forgive them for the futilities of the moment. Later on they will awaken to the effort of spreading the good ... They use their eyes to investigate the surface of things, but their ears have not yet heard the sublime call to redemption. We must carry on. We will be with you in the daily task. It is necessary to forgive and love always, forgetting the dark day in order to arrive at the luminous future. Don't give up! The Eternal Father will bless you."

I noticed that Eulalia had not heard him with her physical ears. Instead, her frontal lobes were filled with intense light. The instructor's moving words remained in her mind and heart like sublime thoughts that had fallen on her from the sky, saturated with comforting and blessed warmth.

"Yes," answered the devoted worker from the bottom of her heart, although her lips were closed in incomprehensive silence. She would work till the end, aware that the service of the truth belongs to the Lord and not to humans. She would ignore offenses. She would receive objections from others and transform them into helpful aids. She would convert depressing opinions into reasons for renewed strength. She would readily acknowledge her own faults, even though they resulted from someone else's weakness, rendering thanks for the opportunity to correct them whenever possible. She would indeed press onward. Her mediumship would be an area of work where she would perfect her sentiments, without being overly concerned with the elements of its manifestation. In fact, why should she worry

about difficulties in psychography if she had a heart beating with love? Yes, she would listen to the suggestions of goodness before anything else. She would be faithful to God and to herself. Even if her human friends couldn't understand her, didn't she have the comfort of being understood by friends on the spirit plane? At the end of her earthly experience, there would be enough light for all. It was her duty to believe, work, love and wait on the Divine Lord.

The Assistant removed his hands, left her side and said to me:

"Our sister has been helped and is all right; thanks be to God!"

Observing the medium's frontal lobes clothed in glowing light, I communicated my wonder to Calderaro.

Explaining further, he stated:

"At this moment Eulalia is mentally in the highest region possible for her. She has retreated calmly to her innermost sanctuary so as to profitably understand and forgive."

Indicating the cerebral region he was referring to, he concluded:

"In the frontal lobes, Andre, the physical exteriorization of important perispiritual centers, there are million of cells waiting for human effort in the area of spiritualization in order to become operative. Not one of the most daring thinkers of humankind from ancient times up till now has ever managed to use a tenth of them. They are energies of a virgin field, which the soul will gain not only through evolutionary continuity but also through self-education, moral improvement and sublime elevation. My friend, only a living and revealing faith can initiate such an endeavor as an indispensable trailblazing light for individual progress."

10
A Bitter Loss

In the middle of the night, we were confronted by an afflicted mother. As she spoke, the entity aroused our compassion by her look of dreadful suffering.

"Calderaro! Calderaro!" she pleaded anxiously, "Please help my daughter, my poor, poor daughter!"

"Oh! Has she taken a turn for the worse?" asked the instructor, showing his familiarity with the situation.

"Yes! A lot worse!" wailed the worried mother with trembling lips; I can see that she's gone completely mad ..."

"Has she missed out on the great opportunity?"

"Not yet," said the mother, "but she's on the verge of extreme disaster."

Calderaro promised to hurry to the sick girl in a few minutes and we resumed our conversation.

Due to my interest in the case, the thoughtful Assistant summarized the facts.

"It is a regrettable instance," he explained kindly, "in which thoughtlessness and hate are the dreadful factors. The sister who came to us a moment ago left a daughter behind on the earth eight years ago. The girl was raised with excessive pampering and grew up not knowing a thing about work and responsibility, although she did belong to a noble social circle. She was an only child and early on was subject to pernicious whims. As soon as she found herself without her mother's guidance in the physical realm, she proceeded to dominate governesses, to bribe servants and to deceive her father's care. Surrounded with material means, at twenty years of age she dived into the follies of worldly life. Thus, left unprotected by circumstances, she wasn't able to prepare herself adequately to face the problems related to her redemption. Without the spiritual protection peculiar to poverty and without the blessed stimuli of material hurdles, but with striking yet transitory physical beauty playing against her inner needs, the poor girl had reincarnated, followed closely not by an enemy per se, but by an accomplice in serious wrongs who had discarnated long ago, and to whom she had linked herself by means of the awful bonds of hatred in a recent past. Thus, abusing her freedom in reproachable idleness, she took on the duties of motherhood outside the bonds of marriage. Now at twenty-five years of age, unwed, rich, and enjoying the prestige of her family name, she regrets too late the responsibility of her situation and is struggling desperately to rid herself of her unborn son: the same accomplice from the past I referred to earlier. 'Thanks to divine mercy,' this wretch hopes to use his former companion's lapse of judgment to accomplish some redemptive service under the supervision of our Superiors."

In light of the amazement that unexpectedly came over me – I knew that reincarnation is always a blessing that

materializes with assistance from higher up – the Assistant reassured me:

"God is a loving and wise Father who always converts our wrongs into a bitter medicine that can heal and strengthen us. Cecilia, the mental case we are about to visit, has thus reaped from her carelessness the very best resource capable of rectifying her life ... However, the unfortunate creature is reacting fiercely against divine help through regrettable and perverse behavior. For some weeks now, I have taken part in assisting her due to her mother's reiterated and moving pleas to our superiors. However, I have little hope that her rehabilitation is close at hand. The bonds between mother and potential son are bonds of bitterness and hatred – both destabilizing energies. Such bonds translate into a circumstance in which the female spirit must seek the sanctuary of resignation and hope if it intends to be successful. That is why the Supreme Lord created the warm and velvety nest of motherly love to level off redeeming pathways and perfect the sentiments. But when the woman rebels, insensitive to the sublime vibrations of divine inspiration, it is difficult, if not impossible, to carry out the plan. Thus, giving in to reprehensible yearnings, the unfortunate creature went looking for help from doctors, who, with support from our plane, refused to satisfy her criminal intentions. She then began taking poisonous drugs, which she has been abusing intensively. Her mental condition is one of pitiable madness."

His brief introduction finished, Calderaro continued:

"We don't have a minute to lose. Let's go."

A few minutes later we entered a comfortable, scented room.

A young woman was stretched out on a bed, writhing in atrocious convulsions. At her side stood her mother in the plane invisible to physical eyes, and an incarnate nurse – one of those who was used to witnessing biological catastrophes and moral dramas and had thus become insensitive to other people's pain.

The sick woman's mother stepped forward and informed us:

"Her situation is dire! Help her, for mercy's sake! My presence here is limited to preventing the entry of disturbing spirits making their sinister rounds."

Calmly and thoughtfully, the Assistant leaned over the patient and suggested that I make a detailed examination of the physiological picture before us.

The organic outlook was most moving.

Fraternal compassion prevents us from relating the sad description of the embryo about to be expelled.

Limited to the topic of medicating hallucinatory minds, we can only say that the young woman's situation was shocking and deplorable.

All the endocrine centers were in disarray and the autonomous organs were working at an alarming rate. Her heart displayed a strange arrhythmia and the sweat glands were working in vain to expel a virtual torrent of invasive toxins. The darkness was complete in the frontal lobes. Disturbance was obvious in the encephalic cortex. Only the basal ganglia registered a notable concentration of mental energies, informing me that the wretched creature had descended into the lowest realm of her being, dominated by the disintegrating impulses of her own deviant, uneducated sentiments. From the basal ganglia, where the strongest radiations of her hallucinatory mind were gathering, dark filaments descended that assaulted the fallopian tubes and ovaries, piercing the womb like tiny spears of darkness and falling upon the four-month-old embryonic organism.

The scene was awful.

As I tuned in to the patient, I heard her cruel statements in the realm of thought:

"I hate! … I hate this intrusive child. I didn't want it in the first place! … I'm going to expel it! … Expel it!"

As if it had been assaulted during its gentle sleep, the mind of her reincarnating child begged her in tears:

"Spare me! Spare me! I want to wake up and work! I want to live and realign my destiny … Help me! I'll settle my debt! … I'll pay you back with love … Please don't expel me! Have mercy!"

"Never! Never! Damn you!" the wretch said mentally. "I'd rather die than receive you in my arms! You're poisoning my life; you're spoiling my plans! I detest you! You're going to die!"

And the dark rays continued their descent.

Calderaro raised his venerable head and asked me:

"Can you grasp the extent of this tragedy?"

Completely at a loss for words, I nodded.

At that moment of anxious expectation, Cecilia addressed the nurse decisively:

"I'm tired and worn out, Liana, but I must insist on the surgery being done tonight!"

"Oh?! Just like that; when you're like this?!" the nurse asked.

"Yes, yes!" the sick woman replied impatiently. "I don't want to put it off any longer. The doctors refused to do it, so I'm counting on you. My father must know nothing about it. I hate this situation and shall rid myself of it."

Calderaro placed his right hand on the nurse's head in an obvious attempt to transmit some conciliatory plan. She stated:

"Try to get some rest, Cecilia. Maybe you'll change your mind."

"No, no," the improvident future mother objected in an obviously bad mood. "My mind's made up. The surgery shall be tonight."

In spite of this explicit refusal, she took the sedative the nurse offered her in response to our indirect influence.

My instructor's course of action had worked.

Partially disconnected from her physical body and obviously drowsy due to the calming effect of the medication,

Calderaro applied magnetic fluids to the photosensitive disc of her visual apparatus. Cecilia could then see us, though imperfectly, and gazed in wonder at her mother.

I noticed, however, that while the mother shed abundant tears of emotion, her daughter remained impassive despite her look of astonishment.

The discarnate mother stepped forward, hugged her and said anxiously:

"Dearest daughter, I've come to you so that you don't go through with this sinister deed. Reconsider your mental attitude and reconcile yourself with life. Receive my tears as an appeal from my heart. For mercy's sake, listen to me! Don't immerse yourself in darkness, when the divine hand holds the portals of light open to you. It's never too late to start over, Cecilia, and in his infinite devotion God turns our wrongs into a web of salvation."

The crazed mind of the listener vaguely recalled social conventions, as if she had lived a moment of indefinable nightmare.

Nevertheless, her mother continued:

"Reach out to your conscience above anything else! Conventions are respectable and society has its just principles, but a time comes in the sphere of destiny and pain when we must hold to God alone. Don't forsake courage, faith, valor … When illuminated by love and sacrifice, motherhood is a happy event anywhere, even when the world is unaware of the cause of our downfalls and denies us the resources for our rehabilitation, relegating us to relapse and helplessness. You might face a storm of tears for now: the storm of incomprehension and intolerance will slap you in the face … Good times will return, however. The way is rocky and arid; thorns will tear at you. But against your heart you will hold a loving son, showing you the future! Truth is, Cecilia, you should have built your nest of happiness in the tree of stability, glorifying in peace the accomplishments of each day and the blessings of each night. But you couldn't wait … You gave in

to unrestrained passion and forsook your ideals at the first impulses of desire. Instead of building upon a sure foundation with serenity and trust, you chose the perilous path of haste. Now it's crucial for you to avoid a fatal downfall, to bypass the treacherous abyss, to cling to the lifesaver of supreme duty. So, my dearest, return to the peace of mind you used to enjoy and resign yourself to the new direction you have given your life by accepting the duty of pain-filled motherhood at the sacrifice of other aspirations. In the silence and darkness of being isolated from society, we often achieve the happiness of getting to know ourselves. Public scorn may incite the weakest to forget themselves, but it uplifts the strongest to God and supports them on the nameless trail of humble obligations that leads to the mount of redemption. Your father might curse you and our dearest relations on earth might despise you and try to debase you. But what kind of torment is there that will not ennoble the spirit that is prepared to redeem its debts with dedication to the good and with serenity in pain? Wouldn't it be better to have a crown of thorns placed on one's brow than to have a mountain of hot coals in one's conscience? Evil can waste us and lead us astray; the good always rectifies. Moreover, if it is certain that the suffering of shame will flog your sensitivity, it is just as certain that the glory of motherhood will shine on your path … Your tears will water a dear and sublime blossom: your son, flesh of your flesh, being of your being. What can't a woman who knows how to resign herself accomplish! The storm will roar, but always outside your heart, since within it, in the divine sanctuary of love, you will find within you the power of peace for your victory."

The sick woman listened, indifferent, unwilling to yield. She received her mother's pleas with an unchanged attitude. Her mom, however, mobilized all the resources within her reach and continued after a longer pause:

"Listen, Cecilia! Don't hold on to this unyielding attitude. Don't isolate your mind from your heart. Let your sentiment

benefit your reason so that you may overcome your harsh trial. Don't concentrate solely on the physical body or think that spiritual and eternal beauty builds its temple in the body of flesh, which is on its way to turning to dust. Death will come no matter what, bringing the reality that confounds illusion. Don't persist in the darkness of lies. Humble yourself in constructive self-denial; take up your cross and move on to higher understanding … Within your ordeal of inner suffering, you will hear the tender voice of a blessed son … If desertion by the world hurts you, he will be at your side as the gentle representative of the Divine One … How will you possibly miss the mantle of fantasy while two soft little arms are placed affectionately and faithfully around you, leading you toward renewal for the greater life?"

At this point, surprising me with her aggressiveness, Cecilia argued in thought:

"Why didn't you say that to me before? While on earth, you always satisfied all my whims. You never allowed me to work; you encouraged my idleness; you led me to believe I was in a higher position than other people and that every kind of special privilege was owed to me. In other words, you didn't prepare me! I'm alone with an afflicting problem … I don't have the courage to humble myself … To beg for paying work sure isn't the ideal you passed on to me, and for me, facing shame and misery would be worse than dying. No! … I won't give in, not even at hearing your voice, which, in spite of everything, I still love! … But I can't go back."

The touching scene was dreadful. There I was, observing the millennia-old conflict between a mother's tenderness and real life.

Weeping more bitterly, the venerable mother clung to her daughter more vehemently and pleaded:

"Forgive me for the wrong I did to you because I loved you so much … Oh dear daughter, human love doesn't always proceed

with the care it should! At times, blindness leads us to commit terrible mistakes, which only the blow of death can expunge. But haven't you considered my pain? I realize my indirect participation in your present misfortune, but I now understand the extent and intricacies of a mother's duties. I don't want you to reap thorns in the same place where I'm now suffering the bitter results of my improvidence. Just because I erred out of excessive tenderness, don't go astray in an escalation of hatred and inconformity. After the grave, the day of the good shines brighter, while one night of evil is especially darker and stormier. Accept humiliation as a blessing and pain as a priceless opportunity. All earthly struggles come and go. They may last a while but not forever. So don't complicate destiny. I submit myself to your accusations. They are deserved by someone who, like me, forgot about the forest of accomplishments for the eternal life, willfully remaining in the garden of ephemeral pleasures, where flowers don't last more than a fleeting minute. Cecilia, I forgot about the blessed hoe of one's own effort, with which I should have worked the soil of our life, sowing the gifts of edifying work. I still haven't wept sufficiently to redeem myself from such a regrettable mistake, but I trust you and hope that the same doesn't happen to you on the harsh path of regeneration. It's better to beg for one's daily bread, to become embittered by the gibes of human cruelty there on earth than to spurn the bread of God's opportunities and allow cruelty to enslave the heart. The suffering of those defeated in human struggles is a storehouse of enlightening experience. The Divine Goodness turns our wounds into illumination for the soul. Blessed are those who reach death covered with the scars that give evidence of the hard battle. For them, an everlasting era of peace will blaze on the horizon, for reality does not surprise them when the coldness of the tomb blows into their hearts. Truth becomes their generous friend; hope and understanding, their loyal companions! Return

to your senses, dear daughter; renew your courage and optimism, in spite of the threatening clouds hovering over your delirious mind ... There's still time! There's still time!"

The sick woman, however, made a huge effort to return to her envelope of flesh, uttering harsh, ungrateful words of refusal.

Shirking off Calderaro's calming influence, she gradually returned to her field of sensory perception in raspy cries.

The instructor approached the tearful mother and said:

"Unfortunately, my friend, the process of madness by insurgence seems complete. Now we must entrust her to the power of Supreme Divine Providence."

While the mother burst into tears, the sick woman, disturbed by her own mental emissions, complained to the nurse:

"I can't! I can't go on! I can't handle it ... The surgery, now! I don't want to waste another minute!"

Staring at the nurse with a horrified expression, she added:

"I just had a dreadful nightmare ... I dreamed that my mother had returned from the dead and asked me to be patient and to have mercy! Not a chance! ... I'm going all the way! I'd rather kill myself!"

Inspired by my instructor, the nurse continued voicing a number of conscientious thoughts.

Wouldn't it be best to wait a bit longer? Mightn't that dream be a timely warning? Shouldn't Cecilia's profound weariness be taken into consideration? Besides, didn't she feel assisted by a spiritual intervention? The nurse continued to find grounds to postpone the decision.

The patient, however, was inflexible. And thus, to our astonishment and in the presence of the tearful discarnate mother, the procedure began. The prognosis was grim as we watched the scene extremely moved.

I had never imagined that an imbalanced mind could inflict such great harm on its own body.

The disarray of the physiological cosmos increased by the minute.

Poignantly surprised, I continued to examine the situation, surprised to see that the embryo reacted at being violated, as if desperately trying to adhere to the placental walls.

The unborn child's mind began to awaken as the removal effort proceeded. Dark rays were coming not only from the mother's encephalon but also from the embryonic organism, establishing even greater disharmony.

After a long and laborious procedure, the little being was finally removed …

Astonished, I noticed, however, that the unlearned abortionist had been able to remove only a small amount of lifeless flesh from the womb, because, as if strong, indefinable powers were keeping the reincarnating spirit connected to her body, it posed a unique situation, adhered as it was to the cellular field that was expelling it. Semi-conscious in a frightful nightmare of suffering, it displayed extreme despair, wailing in screams of affliction and sending off deadly vibrations as it babbled in disconnected sentences.

Weren't we looking at two fiends, shackled dreadfully to each other. The unborn child had become a deadly executioner of the mother's psyche. Pressing the uterine network of vessels with unintentional impulses precisely in the area where the mother and fetus exchange blood, he caused a violent and abundant hemorrhagic process.

I saw even more.

Unduly displaced and kept there by uncontrollable forces, the unborn spirit's perispiritual organism[20] reached the heart

[20] The spirit is surrounded by a substance that might look vaporous to you but which is still quite dense to us [in the spirit world] … As a fruit seed is enveloped by the perisperm,

area in willful movements. Wrapping around the nodules of the right auricle, it interfered with the stimuli channels, causing a tremendous shock to the central nervous system.

This increased the hemorrhagic flow, which reached unexpected intensity, compelling the nurse to ask for immediate help after destroying as best as she could all traces of her wrong.

"I hate you! I hate you!" the mother's mind screamed in delirium, still feeling the presence of her son in her organic body. "I'd never cradle an intruder who would put me to shame!"

To describe it more accurately, both mother and son now seemed to be in sync in the wave of hatred, because, displaying a strange form to my eyes, his mind replied at the height of his wrath:

"I shall avenge myself! You shall pay cent by cent! I shall never forgive you! ... You have failed to let me retake the earthly struggle, where the pain that we would have shared would have taught me to forgive you for your sinful past and to forget my excruciating sorrows ... You have refused the trial that would have led us to the altar of reconciliation. You have slammed the doors of redeeming opportunity in my face. However, the evil power that rules inside you lives in my soul too ... You have brought to the surface of my mind the wicked slime that lay dormant within me. You have denied me the resource of purification, but now we are united again and I shall drag you into the abyss ... You have condemned me to death, and so my sentence regarding you is the same. You have failed to give me rest and have kept me from restoring my peace of mind, so your time on earth is up ... You did not want me for the work of love ... So you shall be mine again to satisfy my hatred. I shall avenge myself! You shall follow me!"

---

the spirit per se is surrounded by an envelope, which by comparison, may be called the perispirit. Question nº 93, *The Spirits' Book*. – Tr.

Destructive mental rays were crisscrossing in a horrendous scene from spirit to spirit.

While I was observing the intensification of toxins along the whole cellular network, Calderaro was praying in silence. He seemed to be invoking outside help. In fact, a small group of spirit workers entered the room a few moments later. The instructor gave them orders. They were to help the unfortunate spirit mother, who would remain with her wretched daughter till the end of the process.

Next, the Assistant asked me to leave with him, adding:

"She will discarnate in a few hours. Every day, Andre, hatred exterminates individuals with an intensity and efficiency more destructive than all the cannons on earth thundering at once. Hatred is mightier at complicating problems and destroying peace than all the wars known to humankind over the course of the centuries. This is no mere theory. You have just witnessed a dreadful event that is repeated every day in the physical realm. With the establishment of such horrible forces over these two imbalanced souls that Providence had sought to unite through reincarnation, one must entrust them henceforth to time so that pain and suffering can perform the indispensable corrective remedy.

"Oh!" I exclaimed, distraught, contemplating the duel between these two tortured minds. "What's going to happen? Are they going to remain intertwined like this? For how long?"

Calderaro gazed at me in the downcast manner of a brave soldier who has temporarily lost the battle, and said:

"Direct intervention would be useless now. We can only cooperate with prayers of fraternal love, followed by the renewing role of daily struggle. The painful process of mutual obsession has begun for both, with bitter consequences in space and time, the extent of which none of us can predict."

11
Sex

Still affected by Cecilia's tragic drama, I accompanied Calderaro to an unusual study center, where high-level instructors taught students devoted to assistance work down on the earth.

"This isn't a temple of advanced instruction," stated the instructor, "but an institution of effective support for the ideas and undertakings of industrious coworkers in workshops of spiritual support; a center of friendship created for disciples ennobled by persevering efforts."

In answer to my inquiry as a learner, he continued benevolently:

"These friends gather once a week to listen to messengers trained in issues that are closely related to our ministry of assistance to humans. I want you to attend this evening because the messenger will be commenting on problems pertaining to sex. Since you are currently studying the enigmas

of insanity, and since you don't have enough time for direct experimentation, this lecture will meet our needs."

There was no time for more preliminary explanations.

The Assistant saw that the session had already started, and thus we proceeded without more ado. In fact, we found the meeting well underway. A little more than two hundred members from our realm were listening attentively to the enlightened instructor of souls.

We sat down and listened respectfully.

Surrounded by a bright glow, the bearer of wisdom lectured without affectation. With resonant words that penetrated our inner being by their inflection of sincerity, he spoke simply:

"In examining the causes of insanity among incarnate or discarnate spirits, ignorance regarding sexual behavior is one of the most crucial factors.

"Human misunderstanding about this subject is like a silent war of extermination and upheaval that greatly exceeds the devastation wrought by the plagues in the history of humankind. You know that in the 6th century the bubonic epidemic, called the "Justinian Plague,"[21] killed almost fifty million people in Europe and Asia ... This impressive number is trifling when compared to the millions of souls that the anguishes of sex assail everyday. A pressing problem that has maddened many fine minds, we cannot attack it with a verbal tirade, addressing it from the outside inward, in the manner of amateurish physicians who prescribe lengthy treatments to

[21] The first outbreak of plague in Europe occurred between 541 and 544 BCE, known as Justinian's Plague. The plague most likely traveled north along the Nile into the Mediterranean Basin. Because this was a central trading region, it quickly branched out along trading routes from Egypt into Central and South Asia, the Middle East, North Africa, and much of Southern Europe. Between 541 and 542, forty percent of Constantinople, then the central port of trade in the Mediterranean, was dead. The plague finally petered out in 544 in Northern and Central Europe due to a lack of ongoing and significant trade to and from the region. (Thomas, 1997). http://fubini.swarthmore.edu. – Tr.

their patients while usually lacking any real knowledge about the disease.

"Now that we have distanced ourselves from the highly rigid impositions of form – without freeing ourselves, however, from the fundamental influences of their laws, which still shape our manifestations – we can understand that the enigmas of sex cannot be reduced to mere physiological factors. They do not result from automatisms in the field of cellular structure, such as those that characterize the male and female genital organs, which are actually identical in most ways, differing only in outward appearance. In this regard, we have formulated more-advanced concepts. If dominant procreative forces reside there in keeping with the statutes of earthly nature – regulators of physical life – then sexual problems are a phenomenon that is peculiar to our psyche as it progresses toward the higher regions of evolution.

"It is painful, however, to see the disharmony that humans have sunk into, which reflects darkly in the spheres closest to the corporeal struggle. Over the centuries, countless liberating movements have risen in hopes for a better life. Bloody wars of nation against nation, and civil conflicts spreading unspeakable suffering, have been fostered over the course of time on behalf of regenerating principles, through which new conquests of world rights were achieved. However, the bondage of ignorance in the area of sex continues to enslave millions.

"It is futile to believe that physical death would offer a peaceful solution to highly imbalanced spirits who hand their bodies over to ungoverned passions. The insanity in which they struggle does not occur from simple changes in the brain: it originates from the dissociation of the perispiritual centers and requires a long, long time to recover.

"For most incarnates, the juvenile phase of their physiological forces undeniably represents a delicate period of

sensations in light of the creative and preserving laws that rule the human family. But this is incidental and does not define the substantial reality. The control center of sex is not located in the dense body, but in the sublime organization of the soul.

"Down on earth, men and women are distinguished according to specific organic features. As for us, in transit to higher spiritual regions, the remembrance of our earthly existence is still preponderant. We know, however, that in such higher regions femininity and masculinity are characteristics of souls that are highly passive or openly active.

"Consequently, we know that, in the variations of our experiences, we gradually acquire divine qualities such as determination and tenderness, strength and humility, power and gentleness, intelligence and sentiment, initiative and intuition, wisdom and love, until we attain our supreme balance in God.

"Convinced of this universal reality, we cannot forget that any exteriorization of the sexual instinct on earth, in whichever way it may express itself, will not be destroyed but transmuted once a state of sublimation is achieved. The sexual expressions of the animals participate in the same ascending impulse. Amongst early peoples, sexual eclosion was expressed by absolute ownership. The fully active personality of the man dominated the completely passive personality of the woman.

"However, the patient work of millennia has transformed these relationships. Woman-mother and man-father gave rise to a new breath of renewal to the spirit. Based on sexual experiences, the tribe became the family; the hut metamorphosed into the home; armed defense gave way to jurisprudence; the wild forest was transformed into the peaceful farm; the heterogeneous character of huge expanses of territory opened the way to the communion of ideals in progressive homelands; barbarism rose to civilization; the crude processes of physical attraction

were transubstantiated into artistic aspirations that dignify the individual, and grunts were elevated to melodies. Stimulated by the creative power of sex, the human community is advancing, albeit slowly, toward the supreme goal of divine love. From the spontaneous, brutal manifestation of the less elevated senses, the soul is traveling toward its glorious initiation.

"Desire, ownership, affinity, fondness, devotion, selflessness and sacrifice constitute aspects of this sublime journey.

"Sometimes, humans take years, centuries and many lifetimes to go from one level to the next. Few individuals are able to keep themselves above the fray with the equilibrium that is required. Very few have crossed the territory of ownership without battling cruelly with the monsters of selfishness and jealousy, to which they have completely surrendered. A small number travel the road of tenderness without shackling themselves for a long stretch to the many chains of exclusiveness. And sometimes, only after millennia of excruciating, purifying trials, can the soul reach the luminous zenith of sacrifice for its final deliverance en route to new cycles of unification with the Divinity.

"The rapture of the saint was once a mere impulse, like the polished diamond – a drop of heaven chosen to reflect the divine light. The diamond lived on the river bed, ignored amongst the unpolished pebbles. It is obvious that, just as the diamond is put to the polishing wheel in order to achieve its ultimate beauty, so it is with the sexual instinct. In order to be crowned with the glories of elation, it must submit itself to the imperatives of responsibility, the demands of discipline and the requirements of selflessness.

"These conclusions, however, should not lead us to plans for compulsory sanctification in the corporeal world. No human being would deny his or her stage of evolution. We cannot expect an uneducated primitive to wear the academic gown of a

university professor and overnight begin to teach Roman Law. Consequently, it would be foolish to expect the behavior of a saint from a person of average evolution. Nature, the representation of Inexhaustible Goodness, is a benign mother who offers work and assistance to all the offspring of creation. Her determination to sustain us is as strong as our determination to progress in the direction of the Supreme Good.

"Therefore, we do not want to profess strict standards of artificial virtue in the world, nor favor any system of unconscious relationships. Above all, our banner is that of fraternal understanding. Let us work so that the light of understanding may be established amongst our incarnate fellow spirits so that their love-related troubles do not lead so many victims to the brink of death, intoxicated by criminal passions.

"Due to a lack of sexual understanding, countless crimes abound on the earth, causing strange and dangerous processes of insanity far and wide.

"From time to time, one or more victims enter a hospital for the mentally afflicted and submit themselves to medical treatment, much like workers who bring their broken tools to a repair shop. However, in these places we find only those who, embittered and defeated, have hit rock bottom. Millions of our brothers and sisters are in a state of semi-madness right in their own homes or in institutions. They fill the ranks of those incapable of commitment or selflessness, immersing themselves little by little in the dark swampland of hallucination ... With their crazed minds fixed in the den of the subconscious, they become lost in debased automatisms and stubbornly hold on to their depressing psychic condition. Jealousy, dissatisfaction, misunderstanding, thoughtlessness and failure to restrain their sexual appetites spread terrible phenomena of instability.

"Disturbing mental images are being projected on the earth, compelling us to perform a strenuous work of assistance so as to limit the circle of misfortune and horror of those who carelessly fling themselves into reckless adventures of animalized sentiment.

"We will not solve such a complex problem by merely using medical interventions. Although the contribution of medical science is admirable in treating effects, it does not address inner causes. Personality is not the work of the internal labor of the glands, but the product of the chemistry of the mind.

"Endocrinology can do much with hormone injections as a first-aid measure at the cellular level, but it cannot repair the lesions of thought. Sooner or later, genetics will be able to interfere in the secret chambers of human life, disturbing chromosomal harmony by imposing gender on the embryo. However, it will not reach the higher regions of the feminine or masculine mind, which will retain its own features regardless of the outer format or established conventions. Medicine will invent thousands of ways to help the body whose internal balance is out of kilter, and for such a constructive endeavor it will continue to deserve our sincere admiration and fervent love. But it is up to us to practice the medicine of the soul, a medicine that upholds the spirit entangled in darkness.

"We must shine the light of fraternal compassion on our incarnate brothers and sisters, and trace out well-defined paths for individual responsibility. If more love would exist in these abysses where the insanity of instinctual behavior abounds, defeat would give way to sanctifying experience.

"How can the blessed service rendered by physicians to the victims of sexual anguish be worthwhile if they have to face the hostility of the family? How can one save the diseased in soul at a charitable institution if the social organism crushes the patient with all the weight of its opinion and authority?

Obviously, it would be foolishly sentimental to expect sociology to transform its codes all at once, or to impose on human society certain standards of tolerance that would be incompatible with its needs for self defense. But we can maintain a praiseworthy deeper understanding, improve the disposition of our incarnate friends and awaken them little by little to the solution that concerns us all.

"Spiritualized love, the offspring of Christian selflessness, is the key that can open the doors of the abyss, into which thousands of individuals have fallen and still fall into everyday.

"Let us distribute the blessing of understanding among humankind; let us extend a strong hand to all spirits who are prisoners of the turmoil of the sensations, enabling them to know that the workshops of regenerating work are open to all God's children, perfecting their sentiments, sublimating their impulses and broadening their spiritual aptitude.

"Let us remind disheartened souls that sex in the realm of love is what the eyes are to sight and the brain is to thought – that is, no more than a device for exteriorization. It is a regrettable error to believe that only perfect sexual normalcy, consonant with respectable human conventions, can serve as an expression of affection. The field of love is infinite in its essence and manifestation. While it is necessary to avoid aberrations and excesses, it is imperative to recognize that all beings were born in the universe to love and to be loved. Sometimes, the imperatives of beneficial trials, the duties of expiation and the demands of specialized work are temporarily in force for many, wherein learners, debtors and missionaries must endure long phases of soul hunger and thirst. But this is not an obstacle to love. Jesus did not share in a normal marriage; nevertheless, the family of his love grows every day. He did not generate transient forms in corporeal circles, but his fecundating energies renewed civilization, altering its course up till now by making the world a better place. Sublime

symbolism is apparent in the conduct of the Master, who, in this way, leaned toward people who were defeated by human convention, the lonely and humiliated, enabling them to realize that it is possible to take part in the expanse of the Infinite Good by loving and denying oneself to the exclusion of selfishness and the inferior purpose of being loved according to one's own whims.

"The construction of true happiness does not depend on satisfying the instincts. The exchange of sexual cells among incarnate beings, guaranteeing the continuity of physical forms in the evolutionary process, is but one aspect of the multiform exchanges of love. It is important to realize that the exchange of harmonious energies, of combined spiritual fluids, of attuned vibrations between souls who love each other, soar above any tangible exteriorization of affection, sustaining imperishable works of life and light in the unlimited spheres of the universe.

"Let us therefore develop a loving assistance to those who despair in the world, feeling themselves caught in the temporary condition of being disinherited. Let us teach them to free their mind from the web of the instincts, opening a pathway for them toward the ideals of sanctifying love. Let us remind them that by setting their thoughts on tormented sex while forgetting other spiritual achievements by means of the organic cosmos is akin to hopelessly paralyzing oneself on the evolutionary track. It is to deliver oneself, defenseless, to the influence of the perilous monsters of the imagination, such as spite and envy, despair and bitterness, which open ruinous wounds in the soul and demand exclusiveness, leading to insanity and unconsciousness. Let us invite them to search for horizons further away in the heart. Love will always find new worlds. And for such discoveries to be crowned with the divine light, it is enough for individuals to abandon idleness, which in turn will combat ignorance. Inside each one of us shines a liberating light, the thought of renewal

for the common good, which we should cultivate and intensify every day of our lives.

"Captivity in the torments of sex is not a problem that may be solved by intellectuals or doctors acting in the outer realm: it is a matter of the soul, which demands an individual process of healing; and the soul can solve it only in the tribunal of its own conscience. Of course, all external help is valuable and respectable, but we have to realize that the slaves of disturbances in the field of sensations will be delivered only by themselves, by increasing their comprehension, by understanding their own difficulties and the suffering of others, and finally, by implementing 'love one another' both in education and in the core of the soul, using the best of the mind's energies and the best sentiments of the heart."

I could see that the lecture had ended in the midst of a general feeling of respect.

The messenger's words had fascinated me. These concepts on sexology were new. They were not repetitions of descriptive compendiums, nor the product of cold observations by scientists and writers concerned with producing effects through empty words. They came from words inflamed with the fraternal love of a guide dedicated to the needs of his still-fragile and less joyous brothers and sisters.

The audience began to stir, and I realized that attendees could now ask questions related to the evening's topic; in fact, several were posed and all received valuable answers that were both enlightening and edifying.

As the instructive inquiries continued profitably, a question was asked that piqued my curiosity.

"Venerable instructor," began the attendee reverently, "down on earth, a considerable number of incarnate psychologists have recently adopted Freudian principles as the basis for

investigating the troubles of the soul. For the great Austrian doctor, almost all psychic disturbances were based on deviant sex. Some of his disciples, however, have modified his theories somewhat. Correcting the thesis of erotic hallucination, which psychoanalysis has broadly applied even to children in the study of dreams and emotions, illustrious scholars have affirmed that every man and every woman is a bearer of the innate desire to feel important, which compels them to sustain primitive impulses of domination. Other exponents of intellectual culture affirm that the human being is a repository of all of the experiences of the race, carrying with him or her a vast arsenal of tendencies toward certain lines of thought."

The questioner paused in the general silence instilled by his valuable inquiry, and then proceeded:

"As we are now far from the dense, incarnate body, we know that the spirit's life is disconcertingly full of surprises for earthly science. Nevertheless, since we have devoted ourselves to the task of aiding our tormented friends down on earth, couldn't you give us some appropriate explanations in that regard so that we can disseminate them later on?"

The wise instructor did not hesitate to clarify:

"I know just what you mean. You are referring to the analytical psychology movement headed by Freud and by two distinct currents of his collaborators. The famous scientist centered his teachings on the sexual impulse, conferring an absolute character on it, whereas the two currents of the psychologists who were at first supportive of him have differed in their interpretation. The first one studies the congenital yearning of the individual, in what is referred to as 'personal relevance', while the second states that, besides sexual satisfaction and the importance of the individual, there is the drive of the higher life, which troubles even the seemingly happiest man or woman. For the circle of essentially

Freudian scholars, all psychic problems of the personality boil down to sexual angst; for a large number of their colleagues, however, the causes extend to the acquisition of power and to the idea of superiority. We will say, on our part, that, although they all bear a certain dose of reason, the three schools are identical in that all of them lack the basic knowledge about reincarnation. They represent the beautiful, costly homes of scientific principles, but they lack the roof of logic. We cannot say that everything in the physical realm is geared toward sex, a wish to be important or aspirations for something higher; however, having arrived at our current level of understanding, we can guarantee that everything in life is a creative impulse. All the beings we know of, from the worm to the angels, are heirs of the Divine One who gives us life, and we are all repositories of creative faculties. Compelled by phototropism, plants appear on the landscape, distributing life and renewing it. The firefly shines in the darkness, seeking to perpetuate itself. The amphibian feels vibrations of love and paternity in the depths of the wetlands. Tiny birds travel long distances, gathering material with which to build a nest. The beast forgets its savage nature when it tenderly licks its newborn offspring. And more than half of the millions of incarnate spirits on the earth, with their minds fixed on instinctive impulses, concentrate their faculties on sex, from which they naturally derive the greatest and most frequent nervous disorders. They constitute enormous legions on the primitive landscape of planetary evolution: our brothers and sisters in the infancy of knowledge, who still do not know how to create feelings and life except by mobilizing the resources arising from sexual forces. A large number of individuals, however, having gone beyond instinct to become endowed with reason, still remain in the madness of prepotency, seduced by despotic caprice, starving for renown and prominence, albeit their sometime involvement in profitable work and noble aspirations … Lastly, a small group of

men and women, governing their own energies in a full regime of individual responsibility after having achieved sexual balance over their instincts, and after having received the rewards of their efforts with which they dominate life, have started focusing on the sublime region in the super-consciousness, no longer finding complete happiness in the physical body or in personal prominence. They are seeking the higher circles of life, absorbed by a higher idealism. They feel they are at the threshold of divine realms, even while still trudging on the hazy road of the flesh, like the traveler, who, after crossing some harsh trails in nocturnal darkness, stops in confusion between the darkness of the night and the indefinable promises of daybreak … For them, sex, individual importance and the advantages of immediate earthly rewards are sacred due to the opportunities they offer for the accomplishment of good deeds. Meanwhile, a new light shines in the sanctuary of their souls … The particularist reasoning has become universal understanding. Their sublimated sentiments have grown in a higher direction. They anticipate Divinity and long to identify with it. They are the men and women, who, having reached the highest human standards, become candidates for angelhood.

"One way or another, however, all of this entails the creative faculties, inherited from God, in permanent play in the scenes of life. Within the organization, conservation and expanse of the universe, every being is driven to create!"

With a meaningful facial expression, the Instructor paused at length and then added in good humor:

"Many a time individuals institute evil, divert the natural current of beneficial circumstances and poison opportunities, thereby remaining for very long periods of time performing reparatory or expiatory work. Nonetheless, even then we can observe the ceaseless manifestation of the creative power that is our own, even in those who go astray … They fall into the abysses of crime

and fling themselves into the valleys of darkness; but by organizing and reorganizing their actions, they acquire the blessed heritage of experience; and with experience, they reach the light, peace, wisdom and love with which they draw near to God. We would thus conclude that, even though Freud's analytical psychology and that of his collaborators have advanced far in the field of investigation and knowledge, partially solving certain enigmas of the human psyche, they lack the key of reincarnation to fully solve the problems of the soul. It is impossible to solve the matter definitively without the concepts of evolution, improvement, responsibility, reparation and eternity. It is not enough to discover complexes and frustrations, to identify psychic lesions and mental deficiencies, without remedying them … In other words, the simple examination of the outer layer is not enough: it is essential to reach the core and set about modifying the causes. To do so, it is essential to confess the reality of reincarnation and immortality. Until then, therefore, let us aid our incarnate friends in their acquisition of confidence in themselves, in the diffusion of divine hope and continuous self-improvement through redemptive efforts."

The messenger concluded with a smile.

Other interesting and opportune questions were presented, receiving clear and edifying replies with real benefit to all listeners.

At the end of the session, I left in silence with Calderaro, who also was quiet, as if digesting the revelatory light of the concepts he had heard. I didn't know what the esteemed Assistant was thinking, immersed in deep meditation. On my part, I realized that, as far as I was concerned, I had discovered a new area of knowledge in the field of sexology. From that moment onward, other concepts of love began to sprout in my awareness, illuminating my entire being.

12
A Strange Illness

Accompanying Calderaro, the selfless brother of sufferers, I entered a comfortable home and was led directly into the presence of a gentleman who was resting.

It was an elegant room decorated in antique gold. A magnificent carpet completed the graceful surroundings. It was covered with whimsical arabesques that matched the designs on the ceiling.

The patient was stretched out on a couch, absorbed in deep thought. At his side, a humble spirit from our realm appeared to be waiting for us.

She approached, greeted us kindly and answered the fraternal inquiries of the Assistant:

"Fabricio is improving but his anguish continues. He has been uneasy and worried."

My instructor glanced expressively at the patient and asked further:

"Is he still in control of himself? Has he completely abandoned himself to destructive thoughts?"

Displaying her contentment, she said:

"Divine Mercy hasn't been lacking. For the time being, complete imbalance hasn't taken over. In Jesus' name, our efforts have been prevailing."

Calderaro turned to me fraternally:

"Have you ever examined a case diagnosed as schizophrenia?"

I hadn't acquired any specialized learning on the subject, but was aware that this particular sickness was one of the most troubling issues in modern psychiatry.

"This unappreciated scientific branch, which studies the pathology of the soul," declared my companion, grasping my lack of knowledge, "has been a battlefield between physiologists and psychologists for quite some time. Such a conflict is regrettable and complex, since both currents have substantial reasons for their arguments. Even so, we must acknowledge the fact that psychology occupies the better position. It gets to the deep causes of the problem, whereas physiology only analyzes the effects and tries to remedy them on the surface."

The Assistant suggested that I examine the patient's mental condition.

I examined him inwardly and was alarmed at the anxieties that occupied his being. The brain displayed strange anomalies. The whole lower surface showed dark spots. Disturbances of the circulation, movement and the senses were quite visible. Calderaro had introduced me to Fabricio, classifying him as schizophrenic; but mightn't this be a case of neurocirculatory asthenia?

The instructor listened patiently and remarked:

"That would be the correct diagnosis of our friend's condition at the moment. Schizophrenia, however, originates in the subtle perturbations of the perispiritual organism, and manifests in the physical vessel as a surprising combination of variable and undefined illnesses. As it stands at present, this is a case of Krishaber's disease[22] with all of its special characteristics.

With a serious look on his face, he added:

"Go beyond the variable effects. Analyze the mind and the sensorial realm."

I launched my probe more deeply into the patient's innermost thoughts and perceived tormenting images on the screen of his memory.

Lost in thought, Fabricio didn't realize what was happening around him in the outer world. Arms motionless, eyes still, he remained distant from the surrounding external stimuli; inside, however, his mind was like a blazing furnace.

His hyper-excited imagination was concentrating on *listening to the past* ... He was recalling the figure of a dying old man, listening to his last words in the physical body as he asked Fabricio to take care of three youths, who were also present in the scenery of his memories. The dying man must have been his father, and the boys, his brothers. They were tearfully talking to each other. Suddenly, his memories changed. The old man and the youths seemed to be rebelling against him, accusing him. They swore at him with uncharitable words.

The patient listened to these inner voices, anxious and embittered. He wanted to undo the past and would pay any price to forget it, eager to escape himself. But it was no use: always the same merciless memories lashing his conscience.

[22] A syndrome characterized by tachycardia, insomnia, lightheadedness or vertigo, hyperesthesia, and a feeling of emptiness in the head; called also cerebrocardiac syndrome. www.merckmedicus.com. – Tr.

I observed the damage to his organs from the intensive use of painkillers. This man must have been dueling with himself for many years.

As I was examining the situation, an elderly lady came into the room and tried to call him back to reality.

"Come on, Fabricio! Aren't you going to eat anything today?"

The man rolled his eyes around the room, mouthed an unspoken negative answer and remained as he was.

The kindly woman insisted, but was unsuccessful at motivating him. Because she continued attentively to try to get him to drink some broth, the patient stood up abruptly as if he had suddenly gone mad, ranting and raving inappropriately and ungratefully. Red with rage, he spurned the offer, surprising me with his uncontrolled outburst.

Drying her eyes, the wife went to another part of the house, while Calderaro, very moved, explained to me:

"He's on the threshold of insanity but hasn't yet entered the land of mental alienation, thanks to the vigilant dedication of an old discarnate relative assisting him."

The Assistant began applying magnetic procedures of comfort to strengthen his endurance.

The patient settled down and Calderaro serenely told his story:

"Our sick brother had the misfortune of unduly seizing a large inheritance after promising his dying father that he would look after his younger brothers, who were watching the exchange between them at the time. But finding himself master of the situation, he threw his brothers out of the house by using one of those well-paid shysters who make an unscrupulous living by falsifying legal documents. No matter how strong and convincing his brothers' justifiable complaints, no matter how moving their appeals to his fraternal protection, Fabricio turned a deaf ear and they were forced into extreme poverty and difficulties of all sorts.

Two of them died on cots in a hospital for the indigent, overcome by tuberculosis due to excessive work on night shifts. The third, relegated to utter abandonment, and not yet thirty years of age, discarnated in a disgraceful state of misfortune, suffering from a severe vitamin deficiency caused by undernourishment. Our wretched friend managed to do all of this while escaping earthly justice. However, he was unable to eliminate the traces of his evil deeds from the hidden corners of his conscience. The memory of this crime remains in his mental organization and become live, hot coals whenever fanned by his remembrances, like embers on a blackened landscape after a devastating fire. As long as he had the endurance provided by a healthy body, this bad son and perverse brother was able to escape himself without much problem. Easy money, solid health, amusements and pleasures served as heavy curtains between his arrogant personality and true reality. However, time wore out his physiological apparatus and consumed most of his illusions. Little by little, he met up with himself; in this *journey back to his inner self,* he had to face the memories he hadn't managed to evade. He tried to find good cheer and well-being, but they hid from him. It was impossible to focus on himself without hearing his father and brothers accusing him and reproaching his villainy … His tormented mind was unable to find a consoling refuge. If he remembered the past, it demanded reparation; if he tried to remain in the present, he found himself unable to acquire the peace of mind to work steadily. And whenever he tried to lift himself to higher realms and pray to the Most High, even then he was surprised by dolorous warnings urging him to right his wrongs. In this spiritual state, he belatedly became interested in the fate of his brothers. The information he received did not allow for immediate restitution – they had all departed the earth, preceding him on the great journey to the beyond. Realizing there was no quick fix for his tortuous destiny, from that time onward he

lost his noble ambitions and healthy ideals. Hope was no longer a consideration. Instead of comforting him, his material advantages now infused him with dreadful boredom and unspeakable disgust. He was chained to the machine of financial responsibilities that he had created without the spirit of possessing wealth in order to spread it in the name of the Universal Good, and as a highly respectable businessman he was unable to avoid the impositions of social life until he collapsed in supreme torpor. Accused by his own conscience, he began seeing persecutors everywhere, which led to dreadful phobias. For him, every plate is poisoned; he distrusts nearly all his family members and cannot tolerate old relationships. The excess of material resources made him skeptical of sincere friendship, gave him notions of privilege he never deserved, emphasized destructive independence and extinguished the blessed light of the verb 'to serve' in his heart. As we can see, his situation is completely unfavorable for recovery. Imposed by the ignoble desires he has always nurtured, his condition is one of apathy and barrenness."

At this point, Calderaro indicated his diseased brain in particular, and explained:

"According to what we have just studied, the nervous system, connected to the encephalic chamber through hard-to-define processes in human science, is nothing more than the representation of an important area of the perispiritual organism. Experiencing insistent remorse and afflictive preoccupations, Fabricio's bankrupt mind has poisoned these vital centers with the incessant emission of corrupting energies. Consequently, what in good psychiatry we might call 'a generalized lesion of the nervous system' has occurred. First of all, this disaster reached the seat of the most recent gains of the personality, that is, the most recent cells and stimuli located in the frontal lobe and motor cortex, thereby temporarily paralyzing our friend's ability

to involve himself in uplifting meditation and salutary work, and obliging him, in spiritual terms, to retreat within himself. Even though his mind is now at a standstill in the instinctive region of his personality, our patient is not yet completely unbalanced, thanks to ongoing assistance from our plane."

When the Assistant had finished, I dared to ask:

"But is there any hope that he can get his equilibrium back any time soon?"

"Absolutely not," Calderaro answered decisively. "In his case, current therapeutic practices would prove futile. The delinquent mind can receive all sorts of assistance, but ultimately it must be its own doctor. Divine Justice acts without fail, although people do not recognize its workings in their daily endeavors. Criminals can escape the punishment of the world's judicial organization for a long time; however, sooner or later they must wander in the lowest regions of their being and suffer punitive afflictions before their brothers and sisters in humanity. To his family and friends, Fabricio is a schizophrenic who is unable to tolerate insulin shock therapy because of his fragile and tired heart. To us, however, he is a fellow spirit injured by ambitions of the lowest kind and has sustained bitter consequences from his purpose of selfish domination in life."

When my instructor paused again, I considered a few further questions.

If the patient offered no hope of substantial improvement, what was the point of our assistance? Why spend so much time on an unsolvable case that held no potential for a reunion between the criminal and his victims in the near future?

Calderaro didn't leave me without an answer.

"We are here," he explained thoughtfully, "to provide him with a dignified death. Insanity will not set in completely.

With our fraternal help, he'll discarnate before the total eclipse of his reason."

And because I appeared startled, my esteemed friend added:

"Fabricio married a woman deserving of heavenly support. This sublime creature gave him three children, to whom he dedicated himself nobly, preparing them for lofty social missions. They are, at present, two teachers and a doctor dedicated to the high ideal of serving the collective good. Fabricio has no right to disturb his family, which was built in the shade of his material support but educated without his despotic personality. For the service he has rendered to his wife and children, he is now receiving help from On High in the form of a transfer of residence through the imposition of death in preparation for a future of readjustment. The prayers of his wife and children have guaranteed him an upcoming 'good death', for which we are organizing his energies. At the same time we are getting the family accustomed to remaining active on its mission of the good without his physical presence."

The Assistant became quiet and prepared to perform magnetic applications on the patient's circulatory system.

He administered energies around the most important arteries for several minutes before progressing to longitudinal passes meant to calm his nerves.

In light of my natural surprise, Calderaro explained:

"We are preparing the access to the thrombosis through the calcification of certain veins. Discarnation will arrive gently in a few days as a compassionate measure, indispensable to the happiness of the patient and those who have closely followed his torment."

The patient seemed to have taken a miraculous painkiller. He settled down, resting his head on the white pillows.

In a moment of silence between us, I inquired curiously:

"Considering his impending death, how will the redemption and liquidation of his debt proceed in the future?"

"The process has already begun," the instructor replied calmly.

"How so?"

Calderaro made an expressive gesture and suggested:

"Just wait."

The patient rang the bell on the headboard. His wife answered right away. Finding him better, she smiled happily.

Now more peaceful, the elderly man asked:

"Ines, can I see little Fabricio?"

"Of course," his companion answered delicately. "I'll go get him."

In a few minutes she returned with a boy eight years of age. He flung himself into his grandfather's skeletal arms with extreme fondness and asked:

"Feeling better, Grandpa?"

The sick man gazed at him tenderly and stated:

"I do feel better, my little grandson … Why didn't you come this morning?"

"Grandma wouldn't let me."

"I guess that's right; I wasn't feeling well."

Ines left the room to observe the scene from the other side of the curtain.

Grandfather and grandson felt more at ease.

Totally transfigured by the boy's presence, our nearly demented friend pleaded:

"My little Fabricio, I want you to pray for me."

The boy didn't hesitate.

He knelt down right there and reverently said the Lord's Prayer.

When the prayer ended, the sick man asked with moist eyes:

"Dear child, don't forget to pray for me when I die."

The boy, now standing, hugged his grandfather and replied, weeping discreetly:

"You're not going to die!"

Appearing relieved, the old man responded to the affectionate gesture, gazed at his grandson and asked with a strange brilliance in his eyes:

"Little Fabricio, do you believe that God forgives sinners like me?"

The tearful and confused boy answered:

"Grandpa, I believe that God forgives all of us."

Displaying the anxieties that populated his soul, he asked further:

"Even a man who betrays his father's trust and steals from his brothers?"

The grandson hesitated, incapable of understanding the full extent of that intentional question. But wishing to please the patient any way he could, he uttered with complete childlike simplicity:

"I think God always forgives."

"That's what I wanted to know," stressed the elderly man, more relieved.

The affectionate and pleasant conversation continued between them.

After a deep examination, Calderaro nodded toward the child and explained:

"This boy is Fabricio's former father. He has returned to the family of his criminal son through the blessed gates of reincarnation. He is his only grandson, and later he will assume control of the material inheritance of the family – the property that was his in the first place. The Law never sleeps."

Astonished by this information, I mulled the questions that surfaced spontaneously.

How would old Fabricio redeem himself? Would he too return in the future to that very home? Would his imbalance continue after the death of the dense body? Would he remain for long in a disturbed state?

Ending our work of assistance in this home, Calderaro smiled, prepared to leave and answered:

"With the residues of his criminal actions in his mind, right after abandoning his physiological domicile, our sick friend will experience the results of his failure for a long time. This will continue up to the point where suffering will finally remove the malignant elements that poison his soul. Once this purgatorial work is complete, then ..."

"Will he return to his family?" I anxiously inquired before he could finish.

"If the current blood-related group raises its spiritual standard to a high level of illumination, he will have to make an intensive effort to join them. Meanwhile, he will never be without support. We are all part of a huge family, of which we've been members from the very beginning – Humankind."

We left the spacious room.

In a few seconds we had returned to nature, enjoying the blessing of a clear blue sky. And while my instructor took refuge within himself, attentive to the responsibilities of his work, I gave expansion to new thoughts related to the breadth and greatness of God's justice.

13
Affective Psychosis

I went with Calderaro in the middle of the night to assist a distressed sister on the verge of suicide.

We entered a comfortable, albeit modest, home and noticed the presence of several unfortunate spirits.

The Assistant seemed like he was in a hurry. He didn't stop to make any comments.

I followed him to a humble room, where we found a young woman weeping convulsively, overcome by immeasurable despair. Her mind displayed an extreme imbalance that had spread to all the vital centers of her physiological make-up.

"Poor thing!" said the instructor very touched. "Divine Kindness will not fail her. She has gotten everything ready in order to escape through suicide tonight. However, Divine Powers will help us to intervene."

He placed his right hand on the weeping sister's forehead and explained:

"This is Antonina, a selfless struggling sister. She lost her father at an early age and when she turned eight she began doing paid work to support her mother and little sister. She spent her childhood and adolescence enduring enormous sacrifices, not knowing what the joys of being a girl and teenager were like. At twenty she lost her mother, snatched away by death. Despite her own dreams of happiness, she was forced to sacrifice herself on behalf of her sister, who was about to get married. Once the wedding was over, Antonina tried to distance herself to take care of her own life, but she soon discovered that her sister's husband was given to terrible behavior. Absorbed in pleasures of the lowest order, he got drunk every day, returning late at night and hitting everything in sight while hurling insults. Our dedicated friend felt sorry for her sister's fate and stayed home with her in silent selflessness to relieve her burden and help her raise her children. The years went by, sad and slow, when Antonina met a certain young man in need of support so that he could continue his studies. They identified with each other through age and similarity of ideas and sentiments. Devoted and noble, she became the young man's selfless sister. His company shed a blessed light on her endless nights of loneliness and sacrifice, somehow. Splitting her time and abilities between her sister, her four small nephews and the object of her dreams, she enthusiastically devoted herself to redemptive work each day, awaiting the future. She imagined that someday she too would receive the crown of motherhood in an unpretentious home, one that was good enough for the happiness of two souls forever united before God. Nevertheless, after graduating, Gustavo, the young man who had benefited from her loving cooperation for seven years, felt that he was too important to share his destiny with the humble girl. Independent and holding a university degree, he

didn't think that Antonina was the companion he envisioned for himself, physically speaking. Having big plans for his social life, flaunting a medical degree and feeling the urgent need to start a family, he married a young woman who owned a huge fortune, scorning the loyal soul who had helped him during uncertain times. Deeply humiliated, our unhappy sister went to visit him but was received with mocking coldness. With repulsive presumption, Gustavo harshly broke the news to her: He needed to organize his business interests and had therefore chosen a more suitable spouse. Furthermore, he stated that his position required a wife who didn't come from an environment of lowly activities. He wanted someone who wasn't employed at a laboratory, who didn't have callused hands or strands of gray hair. The young woman listened to all this in tears without reacting. Since returning home yesterday, she has been harboring a desire to die no matter what. She feels that her hopes have vanished, crushed by the unexpected blow, that her life has been reduced to cinders and dust, and that selflessness opens the doors to ruin and death. She got hold of an amount of a deadly substance and plans to swallow it tonight."

Pausing in his explanation, Calderaro suggested:

"Examine her while I administer first-aid."

I made a detailed examination for several minutes.

Heavy tears were falling from Antonina's eyes. However, her brain was emitting purplish rays, which reached her chest area, particularly her heart. Tormenting thoughts were confusing her mind. Sensing her secret pleas, it was sad to hear her cries of despair and her fervent appeals.

Was it a crime – I wondered – to love someone with so much tenderness? Where was Heaven's Justice that it refused to reward the sacrifices of a woman dedicated to domestic peace? She yearned to be joyful and happy like her childhood friends.

She longed for the tranquility of a noble marriage, with the expectation of little children granted by the Infinite Goodness of God! Was it a blameworthy aspiration to dream of a modest home with the support of a simple and good companion, when even the birds had their own nests? Hadn't she always worked on behalf of the happiness of others? For what unknown reasons had Gustavo relegated her to such abandonment? Didn't the calluses on her hands and the wrinkles on her face prove her dedication to honest work? Had it been worth it to suffer for so many years, seeking to accomplish something that now seemed impossible? No! She would not stay any longer in a world where vice triumphed so easily, trampling on virtue! In spite of the faith that nurtured her heart, she preferred to die, to face the unknown ... She felt disoriented, directionless, almost crazy. Wouldn't it be more reasonable – she asked herself – to seek the darkness of the grave rather than to rot in a nut house?

Stretched out on the bed, the poor woman hid her face in her hands and wept alone, filling us with compassion.

Calderaro stopped his direct assistance, looked at me with a meaningful expression and said:

"I have instructions to impose a deep, deep sleep right after midnight."

Seeing that the clock showed that that time was at hand, the Assistant started to administer fluidic applications throughout her sympathetic nervous system.

The vast network of neurons felt the anesthetizing effect. Antonina tried to sit up and scream, but couldn't: the intervention was too strong for the sick woman to fight.

My instructor proceeded carefully, enveloping her softly in calming fluids. Soon, giving in to the irresistible command, the young woman laid back on her pillow in a state that the common magnetizer would call "deep hypnosis."

Calderaro held her in complete rest for more than half an hour, at which point two spirits surrounded in intense light entered the room. They embraced my instructor, who introduced them cordially.

They were Mariana, who had been Antonina's dedicated mother, and Marcio, an enlightened spirit who had been connected to her for centuries.

Highly moved, they thanked Calderaro, who turned the patient over to her mother's care.

The kind discarnate woman leaned over her daughter and called to her softly, as she used to do while on earth. Partially disconnected from her dense envelope, Antonina arose in her perispiritual body, delighted and happy …

"Mother! Mother!" she cried, opening her heart and seeking refuge in her mother's arms.

Mariana hugged her daughter lovingly, holding her close, speaking words of affection.

"Mom, please help me! I don't want to live anymore! Don't let me return to my body … Fortune has rejected me. I'm so unhappy! Everything is against me … Take me away from here … forever!"

Her noble mother was looking at her sadly, when Marcio approached, becoming visible to the dear woman.

She opened her eyes wide and kneeled instinctively, assisted by her mother. She seemed to be trying to recall someone who had remained in her distant past … One could notice her extreme difficulty to remember precisely. She gazed at the emissary with eyes drenched in different tears: she wasn't weeping with the mournful tears of moments before; she was now touched with sublime comfort, with a mystical joy that was inexplicably welling up inside her from the depths of her heart.

Marcio drew closer, placed his shining right hand on her forehead and said tenderly:

"Antonina, why such discouragement when your redemptive struggle has only just begun? Have you forgotten that we are not orphans? Above all obstacles hovers the Infinite Goodness. Are you refusing the 'narrow door' that will provide us the blessed access to our meeting each other again?"

Perhaps because Antonina was making an enormous effort to recall scenes that had been lost in time, the messenger warned her fraternally:

"Don't force it! Compose yourself! Isn't the present, filled with blessed service and renewing light, enough for us? Someday, you shall regain the blessing of total recall; for the time being, rejoice in your limited gifts. Make use of the minutes to recompose your destiny; take advantage of the hours to redirect your yearnings for the higher realms. What reasons have suggested this crime to you, to cause your own death? What reasons are leading your steps toward the dark abyss? Your mother and I sensed your peril from afar and we are here to help you."

He paused at length, watching her lovingly, and continued:

"My blessed friend, why have you opened your heart to the monsters of despair? Tell me! Don't be silent … I'm not your judge; I'm your friend in eternity. Won't you give me the solace of hearing you?"

The young woman wanted to speak, but the soft rays of light emitted by Marcio surrounded her entirely, stifling her throat in the rapture of those unforgettable moments.

However, as he obviously wanted to give her ample opportunity to respond, he picked her up carefully and insisted:

"Tell me!"

Feeling encouraged, Antonina whispered timidly:

"I'm just worn out."

"But you have never been forgotten. You have received a thousand different resources from Providence that are

essential to the valuable endeavor of redemption. Aren't the earthly body, the sun's blessings, the opportunities for work, the marvels of nature, the bonds of affection and even the pains of the human experience priceless gifts of Divine Supply? Do you ignore the happiness of sacrifice, my dearest; do you deny the potential of love?"

I saw the young woman looking at him more trustingly. Feeling stronger before this undeniable display of tenderness, she opened herself up with sincerity:

"I've dreamed of having a home … I long to live for a man who, in turn, will help me go on living … My ideal is to receive from God a few children whom I can caress! Is it a sin, Heavenly Messenger, to yearn for such things? Is a woman who seeks to sanctify the natural principles of life a criminal? After toiling for endless years on behalf of the happiness of my loved ones, I have seen destiny mock my hopes. Is it a virtue to live among cheerful and happy people, when our own heart has fallen dead?"

Marcio listened to her fraternally, caressing her hands. And demonstrating his achievements of true love, he added more understandingly and tenderly:

"Selfless friend, don't let the darkness of a few hours cast a pall over the light of the centuries to come. Antonina, how can you feel so dreadfully alone, when the Supreme Lord has given you the entire world as your sublime home? Humankind is our family; children in pain belong to all of us. I realize that transitory humiliations to your sentiments are tearing at your soul, that you would like to lean on the loving arm of a worthy and faithful husband. Nevertheless, my dear, it is from the Higher Will that, for now, you receive only the advantages to be found in being single. There are blossoming periods in the human valley, during which we enjoy the full springtime of nature, but there are also other times that are apparently lonely and unhappy, lived in

meditation and self-denial, in whose light we prepare ourselves for new, sanctifying journeys.

"Don't think that the fatal passage of the grave opens the doors to freedom: the Law follows us everywhere, and although the Supreme Lord exerts his infinite compassion, he does not deviate from immutable justice. Eternal Wisdom invariably places us where we can be happiest and the most useful.

"You say that you are destitute and unhappy, but you haven't fathomed the sublime possibilities that surround you. You say that you are unable to embrace your own little ones from God, but why such exclusivity for blood-related offspring? Haven't you seen abandoned children; haven't you seen the offspring of misery and hardship? If you cannot be the mother of children of your own flesh, why not become the spiritual guardian of needy and suffering little ones? Do you believe, Antonina, that we can be totally happy while we hear wailing at our door? Can there be perfect bliss in a heart that beats alongside a heap of tears? The world is not our property. We, the children of the Most High, have been sent here to cooperate in the work that surrounds us. It is true unhappiness to believe oneself to be a favorite of heaven, as if the Compassionate and Wise Father were nothing but a frail and biased dictator! Awaken your slumbering conscience ... Remember that the Almighty is not subject to our characteristics as fallible creatures, and don't forget that, in light of His universality, undeniable duties weigh upon us. We must exercise the priceless resources He has given us in order to someday reach the perfection of wisdom and love.

"In your subjective idealism, you are suffering because of a man, whose psychic pattern fit with yours in many respects, but who later changed the direction of his life and relegated you to oblivion. You weep because you expected to find in his company some of the Divine Presence that would bring serenity

to your anguished hopes as a delicate and sensitive woman … The restlessness of sex has grown in your innermost being, and you are suffering a long siege of tribulations. But … could it be that you consider sex to be the sole source of love? Would you too be a victim of this fatal mistake? Love is a divine sun that radiates through all the splendors of the soul.

"Sometimes, we are deprived of feelings that we have longed for and we are kept from using the creative energies of the physical form so that we can seek higher aspirations. But such obstacles don't keep us from expressing sublime sentiments; to hinder their course would result in extinguishing the universe. What tortures the human mind on such occasions is the prison that we create for ourselves. Caught in haughty selfishness, we don't know how to lose for a few days in order to gain in eternity, or to give up transitory qualities in order to obtain the ultimate gifts of life."

As the young woman gazed at him enraptured through a thick veil of tears, the messenger continued:

"In fact, if you cannot share your life with the man you would choose because of the circumstances that compel you to self-denial, why not give him the pure fraternal love that is always uplifting? Are we by any chance prevented from regarding the people we admire as brothers and sisters? You mustn't forget that, although this groom of your desires is physically handsome for now, in the future he will wear the threadbare garb of fatigue and old age if the mask of death and infirmity doesn't visit him before that. He will experience the disenchantment of the flesh and will value in silence the search for the spirit. If you truly love him, why torment him with the mockery of suicide instead of marshalling your energies to wait for him at the end of mortal existence? If you cannot be the canteen of pure water for the dear traveler, why not be the oasis that will be waiting for him in the desert of his inevitable disillusionment? Besides, how can

you feel such clamorous abandonment, when we ourselves are waiting for you here, eager for your affection and tenderness?"

Antonina smiled in ecstasy in spite of the tears streaming down her face.

Observing the beneficial effect of his encouraging words, Marcio stroked her hair and said:

"Why wait for the offspring of the flesh to exemplify true love? Jesus didn't have them; even so, we all feel sustained by his infinite selflessness. Antonina, do you promise to modify your mental attitude from now on? The worthy and generous, sublime Christian woman forgets evil and loves always."

Moved, we watched as Antonina kneeled down again and exclaimed solemnly:

"In God's name I promise to change my attitude."

The envoy then put his hands on the woman's forehead, enveloping her in streams of light that touched not only the perispiritual matter, but extended further to the dense body, reaching particularly into the areas of the brain, chest and female organs. Delighted by the presence of her mother and the envoy from the higher realms, Antonina immediately departed for a pleasant and restful excursion. Calderaro took it upon himself to help her return to her earthly body in the first hours of the clear morning.

Uplifted by the night's observations, I returned with him to the room of the woman who had been on the verge of suicide.

Between 6:00 and 7:00 a.m., the discarnate mother brought us her daughter, on whose face shone an unknown and incomprehensible happiness.

The instructor helped her repossess her physiological envelope, surrounding her brain with anesthetizing fluidic emanations so that she wouldn't be allowed the bliss of remembering all the details of the night's experience. Calderaro explained that if she retained a complete memory of them, she

would probably go crazy with joy. Thus, the happiness that she had experienced so intensely would be filed away in her organism in the form of new strength, unknown stimuli, courage and satisfaction from an unknown source.

In fact, Antonina did wake up a few minutes later as if she were a new person. She felt inexplicably refreshed, almost happy.

One of her little nephews came into the room and called her. His kind aunt looked at him, enchanted.

Some kind of prodigious, unfathomable energy had reconnected her to an interest in life. She found unspeakable happiness in the sunlight coming through the window; she blessed the humble room where she struggled to tend to God's designs, and she smiled at the thought of the day of purposelessly running away from the learning experience of the world. Hadn't she been rewarded by Providence with a marvelous number of blessings? She contemplated the charming, poorly dressed little child asking her to go with him to the small garden where new flowers were blossoming. How important is an insignificant setback of the heart when compared to the sublime work that she could perform in her condition as a young, healthy woman? Weren't her sister's children hers as well? Wouldn't it be nobler to live in order to be useful, always counting on the Inexhaustible Mercy?

"Aunt Antonina! Aunt Antonina, let's go! Let's go see the new rosebush!" called out the restless boy of five in a joyous invitation to life.

Observing the recovery of her strength, we watched her joyfully get up and answer with a smile:

"Just a sec! I'm coming, my son!"

14
A Saving Measure

We had just finished some work in an uplifting environment dedicated to prayer, when someone approached and asked for the Assistant's help with a particular case.

Calderaro was obviously familiar with the details of the situation, and they were soon engaged in an interesting dialogue.

"Unfortunately," said the informant, "our Antidio hasn't bested the situation; his failure is almost complete. Once again, he has gotten involved with dangerous elements of the darkness and has gone back to making the same nighttime blunders as before, seriously harming our work of assistance."

"Wasn't the recovery of a couple weeks ago beneficial?" the mentor asked fraternally.

"He used it for an even quicker return to recklessness," the other explained sadly.

"But remember that he was almost completely insane."

"Yes, but he managed to regain his health remarkably, thanks to your last intervention; as soon as he felt stronger, he went back to drinking excessively. The parching thirst, brought on both by his own negligence and the instigation of the voracious vampires crowding around him, has undermined his nervous system. Due to his perispiritual body having become semi-freed from the physical body by the pernicious processes of drunkenness, his mind is filled with atrocious nightmares that are aggravated by the perverse spirits who follow his every move."

"Is he home right now?" asked Calderaro.

"No," said the other, disheartened. "I've just left our sick friend at a degrading place, where his condition has sunken to a regrettable level."

My instructor analyzed the case silently for a few moments and then considered:

"We might be able to do something; but whereas last time our assistance entailed restoring him to organic balance as far as was possible for him, this time we'll have to act otherwise. We'll have to bring about a temporary, more accentuated imbalance in his body. In this sort of process, as in other difficult ones, illness always rectifies."

And looking the patient's benefactor in the eye, he asked:

"Don't you agree?"

"Absolutely," he replied, without hesitation. "You are a specialist in assistance and I respect your decisions. Our interest lies in the stable health of our unfortunate brother, who has given in to the appeals of vice without a fight."

We headed for the place where we would be helping our wayward friend.

We entered a building that had spacious windows and was well lit.

The environment was stifling. Unpleasant emanations grew thicker as we proceeded inside.

In the building's main hall, adorned with extravagant decorations, a few dozen couples were dancing as their minds absorbed the atmosphere's abundant low vibrations.

I was overwhelmed by an indefinable and excruciating feeling, but it wasn't caused by the strangeness at observing the men's indifference and the women's frivolousness. Instead, what astonished me was the scene that they were unable to see. The number of troubled and addicted spirits moving about was enormous. The dancers were not dancing alone; rather, to the fast beat of the degrading music, they were unconsciously responding to the ridiculous gestures of their unseen, irresponsible companions. Apish postures were to be seen here and there, and hysterical screams struck the air now and then.

Calderaro didn't hesitate. He was used to this sort of scene. I, on the other hand, was unable to repress the stupefaction that had taken hold of me, so I asked for some clarification:

"My friend, what are we looking at? Cheerful people surrounded by such unconscious and perverse beings? So is dancing a crime? Is looking for joy a serious wrong?"

The instructor listened patiently to my naive questions, asked in the fright that had suddenly overpowered me, and explained:

"Such questions, Andre! Dancing can be as sanctifying as praying, because true joy is a sublime inheritance from God. But here the picture is otherwise. Dancing and enjoying oneself in this place means an outright return to the primitive states of the being, with circumstances that increase the perversion of the senses. These are men and women who are endowed with a lot of intelligence, but they are assuming postures that even apes would perhaps be ashamed of. Even so, rather than being judgmental, we should simply feel sorry for them. They are social trespassers, and most of

them are rebelling against the discipline established by the Superior Designs for their earthly pathways. Many of them are profoundly unhappy and in need of our help and compassion. They try to use wine or pleasure to drown certain notions of responsibility which they couldn't forget otherwise. Weak in the face of struggle but worthy of compassion because of the remorse and tribulations that are devouring them, they deserve our fraternal help."

And glancing over the crowd of troubled discarnates engulfed in vampirism and sarcasm, he stated:

"As for these unfortunate ones, what can one do but entrust them to the Divine Power? They too are trying to make the impossible escape from themselves. In their delusion, they are only postponing the dreadful moment of self-acknowledgment. It will arrive when they least expect it through thousands of painful processes, once the resources of divine love from our Supreme Father have been depleted. Furthermore, their minds are attached to the primitive instincts. Fragile and hesitant, they are afraid of the responsibility entailed in the endeavor of regeneration."

Seeing that I was dumbfounded and eager for additional explanations, the Assistant proposed:

"Let's go! Let them enjoy themselves. Actually, dancing in this place ends up being a benefit to them. Our incarnate and discarnate friends here have reached such a degrading level that, if it weren't for the dancing, they would be out there committing extremely reprehensible acts, such is their predisposition toward crime. May the Father have mercy on all of us."

We hurriedly went further inside.

In a small, stuffy room, a gentleman who looked to be about forty-five lay trembling. He couldn't even stand up.

Calderaro examined him carefully and asked the new friend that had come with us:

"Has it been many days since he started drinking again?"

"Exactly one week."

"He has obviously worn himself out."

As he began applying magnetic fluids, Calderaro advised me to observe the characteristics of the dantesque scene in front of us.

Sick and miserable, and in spite of his precarious state, Antidio ordered one more glass – always just one more – which was dutifully brought to him by a waiter. His hands trembled, denoting his weariness. Cold sweat beaded on his forehead, and from time to time he screamed in wild terror. Around him were four beastly spirits subjecting him to their desires. They took turns seizing his body in order to experience the absorption of alcoholic emanations, from which they derived a singular pleasure. In particular, they stuck to the "gastric path," inhaling the drink that vaporized from the cardia to the pylorus.

The scene brought anguish and astonishment.

Was this a drunkard or a living goblet, whose contents were being sipped by satanic spirits of vice?

Antidio's stomach was full of liquid and his head was clouded with fumes.

Semi-disconnected from his body by the numbing effect of the toxin, he had begun to attune himself more closely to the spirits persecuting him.

The minds of the four wretched discarnates were filled with terrifying visions of the grave they had passed through as alcoholics. Thirsty and afflicted, they brought with them spectral images of vipers and bats from the dark places where they had wound up.

Attuning magnetically to the imbalanced psyche of these vampires, the drunkard started to beg loudly:

"Save me! Save me, for God's sake!"

And pointing to the walls, he shouted in unspeakable terror:

"Oh! The bats! … The bats! Get them out of here! Stop them! … Mercy! Who's going to save me?! Help! Help!"

Two men, whose minds were also fogged by wine, approached in astonishment. One of them, however, reassured the other:

"No big deal. It's Antidio again. He's having another fit. Let's leave him be."

Meanwhile, the wretched drunkard kept on screaming:

"Oh! Oh! A snake … It's squeezing me, suffocating me … What will become of me? Help!"

The perturbing spirits emphasized their sarcastic gestures, laughing wickedly. The poor wretch could hear them in the innermost part of his being, and trying to fight against his unseen tormentors, he shouted:

"Who's mocking me? Who?!"

Clenching his fists, he added:

"Damn you! Damn you!"

The heartrending scene was proceeding, when Calderaro began to explain:

"He's a deplorable family man, who was incapable of fighting against the attractions of this addiction and thus surrendered defenselessly to the influence of discarnate villains compatible with his destabilized condition. In answer to the prayers of his loving wife and two young sons, we have assisted him with all the resources within our reach. Even so, our improvident brother hasn't responded favorably to our efforts. He emerges from every attempt of assistance even more inclined to the perversion of the senses. Above all, he seeks to escape from himself. He hates responsibility and isn't eager to grasp the value of work. In reducing his uncontrollable desire to drink, we hope he can be reeducated. So, we will now use a drastic measure, since the unfortunate man has shown himself to be resistant to all our processes of assistance."

Gazing at me meaningfully, he concluded:

"Starting today, Antidio shall be aided by his disease for some time to come. He will be confined to his bed for a few months in lieu of his body rotting away in a mental hospital – something that would have happened in a few days otherwise, and would have thrown a noble woman and two children into painful uncertainty about the future.

That said, Calderaro began a complex procedure with the application of passes along the man's spine.

Little by little, the patient calmed down in the old armchair where he had been slouching.

The Assistant applied luminous emissions to his heart for several minutes. I noticed that they gradually concentrated in the middle of the organ, which then stopped suddenly.

Antidio seemed ready to discarnate, when Calderaro restored his energies with a quick movement. Forced by the circulatory phenomenon, which had given him a tremendous jolt, the wretch man began screaming for help. There was such a great inflection of pain in his voice that a crowd approached him compassionately.

A kind gentleman felt his pulse, checked his heart and immediately requested an ambulance. In a few minutes, Antidio was taken to the hospital emergency room, followed closely by his attentive spirit benefactor.

Leaving in my company, Calderaro added sadly:

"Our unhappy friend will have to bear a cardiac neurosis[23] for around two to three months. He will use valerian and other

---

[23] "Cardiac Neurosis is an outdated term for Panic Disorder. This term appears in texts from the early 1800s to mid 1900s to designate a condition characterized by palpitations, shortness of breath, sweating and anxiety, which are symptoms frequently observed in heart attack (myocardial infarction). A medication often used to treat Cardiac Neurosis in the past was based on oil extracted from the roots of a plant called Valerian (Valeriana officinalis). Research performed to study the mechanism by which Valerian decreases palpitations and tranquilizes the patient suggests that this compound acts on the central nervous system like benzodiazepine (a sedative discovered in 1955 that can be used to treat Panic Disorder). However, the benzodiazepine-like effect of Valerian remains controversial." Dr. Sonia Doi, U.S. Spiritist Medical Association. – Tr.

medical substances to no avail, and in vain he will try pain killers and detoxicants. Over the course of a few weeks, he will experience unbelievable unrest until the harmony of his psychological cosmos is reestablished. He will experience unspeakable anguish and will subject himself to medications and diets, which will reduce his tendency to forget his sacred obligations, very slowly awakening his sentiments to the noble act of living."

Noticing my surprise, the Assistant concluded:

"What is one to do, my friend? The same Divine Powers that grant humans the caressing breeze also inflicts them with the devastating storm … Both, however, are essential elements for the glory of life."

15
A Christian Plea

My opportunity to study with Calderaro was coming to an end, when, on the eve of my promised visit to the caverns of suffering, the dear Assistant invited me to hear a presentation by Instructor Eusebio. That night, he would be addressing hundreds of Catholics and Protestants who were still at work in the physical realm.

"They will consist of less-dogmatic, more-liberal brothers and sisters who are open to our more-direct influence during sleep. Due to their virtue, they have become worthy of directives from the higher planes."

I couldn't hide my surprise at what he was telling me, but he added quickly:

"It's important to understand that Divine Protection shows no privileges. Heavenly grace is like the fruit that always results from earthly effort: wherever there is human cooperation, there too will be Divine support. It's not the outward expression of a particular religious belief that interests

us fundamentally, but the display of living faith, the soul's positive attitude on its evolutionary journey. Of course, the schools of belief vary, each within its own circle. It's a fact that the more rudimentary the religious understanding, the greater the combativeness arising from the lower circles of spirituality, establishing unfortunate boundaries of opinion and aggravating deplorable hostilities – as if God were nothing but a dictator having a hard time keeping himself in power. Since evangelical Spiritism is a prodigious nucleus of sublime understanding, it is reasonable to regard it as a more elevated and richer Christian school. Since it possesses such blessings of knowledge and love, it should extend them to all fellow spirits, even if they are rebellious and ungrateful as a consequence of the ignorance they haven't yet left behind. Jesus' compassion could be gauged by the evolutionary state of those who followed him closely. As he faced minds imprisoned in the vain intellectualism characteristic of many important personalities of his time, we see him inflamed with divine energy; in contrast, on his final day in Jerusalem before the impassioned and ignorant people – although they were adhering to the principles of their belief system – we find him silent and humble, asking forgiveness for all who smote him."

Impressing his words with a softer inflexion, he added kindly:

"Let's not forget that, above all, we are devoted to an educational endeavor. To save or rescue certain individuals does not mean to take away their opportunity to develop through struggle, to grow and to edify themselves. Instead, it implies fraternal assistance so that they may awaken and evolve, acquiring the same balance that characterizes those who have helped them. It doesn't please the Supreme Lord to have miserable and unhappy children in his Creation; he spreads blessings and talents, riches and eternal amenities all around, expecting only that each of us

be determined to manage our own patrimony wisely. As we have seen, all sectors of spiritual work require divine assistance."

Before he could explain the matter more fully, we reached the peaceful place where the esteemed emissary was speaking.

Glancing around, I could see that there were only a few hundred incarnates at the gathering, assisted by a substantial number of coworkers from our realm.

The moonlight shone gently on the trees, which were swaying in the breeze.

Majestic in the sublime light haloing his venerable figure, it looked like Eusebio's lecture had been going on for a quite a while. Enraptured, his audience listened to his words touched with heavenly light; everyone's faces displayed obvious wonder. Mixed together and kneeling in large numbers on the fresh grass, they felt as if they had suddenly been transported to paradise …

Enveloped in sapphirine reflections, the Instructor spoke with an irresistible power of attraction:

"If the heritage of religious faith represents the undeniable factor of mental balance in the world, what are you doing with this treasure, forgetting to use it in an age when instability and uncertainty threaten all the institutions of order and labor, of understanding and edification? Doesn't the storm of renewal that is redefining principles and nations amaze you, awakening your conscience? Do you believe that an era of peace on the outside is possible without people preparing themselves on the inside to observe and practice the Divine Laws? By admitting such foolishness, the machine – that offspring of your intelligence – has annulled any possibility for you to make a greater incursion into the realm of the Eternal Spirit.

"Being a Christian in days gone by meant choosing the noblest of all experiences, and it entailed the duty of exemplifying the standard of conduct consecrated by the Divine Master. It

consisted in a continuous fight against evil with the weapons of the good, the active manifestation of love against hatred, the certainty of the victory of the light over the darkness, the undeniable triumph of constructive peace over destructive dissention.

"When faced with the Moloch[24] of the imperialism and corruption of the Roman Empire, the adherents of the Gospel did not indulge in bitter arguments; they did not get entangled in the web of detrimental self-centeredness, nor did they squander their precious abilities in order to erect dogmatic boundaries … They loved each other in the name of the Lord and offered their lives as a token of gratitude to the One who did not hesitate to go to the Cross out of love for all of us. They built their most-sublime sanctuaries in communion with the sanctifying principles that identified them with the Savior of the World. They knew how to forfeit temporary advantages in order to gain the imperishable treasures of heaven. They sacrificed themselves for each other in a living display of fraternal devotion. They shared the suffering and multiplied the joy amongst themselves. They died in an anguished testimony of faith in order to reach the life eternal. They fought the imbalances of their time and of their contemporaries, not with cursing blows, not with the edge of the sword, but with the practice of self-denial, submitting themselves to harsh discipline and displaying in their words, thoughts and actions the sublime message of the Master who had renewed their hearts.

"However, as heirs to those nameless heroes who lived in affliction, of minds built up in the promises of Christ, what have you done with transforming hope, with unwavering trust? What have you done with the living faith that your forbearers acquired at the price of blood and tears? What has happened to

[24] A Semitic god to whom children were sacrificed. – Tr.

the spirit of fraternity that characterized the followers of the New Doctrine? Enriched by the grace of heaven, you have gradually forgotten the doors to Divine Revelation and have exchanged them for human amenities.

"You have erected barriers against each other that are difficult to cross. Dogmatism poisons you; schism corrupts you. Narrow interpretations of the divine plan darken your mental horizons.

"You start hostilities in the name of the Kingdom of Heaven, even though it stands for universal love and eternal unity.

"You profane the fount of blessings, damning one another in the name of the Prince of Peace, who, in order to help us, did not waver before his own insulting death.

"What delirium has taken you as you involve yourselves in a mutual competition for the imaginary obtainment of divine privileges?

"In times of old, Christ's disciples competed for opportunities to serve, whereas today, you look for every little opportunity to be served.

"You honor the Light of the Centuries of the Lord, yet you remain in the darkness of an atrocious selfishness.

"You proclaim the glory of peace in him, yet you encourage fratricidal war, in which humans and governments mutually slaughter one another.

"You appeal to the Divine Master, centralizing the inexhaustible fountain of love in his infinite goodness, yet you cultivate disharmony in the depths of your being.

"By what strange convictions do you think you can earn paradise with the power of lip service?

"Have you forgotten that the Word, divine in nature, is always creative? How can you believe in salvation at the price of mere words that you render meaningless by your attitudes?

"Nonetheless, it is imperative to acknowledge the sublime character of your task in the world.

"Jesus founded the Religion of Universal Love, which politically-minded clergy have divided into many schools guided by unjustifiable sectarianism. Regardless of this lamentable human error, the essence of your principles is the same essence that upheld the courage and worthiness of the selfless workers in the early days of Christianity.

"Just because a few missionaries of religious truths may have forgotten the Divine Paternity and let themselves be carried away by extremes of authority, in a preference for oppression and tyranny, you yourselves are no less responsible at this time for the sacred concepts entrusted to us by Jesus, concepts intended for human evolution and the sanctification of the earth.

"At its roots, the Gospel has retained the beauty of its first day. No sophism has managed to dim the luster of 'love one another as I have loved you.'

"In the face of the challenges of heaven, do you actually believe that you are serving God by confining the work of faith within ornate churches? The pomp of outward worship only heightens the foolishness of your dangerous illusions about spiritual life.

"The Divine Master's mission would be fruitless if the Good Tidings were to remain confined to denominational trenches, where you have presumptuously taken shelter with the aim of igniting the abominable bonfire of falsely cordial hostilities.

"Can't you find a different formula with which to express your belief other than by ignoble competition?

"In vain you erect castles of opinion, filled with words without deeds. Remember, however, that just as death surprises rebellious materialists and reveals the reality of life to them, it also opens the court of true justice to try all those

who used religion to disguise the indifference that resides in their inner world.

"Do not believe that faith can be consecrated with very little effort.

"As is the case with science, religion has its specific role in the world. As the balancing power of thought, its servants are called to work together in the harmony of the human mind.

"In the manifestation of positive faith resides the power that regulates the passions and the irresistible impulses of animalism, from which we all have emerged in the evolutionary process that presides over our existence.

"Jesus did not confine his teachings to the narrow confines of temples made of stone. It is true that he revered the monuments that would recall the 'sanctified places of prayer' dedicated to the higher manifestations of the spirit, but he did not remain inert in a posture of worship: he lived winning friends for the Kingdom of Heaven.

"He did not impose rigid norms of action on his followers; what he asked for was love and understanding, sincere faith and good will for spiritually constructive work.

"When he approaches Magdalene, he does not engage in pointless conversation; he interests her heart in the sublime, renewing task. When he visits Zacchaeus, he blesses him for his noble and constructive effort. When he addresses the Samaritan woman, he does not engage in worthless arguments: he impresses her through contact with his divine soul, causing her to abandon the old amphora of fantasy in order to search for the eternal founts. Living with the blind and lepers, the insane and the sick of all kinds, he exemplified a social life based on the purest fraternity and the most elevated incentives for sanctification. Finally, sacrificed on the cross, his last two companions were avowed thieves, to whom he did not hesitate to direct his fraternal love-inflamed word.

"How can one invoke his name to justify the madness of separation on the basis of faith? How can one lean on the Friend of All in order to launch battles of opinion, lighting fires of hatred to the detriment of the common solidarity that he exemplified up to his ultimate sacrifice? Doesn't it vilify his memory to spread dissension in his name?"

I could see that the speaker's words were making a deep impression. The majority of listeners wept with unrestrained emotion, feeling touched by the Judgment of Heaven.

Holding everyone's attention, Eusebio continued intrepidly:

"You are not expected to give up the spiritual deposit of your age-old beliefs. In every area, wherever the sowing of Christ blooms, it is possible to honor the Divine Law, engraving its sublime concepts in the heart. What is asked of your believing spirit is that you utilize the heavenly blessings distributed to you in abundant currents of light.

"Therefore, do not limit your demonstration of trust in the Most High to the ceremonies of outward worship. Get rid of the indifference that chills your ornate cathedrals. Let us make ourselves each other's true brothers and sisters. Let us transform the church into the sweet home of the Christian family, whatever our interpretations might be. Let us forget the erroneous statement that the apostolic times are in the past. In their own lives, all disciples of the Gospel have a bastion destined for the living worship of the Divine Master, before which the multitudes of the needy pass by every day.

"Loving and helping, believing and acting, Jesus supported the imbalanced mind of the Greco-Roman world, infusing it with a new life for a happier humankind. Likewise, all disciples of the redemptive faith can and must cooperate to uplift their fragile and wavering brothers and sisters.

"Flee the Pharisaism of modern times, which refuses fraternal help in the name of the satanic spirit of dogmatic schism. Jesus was never a preacher of discord; he never endorsed the arrogant vanity of those, who, with their lips, declared themselves to be clean, while keeping their hearts clogged with the miasmatic grime of pride and deadly selfishness!

"Let us mobilize our trust in the All-Merciful to spread his blessed kingdom of redemption.

"To wait for heaven while scorning the earth is a work of foolishness.

"No one can bribe Divine Justice, although you often foster the idea of a ridiculous business with the Divinity."

"If a farmer can never stay idle when there is an untilled field or a perilous marsh to tend to, how can we remain idle on the land of crime and darkness, unrest and suffering?!

"The fallen brother or sister is our precious burden; difficulty is our holy incentive; pain our purifying school.

"Let us embrace one another, therefore, in the name of the Lamb of God, who has renewed our mind, uplifting it to the higher realms by means of glorious ascension through sacrifice.

"Only in this way, my friends, can we respond to the lofty destiny reserved for us.

"Faced with a world in jeopardy, crazed by lower ambitions, dominated by hate and misery, and involved in a series of unending and exterminating wars, let us harmonize ourselves in Jesus Christ in order to bring balance to the physical realm.

"Disquieting darkness stalks your steps and institutions as it makes its sinister rounds.

"Avoid the subversion of spiritual values; drive away the darkness that threatens your political-religious organizations. Fear the science that parades without wisdom; free yourselves

from the reason that calculates without love; revise your faith so that its impulses do not become muddled for lack of edification.

"The earth is presently a harsh, dolorous battlefield.

"Awaken your sleeping conscience and love the Divine Law, forgetting the age-old slavery of illusion.

"Salvation is a continual work of renewal and improvement.

"Let us proclaim our faith in Christ Jesus to the troubled world forever!"

Upon finishing his exhortation, Eusebio was haloed with prodigious emissions of light.

The reverent assembly displayed faces pale with bewilderment.

A large group of coworkers from our realm raised their voices in harmony, singing a moving hymn of glorification to the Supreme Lord.

The melodious notes extended into the distance among the trees on the wings of a soft breeze.

When the service ended, I noticed that the incarnate spirits, supported by workers from our assistance activities, were not leaving cheerfully and optimistically. Outside the physical body, and thus perhaps understanding the errors of their wayward belief with greater lucidity, many of them left weeping and downcast ...

16
The Mentally Alienated

Before we visited the caverns of suffering, Calderaro urged me to pay a quick visit with him to a large institute for the mentally alienated down on the earth.

"Then you will understand more precisely," he explained, addressing me with his usual courtesy, "the tragedy of discarnates whose senses are in complete disarray. Except for the purely organic cases, the mentally ill person is someone, who, out of indiscipline or ignorance, has tried to force his or her release from the earthly learning experience. Such a case is actually a type of cleverly disguised suicide, the self-elimination of mental harmony due to the soul's inconformity to the struggles of human existence. Faced with pain, problems or death, thousands of people capitulate, giving in without resistance to the fatal disturbance that ends up opening the door of the grave. At first, they are merely discontent and desperate, which goes unnoticed even by those closely associated with them. Little by little, however, they become the

many degrees of the mentally ill and nearly impossible to cure because they harbor inextricable and overwhelming problems. Imperceptible products of their own disobedience, they start by ruining the physiological patrimony that was entrusted to them, and end up impoverished and wretched. Alone in a living hell, afflicted and half-dead, these are men and women whose suffering started with their earthly existence for having rebelled against the divine purposes, ignoring them and choosing their own foolish caprices while enrolled in the blessed school of the perfecting struggle."

Bearing these comments in mind, I accompanied Calderaro on that morning's outing to a large establishment that housed a huge number of the mentally ill.

In the first courtyard, a number of mentally disturbed women were talking with one another.

With a fierceness in her eyes and wearing the institution's uniform as if it were a royal gown, one grey-haired woman was saying to two listless companions:

"I am a marquise, so I just won't put up with the meddling of these unconscionable doctors. I'm sure I'm being held here for secret family reasons, which I shall investigate the first chance I get. I may have powerful enemies in the royal court, but my friends are even more prestigious and loyal."

She lowered her voice as if fearing hidden spies and whispered to one of her sisters-in-suffering:

"The Emperor is interested in my case and he's going to punish the culprits. They've cloistered me away because of petty money matters."

Raising her pitch, she shouted unexpectedly:

"All of them shall pay! All of them shall pay!"

And she kept explaining herself with the hand motions of a grand dame.

It pained me to observe the interaction between these incarnate patients and the pitiful discarnates crowding around them. Still prey to my old habit of curiosity, I wanted to hear the demented woman out, but the Assistant rushed to say:

"Let's move on. Unfortunately, we must pass by a vast display of expiatory suffering that is impervious to our immediate assistance at the moment. Here, almost all the mentally ill have abdicated reality and are stuck in past circumstances that no longer have reason to be. This unfortunate sister, for instance, held titles of nobility in her previous existence. She gave in to the negative energies of pride and vanity and perpetrated clamorous wrongs. She was reborn into a humble learning experience for readjustment, but at the initial, harsh trials of the beneficial correction process, she became frightened. She reacted against the results of her own sowing, surrendered her body to disastrous experiences, wound up placing herself mentally in the lowest realms of the personality, and began dwelling on her past of grand illusions. She has desperately clung to the memories of the vain marquise of ballrooms that have long since disappeared, and she roams the valleys of dementia in a dreadful state."

We hadn't gone far, when we came across a new gathering in which an odd, extremely nervous woman stood out.

"God, deliver me from all of them! God, deliver me from all of them!" she shouted. I shall never go back! Never! Never!"

An amiable nurse approached and asked:

"Ma'am, calm down! Your husband is coming for a visit. Let's choose some clothes to wear."

And smilingly:

"Aren't you happy about that?"

"No, I'm not!" shouted the demented lady in an amazing expression of anguish. "I don't want to see him! I hate him! I hate him and everything that belongs to him!"

Repeating expressions of scorn, her body stiffened and a lamentable attack of nerves ensued, prompting the nurse to request immediate help.

I wanted to stay and study the situation, but the Assistant stopped me:

"Don't waste your time. You wouldn't be of any help. We'll only be here a little while, so I suggest that you only take note of the refuge of the ones who have shirked their present duties in an attempt to flee the imperatives of instructive reality."

He changed his tone of voice and continued:

"We're not saying that all mental hospital cases are related exclusively to this factor. Many people go through this terrifying tunnel, pressed by the demands of rectifying trials. However, we have to realize that most have inflicted the punishing drama on themselves. They are our brothers and sisters rebelling against the higher purposes that led them to recapitulate difficult lessons such as meeting old enemies again through blood ties, or facing apparently insurmountable obstacles.

"For the spirit's enlightening journey to continue, it is essential that we change our mindset, examine ideas and renew concepts, and for the greater good, invariably modify our inner way of being, just as we do with soil in the revivification of productive farming or with restructuring any human institution for overall progress. However, if the soul refuses to receive divine help through the unceasing transformation processes that are offered for its benefit by means of the various situations that make up the days of the physical learning experience, it withdraws to the edge of the road, creating a disturbing landscape filled with unjustifiable wishes.

"We could say that nearly ninety out of one hundred cases of insanity – except for those that originate from a microbial assault on the brain – begin as a consequence of the grave

wrongs we commit due to our impatience or despair, i.e., by means of mental attitudes that imprint deplorable responses on the pathway of those who welcome and nurture them. Once such destabilizing forces become fixated in the inner being, the disintegration of mental harmony begins. This disintegration doesn't last for only one lifetime but many, until such persons are fully prepared to make use of the divine blessings that flow over them to restore their peace of mind and the capacity for renewal inherent to their individuality in the blessed work of evolution. Because of rebelliousness, the soul can set out on the road to many crimes, enslaving itself to their disastrous results indefinitely. Moreover, because it gets discouraged, it is prone to falling into the abysses of inertia, causing a ruinous delay in the spiritual growth for which it must strive."

At this point, we entered a large patio in the men's area and met a man who certainly fit the description of a complete schizophrenic. He was surrounded by a number of gloomy spirits. The patient was like a perfect robot under their control. His gestures were mechanical, and in a very serious tone he explained to a guard who was approaching cautiously:

"Come here, Joao. Don't be afraid. Yesterday I was a lion, but do you know what I am today?"

Looking at the hesitant attendant, he concluded:

"Today I'm a banana tree."

I would undoubtedly have found this case to be an excellent opportunity for enriching my experience, since I immediately recognized the complete integration between the victim and his unseen obsessors. The poor wretch had ended up as a puppet in the hands of typically wicked torturers.

Calderaro did not allow me to stop, however.

"The process of imbalance is complete," he stated, "and there would be no way for you to immediately recompose his

mental energies because they are centralized in the lower region. The wretch has been the object of the hypnotic practices of relentless persecutors and is exposed to a continuous emission of energies that depress and drive him mad."

"Good heavens!" I exclaimed, confused. "What could help him?"

"He's someone," Calderaro added, "who abused his personal magnetism in previous incarnations."

I couldn't repress a spontaneous objection:

"How so? Magnetism has just come to light …"

Calderaro, with his typical indulgent look, replied:

"Do you think it all started with Mesmer[25]?"

And smiling, he added:

"If we were to take the scriptures literally, the abuse of personal magnetism would have begun with Eve, in Paradise."

He nodded toward the patient and continued:

"In the past, not too long ago, our thoughtless friend took his abilities to allure too far and used them for degrading adventures. Several women who suffered his corrupting actions started sending him constant explosions of noxious hatred, extravasations that our poor friend deserved as a consequence of his many years of reproachable activity. Tormented by this persistent action, his power to resist weakened. He thus became a plaything, so to speak, of the destructive forces to which he had willingly attached himself when he enthusiastically embraced the outright practice of evil. It is impossible to say how long he will remain like this. Generally speaking, when we commit a wrong we can determine the precise moment when we fell into disharmony. We never know, however, when the moment has

---

[25] Franz Anton Mesmer – (1734 – 1815). German physician whose system of therapeutics, known as mesmerism, was the forerunner of the modern practice of hypnotism. www.britannica.com. – Tr.

come to abandon it. On returning to the straight and narrow pathway through the mire in which we wallow because of our indifference or bad faith, we cannot set a date for our return: we entangle ourselves in games of circumstance, from which we can free ourselves only after a painful readjustment."

Noticing my amazement at the cold torturers' hypnotic action, the Assistant considered:

"Don't let it get to you. Physical death doesn't suddenly modify minds that have been devoted to evil, nor is the duel between the light and the darkness restricted to the narrow circles of the flesh."

Soon afterwards, we came across two elderly silly men speaking in disconnected sentences.

"Time," explained the instructor, nodding toward them, "always ends up revealing our true condition. Whenever people have failed to make their lives a priesthood of constructive work – as is our duty on earth – senility of the body is even sadder for the soul because they are no longer in control of the social rules forged for human living; their minds become fixated on the lower impulses. Millions of our brothers and sisters remain stuck at the infantile stage of comprehension for centuries, unmotivated to make efforts at self-improvement. As long as they are supported by the transitory cooperation of relative physical health, earthly conventions, financial means and other temporary circumstances that life on earth offers to those enduring the corporeal experience, they live with the rights that society has granted them as citizens. However, as soon as they are visited by mental illness, a lack of resources, or decrepitude, they reveal their true spiritual infancy. In spite of the advanced age displayed by their 'vehicle of bones', they become like children again for having dwelled too long in the superficial terrain of life."

This exposition couldn't have been more logical. Nevertheless, as I examined that vast environment where so many disturbed individuals of both sexes were staggering about, completely out of touch with the reality of the world and without the slightest prospects for an imminent discarnation, I thought about the people who are reborn already impaired and disturbed; about the mentally disabled children and the young people who struggle with juvenile insanity; about the many phobias that vex respectable and helpful persons. So, I asked the instructor to explain these types of suffering, which can suddenly assail the most upstanding homes.

The Assistant wasn't caught off guard at all:

"Andre, this is a study of sowing in the present as well as in the past. Not only are we considering the learning experience of one ephemeral existence, but also the soul's pilgrimage on the infinite pathways of life, the imperishable life that continually moves onward, overcoming the impositions and injunctions of form as it purifies and sanctifies itself each day. While with us, you will witness a heartrending picture of spiritual sufferings, and it is most likely that, in a mental hospital, you will learn something of the imbalances that affect the mind that has strayed from the Universal Laws. In fact, 'the soul's descent into the lower regions of death' starts with mental alienation. In a mental hospital it is possible to understand a little bit of the insanity of men and women who are apparently mentally stable within the context of earthly society – where they exchange the eternal divine values for immediate illusory satisfactions – but who later, beyond the grave, are relegated to unspeakable despair. As for the disturbances that accompany the soul from earthly birth or childhood, adolescence or old age, it is crucial to realize that imbalance begins with disregarding the Law, just as expiation begins with the misdeed. If a behavior has been

adopted in disaccord with this reality, the spirit will invariably encounter the effects of its own action in every circle in which it finds itself. Whether within the mechanisms of physiological heredity or outside its influence, the mind, whether incarnate or not, will reveal itself in the reaping of what it has sown in the evolutionary field of daily effort. It will find itself on the mountain of advancement for having practiced the greater good, or in the valley of expiation for having practiced evil."

As he prepared to leave, the Assistant contemplated me for a while and concluded:

"Taking into account not only the present but also the distant past, the mentally ill are generally those who have loathed the blessings of the human experience, preferring to isolate themselves in their mental whims. The spirit tormented after death is always someone who deliberately avoided the realities of life and the universe, creating purgatorial regions for itself. Understand?"

I nodded.

Yes, I had understood. And thinking about that morning's lesson, I followed the instructor as he silently left the area of observation; later, we would meet with the benefactors who would visit the caverns on a mission of love and peace.

17
On the Doorstep of the Caverns

Calderaro and I were now with the aid unit that would be working in the caverns of suffering. Sister Cipriana, who headed the activities of this nature, surprised me with a question.

The group was comprised of a small number of coworkers: seven in all.

When she saw me with the Assistant, Cipriana asked kindly after greeting us:

"Is our brother Andre planning on coming with us?"

My selfless friend answered that Instructor Eusebio himself had suggested that it would be appropriate for me to visit the purgatorial abysses. He explained that I was interested in getting information about life in the lower zones so that I could relay it to incarnate friends, thereby aiding them with the preparation they needed for the science of living rightly.

The director listened benevolently, but objected:

"Yes, Eusebio's suggestion is reasonable regarding preliminary observations in the Lower Umbral. Even so, as the person responsible for the expedition's direct work, I cannot give him access to all the particularities for now."

She looked at me with her lucid and gentle eyes, as if she were sorry, and added:

"Our esteemed Andre hasn't taken the course on assisting sufferers in the thick darkness."

She touched me lightly with her caring hand and added:

"Just as it is crucial to garner difficult preparatory accomplishments in order to reap the benefits of the Great Light, it is indispensable to be taught how to administer this same benefit in the 'great darkness'.

Seeing that I was obviously disappointed, the venerable benefactress continued:

"We should remember that our brother is with us because he has substantial problems to resolve. Each situation to which we are led harbors a hidden lesson for our benefit. The higher designs never confront us with issues that are unnecessary in the arena of the circumstances. If Eusebio felt compelled to recommend this opportunity, it is because Andre Luiz has urgent services to render in such an environment. Considering my own responsibilities, however, I cannot authorize him to accompany us everywhere we go. So, I would ask Brother Calderaro to remain with our esteemed student on the doorstep of the caverns without descending into them with us. Even there, studious as he is, he will find an inexhaustible supply of observational material without having to face upsetting situations for which he has not been prepared appropriately."

In view of this solution, all three of us felt better. I thanked her, contented. Calderaro was also grateful. And so, as

workers overjoyed with the opportunity of continued learning for the good, we headed for a terrifyingly dark region.

Ah! I had already seen deep abysses where guilty spirits accused one another in deplorable behavior; I had seen jets of flame coming down from the sky upon the valleys of rebelliousness; I had witnessed countless spirits under the influence of strange hallucinations in chambers of rectification; here, however ...

Were we perchance coming to the "dark forest" referred to by Dante Alighieri in his immortal poem?

The scattered, lamenting voices rising toward the foggy sky tore at my soul! No, there were not only lamentations. As we descended, the outbursts changed: we also heard bursts of laughter and profanity.

We stopped on an enormous, marshy plain, where numerous groups of discarnate spirits extended beyond view in astonishing disorder, like thousands of deranged individuals either separated from one another or in swarms, depending on their specific type of imbalance.

I could not possibly calculate the extent of the enormous marsh, and even if I had had topographical charts, the fog was too dense for distances to be computed.

We traveled a few miles horizontally, and when the terrain began sloping downward again to reveal other abysmal sights, Sister Cipriana and her colleagues cheerfully said goodbye, telling the Assistant and me that they would come to get us in about six hours.

Embracing me, the director said kindly:

"My friend, I wish you happy success in your studies. I'm sure that when we return, you will convey your comforting impressions."

I smiled, delighted at such a generous demonstration of esteem.

Calderaro and I found ourselves alone in the utter expanse populated by strange inhabitants.

The conversations around us were countless and complex. It seemed at first sight that the "discarnate folk" were not aware of their situation.

While large crowds of tortured souls thrashed about in a viscous substance on the ground where we were walking, assemblies of demented spirits swarmed not far away, engaged in endless arguments about petty subjects.

The landscape was obviously extraordinary due to the hellish characteristics surrounding us. Noting the heedlessness of many of those miserable brothers and sisters, I couldn't silence the questions assailing me.

The groups of wretches were completely unaware of each other's suffering. Certain groups volitated a little above the ground like flocks of black crows that were even darker than the darkness that engulfed us, while large throngs of wretched spirits remained stuck to the ground like unfortunate birds with broken wings … How to explain it all?

I started my questions by addressing the instructor:

"Can't these woeful beings see us?"

"Some can, but they don't care – they are too concerned about themselves. They harbor contemptible sentiments in their hearts and it will be a long time before they are free of them."

"Are all these souls forsaken, left to themselves?"

"No," replied Calderaro patiently. "There are several rescue outposts around here, and several schools with many dedicated selfless aids. Sufferers and tortured personages are cared for according to their potential to benefit from it."

He had an understanding look on his face as he considered:

"The lower zones will never lack nurses and teachers, because one of the greatest joys of heaven is that of emptying infernal places such as this."

As I watched throngs of beings moving through the air very near to us, I remembered that in our colony the faculty of volitation was not commonly used so as not to offend those who had not yet developed it; but ... what about here? Low order spirits were volitating, even though just a few yards off the ground.

Calderaro explained:

"Don't be so surprised. Basically, volitation depends on the mental power that the mind has stored up; in any case, though, it is important to remember that the highest flights of the soul are only possible when an elevated intellect is combined with sublime love. There are perverse spirits with a strong volitative capacity even though it is limited to lower realms. They have an immense mental capacity and can manipulate certain forces of nature, but they lack qualities connected with the sublimation of the sentiments, and this keeps them from going higher. As far as the spirits in our colony are concerned, a large number of individuals are still unable to use such an advantage, but that is natural. In the common evolutionary process, it is easier to rescue and live with individuals who have a greater supply of love and a reduced amount of intelligence than it is to harbor highly intelligent individuals who have no love for their fellow beings; as for the latter, a constructive community life is almost impracticable. Concerning volitation, it is important to observe the examples found in nature, remembering that crows fly low, looking for scraps, whereas swallows fly high, seeking the springtime."

After this explanation, I recalled earthly conditions and asked:

"But ... what about the need for food?"

The Instructor didn't hesitate:

"They lack nothing as far as the essential necessities of help and maintenance are concerned; it's just like any mental hospital in the physical realm."

The Assistant paused briefly and then proceeded:

"Speaking of mental hospitals, I must tell you now that my aim for having taken you to one was to prepare you for this excursion. In these groups of incomprehension and pain, there are endless ranks of insane individuals who intentionally avoided the realities of life. They fixated their minds in the lowest zones of the self, and forgetting the sacred patrimony of reason, they committed grievous wrongs, acquiring enormous debts.

"Within our own spirit community, you have seen suffering brothers and sisters receiving proper assistance. Some are still suffering strange hallucinatory disturbances; others are kept like perispiritual mummies in deep lethargy, waiting to wake up; still others populate vast infirmaries, gradually recovering spiritually ... Here, however, veritable tribes of criminals and moral delinquents congregate, attracted to each other according to the nature of the wrongs they hold in common. Many are intelligent and, intellectually speaking, enlightened, but they don't have one speck of love to exalt their hearts. They roam from obstacle to obstacle, from nightmare to nightmare ... Still insensitive to spiritual help due to the hardness of their sentiments, the shock of discarnation seems to have galvanized them in the mental state they were in at the moment of their transition between the two spheres; thus, it's not easy to extricate them right away from the instability into which they thoughtlessly fell. They remain at a standstill, sometimes for years on end, stuck in the errors they had gotten accustomed to. By strengthening base impulses through the incessant, mutual exchange of energies, they usually begin to experience not only their own instability but also that of their companions in misery."

In view of the pandemonium we were witnessing, the instructor continued:

"The ancient concept of Erebus[26] burning in the eternal flames of divine vengeance is a dangerous illusion; nevertheless, the purgatorial places of criminal desires and actions, awaiting souls tainted by their excesses, are logical realities in the spirit-inhabited regions. Here, misers, murderers, the greedy and addicts of all kinds assemble in a deplorable state of inner blindness. They form compact lines that gradually make their way toward the abysses. Each one possesses an ugly story filled with anguished details. Prisoners of themselves, they have shut their minds to life's revelations and have restricted their mental horizons. They move within themselves in exclusive actions of their base impulses, holding on to the past that they should be expunging. When they begin to show signs of improvement, they are assisted by the industrious and selfless congregations of helpers who work here. In response to imperatives from above, higher authorities from our realm set up tribunals for instructional purposes. Their rulings manifest love and wisdom and always end up ordering either regenerative work by means of reincarnation on the earth or laborious tasks in the bosom of nature, once those who violated the Law to their own harm show enough comprehension and repentance.

"From this vast warehouse of guilt-tinged mental alienation originates the largest quotient of the dolorous reincarnations that populate the corporeal circles. From here as well as from other similar zones, millions of brothers and sisters enduring arduous trials proceed to the denser physical realm so that they get rid of their debts and re-harmonize their disturbed inner self. Few, however, manage to profit from the earthly opportunity in the sense of restoring their own energies. It is always easy to flee the upright path but very difficult to return to it."

[26] A personification of darkness in Greek mythology. www.merriam-webster.com. – Tr.

Just then, a huge, noisy beehive of sufferers approached us. It was a frightening group of brothers and sisters who were positively crazy. They spoke haphazardly, discussing murders; they used cruel words to tell about indescribable scenes of pain and perversity.

Not one of them knew we were there.

Very serene and knowing my engrained curiosity, Calderaro explained:

"These poor wretches are yoked to one another by nearly-perfect affinities and are constrained only by the vibratory laws that govern them. But if you'd like to get to know the history of some of them, probe the mind of the one that interests you the most."

Taking advantage of a moment in which their quarrel had abated, I approached an unfortunate brother who impressed me with his sickly face.

I tuned in to the mental wave he was emitting, but the picture I saw didn't allow an extended inquiry.

I could see the reason behind his insanity: he had murdered his wife in dreadful circumstances. He showed no remorse, however. In fact, he wanted to see his victim again so that he could torture her as many times as possible.

What tragedy lay buried in those disturbing recollections?

Astonished, I looked at the Assistant in mute questioning. At that point, however, an onerous group of monstrous beings had neared us, levitating and making a deafening noise. I immediately forget about the wife murderer. Perceiving my perplexity, Calderaro explained:

"This gang of miserable spirits, which moves about the best it can, is composed of former merchants whose sole desire was to amass money to satisfy their own greed but without benefiting anyone else. The gold that belonged to them temporarily was never used to sow thankfulness in one single

companion of their human journey. Eager for an easy fortune, they invented a thousand ways to monopolize both large and small profits, without being the least bit concerned about their neighbors' welfare. They were men of agile minds; they knew how to mentally soar long distances, ensuring the total success of the material businesses they operated with exclusively selfish goals. Their neighbors' suffering didn't phase them, they ignored others' problems, and they didn't care about the value of time in relation to the perfecting of their souls. They only wanted to accumulate financial advantages; nothing more. Divorced from charity, comprehension and the divine light, they created for themselves the cold and unyielding myth of gold, combined with a strong mind and an avaricious heart ... Enslaved now to the fixed idea of continuing to amass wealth, they fly heavily here and there, demented and confused, seeking the monopolies and profits that they can no longer find."

I felt sorry for them. I wanted to stop some of them and talk to them fraternally so as to enlighten them, but the instructor held me back and asked:

"What are you doing? It would be useless. It's impossible to use only words to suddenly readjust so many cruelly imbalanced minds."

And urging me ahead, he concluded:

"Let's go. It would take you many weeks to get to know the landscape of pain that is spread out before us, and we have only a few hours."

18
An Old Affection

We hadn't gone far, when an odd group of little old men stopped beside us.

Their distorted faces had dreadful features and they were ragged and skeletal. They were carrying handfuls of a mud-like substance, and at the slightest breeze, they would clutch it anxiously against their hearts as if they were terrified of losing it. They were looking at each other terrified as if they feared an impending disaster, and they were whispering amongst themselves in a spiteful and suspicious manner. At times they seemed ready to flee, but out fear and suspicion, they stayed put.

One of them remarked in a raspy voice:

"We've got to find a way out! We can't hang around here. What about our businesses? Our homes? The wealth we've discovered is incalculable."

And he would boastfully hold up the handfuls of mud oozing through his warped fingers.

"But ..." he continued thoughtfully, "all this gold is at the mercy of thieves in this miserable marshland. We absolutely have to find a way back. This place would scare anyone."

Listening to this odd character, I looked at Calderaro questioningly, who explained:

"These are misers who discarnated many years ago. They lowered themselves to such a profound degree of attachment to transitory material wealth that they became incapable of reaching the equilibrium of the mental zone of dignified work and were unable to access the inner sanctuary of the higher aspirations. While on the earth, they couldn't see how they could support themselves by being moderately ambitious, nor did they give any thought to the methods they used to reach their selfish ends. They scorned other people's rights and mocked their afflictions. They took advantage of the naivety and blind trust of imprudent acquaintances, and laid veritable traps for them in order to drain their savings and enrich themselves. As a consequence of having spread so much suffering through their thoughtless actions, the mental matter of their victims sends out malevolent emissions of vengeance and cursing, imposing ethereal armor around their field of thought. They are completely numbed with their minds fixated on their wrongs of the past, and they have become true ghosts of greed, tormented by mirages of gold in this wasteland of suffering. We can't tell when they will finally wake up, given their situation."

I felt truly sorry for them, to which Calderaro stated:

"They went mad in the fever of possessing and ended their sinister enterprise enslaved by mental monsters of indefinable shape."

I was about to reply, when one of the elderly men raised his voice amid the strange concert and exclaimed:

"My friends, aren't we victims of a nightmare? Sometimes, I think that we might actually be wrong. How long have we been wandering around away from home? Where are we, anyway? Have we gone mad?"

Oh! That voice! Listening to it, a terrible doubt took hold of me. Who was going mad? I asked myself. Me or that old man?

I gazed at his features. Oh, no! Could it be? That wretched spirit reminded me of my paternal grandfather, Claudio. He had been affectionate toward me from my early childhood. He had been ice cold toward others, but had been gentle with me, often patting my toddler's head with his age-wrinkled hand. His eyes would sparkle when they met mine, and my mother always said that only in my company could he find calm from the attacks of nerves that preceded his demise. I couldn't recall his life's story in detail, but I did know that he had made a considerable fortune in scandalous profits, and experienced a very difficult old age because of his excessive attachment to money. Greatly troubled in his final years, he saw conspirators and thieves everywhere. My father was extremely worried and brought him to our house, where my mother helped him through his final suffering.

In an instant, I remembered his death. I came home from school to kiss his cold hands for the last time. I never forgot how he looked in death. His hands were curled on his chest is if he were greedily guarding a secret treasure, and in his glassy eyes – which merciful hands had been unable to close – roamed the terror of the unknown, as if he were being attacked by tragic visions in the Beyond, to which he had been snatched against his will.

Over the course of time, I found out that my grandfather had left a significant financial inheritance, which we, his relatives, wasted on opulent fancies ... As I looked back at the past, I realized that a strong tie bound me to that wretch who was still

suffering the nightmare of earthly gold, carrying handfuls of mud that he pressed affectionately to his heart.

Just then, while the memories were filling my mind, one of his miserable companions shouted:

"Nightmare? No, no! Claudio, don't be so dramatic!"

His name had been spoken! The confirmation horrified me. I wanted to scream but could not. Understanding what was going on inside, the helpful Calderaro assured me:

"Andre, now I understand the meaning of your coming here: Sister Cipriana was right. There's no time to lose. The old man is showing himself receptive. He has begun to understand that he's probably in the wrong, that perhaps he's been living a cruel nightmare. Let's help him. We have to get him to see us."

Highly concerned, I watched as the dedicated instructor began applying fluidic energies to the dim eyes of my unfortunate forefather. With this providential afflux, he received temporary lucidity and was finally able to see us.

"Oh!" he cried out before his terrified colleagues. "What a different light!"

And rubbing his eyes, he asked us:

"Where have you come from? Are you priests?"

He was obviously alluding to our snow-white tunics.

I took a slight step forward and asked:

"My friend, are you Claudio M, ... an old landholder from around V ...?"

"Yes. You know me? Who are you?"

With a sigh of relief, he added emotionally:

"I've been imprisoned in this mysterious region for so long. It's rife with dangers and monsters, but it's got a lot of gold – a lot of gold ... Your words are encouraging ... Oh! For God's sake! Help me get out ... I want to go back."

He kneeled with arms stretched out to me and repeated:

"To go back ... to see my family again; to feel at home again!"

Moved, I embraced him. Not wanting to shock him with untimely revelations, I explained:

"Claudio M ... you are the victim of a regrettable error. Your former home closed to you along with your physical eyes! You imprisoned your spirit in an empty dream of deceitful riches. Death snatched your soul from its corporeal abode over forty years ago."

The old man's distraught eyes popped out. He didn't fight it. He immediately began to weep convulsively, tearing at my most innermost fibers.

"I really can feel it!" he gasped, inspiring compassion. "My head's ablaze; I can't think straight; but ... what about the gold, the gold that I piled up with so much sweat?"

"Look at your hands, now that divine clarity is inspiring your spirit! The treasure you accumulated at the expense of others' difficulties has turned to mud-like refuse. Look!"

My grandfather began to contemplate the wads of mud he had been carrying and cried out in horror. He rested his tear-filled eyes on me and considered:

"Could this be my punishment? My wrongs toward Ismenia demanded punishment."

While the sobs choked him, I asked:

"Who's Ismenia?"

"My sister. I trampled on her rights."

Moving us deeply, he continued:

"God sent you; please hear my confession. As he lay dying, my father entrusted me with a sister, who was not a legitimate daughter of our family. My devoted and saintly mother raised her with the same boundless dedication that she gave to me. But when I found myself alone, I kicked her out. I proved that we weren't related by blood so that I could more easily inherit

the fortune that my father had bequeathed us. The poor woman pleaded and suffered, but I relegated her to a miserable fate so I could protect the solid financial base I had received. I was rich; I increased my wealth and continued to do so."

Gazing at his soiled hands, he continued bitterly:

"And now?!"

I was going to console him, to open my tear-moved heart to him; however, Calderaro made a foreboding gesture that suggested silence.

My grief-filled grandfather continued, unveiling new horizons of sentiment:

"Where are my family members, whose future I so worried about? Where's the money I piled up so painstakingly to the detriment of my own soul? Where's my sister, whose resources I snatched away? Why wasn't I taught that life would go on beyond the grave? Am I really 'dead' to the world, or crazy and blind? Oh! I'm so miserable! Who's going to help me?"

Extending his withered arms, he pleaded:

"Have pity on me! My parents were put in the grave many years ago, and my children have surely forgotten me … I'm despised; I have no one. Help me, emissaries of the Eternal One! Please don't forsake an old man betrayed by his ambitions and purposes! Now that I can see what I am, I'm afraid, I'm so afraid."

His tear-veiled gaze lingered on me as he remarked:

"My family has forgotten how devoted I used to be. Only one person in the world would remember me and would hold out his protective hands if he knew where I was."

His dolorous mask displayed an expression of kindness as he clarified:

"My grandson, Andre Luiz, was the apple of my eye. Many times, his affection comforted my tortured mind. At home, on

many occasions I expressed my hopes that he would dedicate himself to Medicine. I left him an inheritance in my will for this purpose. I had hopes of seeing him do the good that I, an ignorant man, was unable to do. Remorse frequently assailed me for the extortion I had inflicted on my sister. But I was comforted by the idea that the grandson of my heart would in some way spend the money I had inappropriately hoarded by educating himself suitably for the benefit of others … He would be the benefactor of the poor and the sick; he would sow generous seeds where my useless existence had scattered stones and thorns of foolishness. My grandson would be handsome, beloved and respected."

Fixing his attention on my gestures and wiping away copious tears, he asked in a pleading voice:

"As God's messengers, mightn't you take the awful news to my grandson about the evils that consume me? I don't deserve to be delivered from these dungeons in which I have gone mad, but it would be of some relief to know that Andre is aware of my suffering!"

Assistant Calderaro's signals for me to restrain myself while waiting for more clarification were unable to hold me back. My chest burst in a torrent of irrepressible weeping. In this place I was not in the presence of higher assemblies, whose emissions of energy would support me to the end of my instructive struggle for self-discipline, but was, instead, in the presence of the regrettable vestiges of earthly passions. I recalled my grandfather patting me on the head. I remembered my father always alluding to the old man's wishes concerning my academic preparation … I thought about the long years the poor man had spent there, hanging on to ideas of financial possession. I understood the extent of my debt to him concerning the medical degree that I hadn't used honorably while in the world … I directed a pleading look at Calderaro, begging him to forgive me.

The Assistant smiled and understood everything.

Who could lose their childlikeness completely, if Christ himself, the Supreme Guide of the Earth, had once opened his tender arms in the manger?

Mentally returning to the scenes of a distant childhood, I felt like a little boy again. I leaped over the space that separated us and kneeled down at the feet of my unfortunate benefactor, who looked at me, trembling and frightened. I covered his hands with kisses, and raising my tear-filled eyes, I asked:

"Grandpa Claudio, don't you recognize me?"

I couldn't even begin to describe what happened next.

For a moment I forgot about the study I had intended to conduct; I disregarded the images of that environment that provoked curiosity and dread. My spirit breathed sincere recognition and the purest love. And while the wretched, miserly spirits cried out – some in rebelliousness, others laughing furtively, incapable of understanding this unexpected scene – I, supported by Calderaro, who also wiped away discreet tears because of the emotion that had overcome me, held my grandfather in my arms as if I were mad with joy, carrying a precious burden that was sweet and light to my heart.

19
Together Again

When Cipriana returned with the other friends, she found me drenched in tears as she listened to the extraordinary story about my semi-lucid grandfather. Indicating that she understood, she said benevolently:

"Andre, I knew there had to be a purpose for your coming here."

I took a few minutes to describe the incident, providing her with all the information about the past.

The director calmly pondered my revisit to the past and then replied:

"We don't have much time; and since he's too sick to come with us, we'll have to intern him nearby."

In spite of his joy at having recognized me, my grandfather was far from coherent: he spoke in rambling sentences and kept repeating Ismenia's name.

"We mustn't forget," the venerable instructor pointed out, "that brother Claudio needs treatment and care. It's impossible to tell when he'll be able to breathe a more elevated atmosphere."

That said, she examined the half-mad old man with maternal care.

After a few moments, she said:

"Andre, for our patient to improve more quickly and efficiently, he needs to return to the corporeal experience."

"Then, in that case," I asked humbly, "can we count on your help, Sister?"

"Of course. Since it will be a reincarnation merely for reparatory activities and with no involvement in communal interests, our personal cooperation can be more decisive and immediate. There are many benefactors in this area who provide for a large number of reincarnations in regenerative circles. Let's see if we can examine our brother's future situation."

She submitted the sick man to a gentle inquiry.

In an emotional tone, the old man explained that when his father got married, he brought with him from his turbulent youth a daughter, whom his mother had welcomed kindly. Later, this sister had been Claudio's devoted nanny, becoming a creditor of his gratitude. However, when his parents died from a malignant fever, he became blinded by the desire to possess money in excess, and thus stripped her of her inheritance the day before his marriage. Robbed of her assets, and after much weeping and complaining in vain, Ismenia was forced to work in the home of a wealthy family, who gave her a job as a kitchen maid earning a pitiable wage. He later learned that, pressured by material difficulties of all kinds, she had married an illiterate, rude and cruel man who physically abused her, and that she had had a few daughters in a dire condition of poverty. After exposing this major deviation from his path, Claudio shook

our hearts as he continued listing the unworthy ideals he had nurtured in the grips of avarice.

Showing me that she was used to problems of this nature, Cipriana explained:

"We have identified two essential points for the work ahead of him. One is the need to reestablish a relationship with Ismenia. But we don't know where she is and whether she is incarnate or not. The other is the imperative of extreme poverty, with hard work so that he can reeducate his aspirations."

With the likely address of the mistreated sister's descendants in hand, Cipriana ordered two of our companions to conduct a quick investigation on the earth in order to provide us a course of action in this unexpected turn of events.

The emissaries were gone only about ninety minutes.

They had some great news, which comforted me.

They had located the family the unhappy old man had referred to in his anguished reminiscing. As for Ismenia, the friends from our realm explained that she had indeed reincarnated and was in the juvenile phase of her new body. She had been reborn into the same family for whom she had worked when my grandfather had kicked her out.

Cipriana was very excited upon hearing this, and showing further interest in our case, she suggested that we immediately begin laying the groundwork for the future by winning the girl's sympathies.

By then, we were inside an aid organization, which responded very favorably to our director's request on behalf of the sick man.

Focusing all her attention on my old creditor, the esteemed benefactor told me:

"Our friend won't be able to leave this place of fraternal assistance for about two years because he is deeply attuned to the

outside atmosphere of the lower zone. We will visit him often and give him the support of our resources until he can once again breathe the air of earth. His mind cannot easily free itself from its web of incomprehension, and in such a state he wouldn't return successfully to the physical learning experience."

I accepted her suggestion, following the steps recommended for the case.

Cipriana gazed tenderly at the demented man, and continued benevolently:

"Now, Andre, to finish this week's work, let's try to bring Ismenia here for the preparatory work of bringing them together. Since she is presently in her youth, she'll probably help us at the right time and receive her disturbed brother into her home. But before anything else, we need her sympathy regarding our plans for restoring him.

"If Ismenia accepts; if she agrees ..." I added hesitantly.

"We'll take care of the rest," Cipriana promised decisively. "Claudio's return to the physical realm will entail highly personal aspects, without major implications for society in general. Thus, we can coordinate most everything ourselves."

Entrusting the sick man to the care of the benevolent workers in charge of that house of Christian love, we headed for Rio de Janeiro and found Ismenia in a modest home in the Bangu district.

We respectfully entered the modest home at dawn.

My grandfather's sister was now the sixth daughter of the woman known in her physical existence as the granddaughter of the former Ismenia, whose personality, for her earthly family, had been lost in time. To us, however, she was none other than the same child and young girl as before, who had come back for the perfecting endeavor of the corporeal struggle.

Everything there breathed of noble poverty and endearing simplicity.

Cipriana placed her right hand on the sleeping girl's forehead, as if to call her to us. In fact, a few instants later she was with us. Seeing our leader enveloped in an intense light as she greeted her with a gesture of blessing, she kneeled down, exclaiming in tears of jubilation:

"Heavenly Mother, who am I to receive the grace of your visit? I am an unworthy servant."

She covered her face with her hands, feeling perhaps dazzled by Cipriana's sublime light and barely able to repress the turmoil in her heart. But our venerable benefactor approached, rested her caring hands on her thick black hair and said compassionately:

"My daughter, I am only your sister, your friend ... But listen! What is your purpose in life?"

As the girl lifted her tearful eyes, the noble messenger added:

"We need your help but we do not want to be useless friends. How can we be of service?"

Heavy moments of expectation passed.

"Don't be afraid to speak up!" added Cipriana helpfully."

With her voice choking with emotion, she stated with youthful naivety:

"Mother, if I can ask anything of you, please help Nicanor. We've been engaged for almost two years, but we are poor. I earn a small salary working in the textile industry in order to help maintain our home, and Nicanor is a bricklayer ... We have been dreaming of having a small, modest home under the watch-care of Divine Providence. Can we hope for God's approval?"

With an expression of motherly tenderness, Cipriana considered:

"Why not? Your wishes are just and sanctifying. Nicanor shall have our assistance and your hopes our strong support. However, we need something in turn."

"Oh! I'm just a lowly servant; how could I serve you?"

The director didn't prolong the conversation, but stated only:

"Come with us!"

Then, to my great surprise, Cipriana covered Ismenia's face with a thin veil made of a substance similar to gauze so that she wouldn't see the sorrowful landscapes that we would be crossing.

With our support, the young woman was soon kneeling curiously and emotionally before my grandfather. Upon seeing her, he broke into exclamations filled with anxiety:

"Ismenia! Ismenia! My sister, forgive me!"

Tormented, he caressed her hands while gazing at her humble face:

"Oh! It really is her," he insisted, obviously amazed. "She has the same look of grief as on the day I threw her out! … But what has she done to look so much younger and more beautiful?"

Since the visitor remained silent and bewildered, he urged, afflicted:

"Tell me; tell me that you forgive me; that you will forget the evil I did to you!" At that point of the unexpected meeting, Cipriana intervened and asked her:

"Did you know that your great-grandmother had a brother …"

The young woman did not let her finish, and asked:

" … Who threw her out of the house?"

"Yes."

"My mother once mentioned that distant past," she added sadly.

"Don't you recognize him?" her benefactor asked warmly. "Don't you remember?"

The old man interrupted to refresh her memory:

"Ismenia, Ismenia! It's me, Claudio, your wretched brother."

The girl didn't know what to make of such words. Cipriana, however, touched her frontal lobe with her hands and enveloped her in abundant magnetic radiations, causing the emergence of memory in the most important perispiritual centers. She insisted gently:

"See the past once again, my friend, so that we may better serve the Divine Work."

Astonished, I watched as something extraordinary happened to the young woman's mind: her previously sweet and peaceful eyes dilated and became troubled. She tried to withdraw before my grandfather's pleading look, but Cipriana's energy stopped her, preventing the expansion of her initial impulses of fear and repulsion."

"Yes, now I remember!" she groaned in horror.

Our instructor then released her forehead, and nodding toward the sick man, she asked movingly:

"And don't you feel any compassion?"

There were a few tense moments of expectation; love, however, always divine in women with high aspirations, triumphed in Ismenia's loving gaze. Completely changed, she embraced the sick man, saying:

"So, it is you Claudio? What happened to you?"

The old man described his suffering at length, disclosing his past wrongs, and then spoke more lucidly and happily of the comfort that meeting her again had brought him.

She held him close for a long time, enabling him to feel her immense tenderness, dedication and unlimited understanding.

When both seemed fully reconciled, Cipriana approached her and considered:

"My friend, we would love to hear you promise to help our friend Claudio in the near future. Will you cooperate with us on

his behalf and receive him with the selfless arms of a mother if Divine Law authorizes your marriage to Nicanor?"

Displaying the treasures of a simple and humble existence, Ismenia respectfully replied:

"If Heaven grants me the happiness of contributing something on Claudio's behalf, the real benefit will be mine. And if someday I receive the conjugal blessing, he will be our first, beloved little son. I know even now that Nicanor will be overjoyed with this, my promise."

Gazing blissfully at the wretched prisoner of the darkness, she promised:

"He will share our poor and honorable life; he will know the joys of earning a living with his sweat and Divine Watch-Care. In our company, he will forget the illusions that have separated us for such a long time."

Displaying a delightful simplicity of heart, she planned in rapture:

"He will be a happy bricklayer like Nicanor! He will bless the worthy struggle that we presently bless!"

While she wept emotionally, Cipriana embraced her, also touched. With moist eyes, she assured Ismenia:

"Blessed are you, dear daughter, for, like us, you understand the heavenly ministry of the worthy woman who is always ready for sublime motherhood."

A few more moments went by in wholesome understandings, and as the sun garlanded the horizon with diamond-like hues, we were once again in Ismenia's modest room, helping her return to her body and to forget what she had experienced with us in the spirit realm.

She woke up in her body feeling an unknown elation. Her mind was refreshed with happy ideas. She had the clear impression of returning from a marvelous excursion, whose details she could

not define. Without knowing how, she was absolutely certain that she would marry and that God was holding a happy future for her.

Who could describe our appreciation and wonder of those moments? My companions blessed her, and I, in my turn, bid her an emotional farewell, silently kissing her tiny hand in profound friendship and inexpressible gratitude.

20
At Cipriana's Home

After my week of study, and harboring new values in my spirit, I accompanied Calderaro at twilight to the laudable institution in the lower zones that the Assistant called "Cipriana's Home."

I was feeling extremely confused by the problem that was demanding my full attention – unexpectedly meeting my grandfather again – so there was no longer any reason for extensive investigations of a philosophical-scientific nature based on the privileged knowledge of my instructor, who was soon to take his leave.

My research had given way to meditation, my reasoning to sentiment. I had gathered extensive material regarding the manifestations of the mind and had obtained invaluable deductions for defining the imbalances of the soul. I had examined several patients. I had identified diseases whose causes were connected to the most-profound and least-known roots of the spirit. Amidst all that information, however, I had found

a patient who had shifted me from my burning intellectual curiosity towards more-defined reflections on destiny and being.

I now realized that, in order to acquire profitable wisdom, love is essential.

The profuse questions had gone silent, repressed in my aching soul.

It is true that I could have advanced much farther in the area of new knowledge. I could have won prestigious friendships. I could have renewed and improved my concepts of life and the universe. But what would such trophies mean if I could not help a benefactor in trouble?

With my focus set on the remarkable issue of the moment, I arrived with Calderaro at the enormous institution where Cipriana administered the constant benefit of her sisterly dedication.

As far as I could tell, it was a place of assistance that was different from all the others that I was familiar with - it seemed like a large center of an essentially earthly endeavor.

Most of the spirits working there were not of an elevated order, but were normal human personalities in the process of regeneration. With the exception of Cipriana and the advisors in her group, the large community consisted of obviously little-evolved individuals: men and women similar in aspect to those who populate the corporeal circles.

As usual, Calderaro came to my rescue and explained:

"Sister Cipriana visualized this loving shelter of spiritual restoration and made it real by using the actual suffering and disturbed brothers and sisters roaming the surrounding areas.

"Of course, strictly speaking, she doesn't actually live here, in this regenerative school; however, she does dedicate a great deal of her time to her sanctifying ministry in the low spheres of evolution. Basically, the organization operates under

the supervision of fellow spirits who have shown improvement. It is an important school of readjustment for the soul, of self-examination and preparation for individuals of good will. Our commendable friend is the one who began the work and she remains its most faithful provider. Nevertheless, the institute is in the lower zones for individuals who want to improve their existential conditions. It is a transitory school that has become a valuable center of instruction and support under the direct operation of those who benefit from it. Individuals who were freed from the flesh in a pain-filled inner state – as far as their understanding is concerned – receive precious help in order to readapt to life appropriately."

Diverse groups composed of average spirits were headed towards a building in the center of the huge organization, which I guessed to be a temple devoted to prayer.

Many residents were walking quickly alongside us, talking. There were both happy and worried people just like on any big-city public street on the earth. I felt like we were visiting an enormous university situated in a gloomy environment.

Although there were differences between the small or large groups of brothers and sisters as far as appearance is concerned, they were identical to one another in the lively look of hope glowing in their piercing eyes. Everyone we came across showed a discernible attitude of industriousness and renewal. Even the large numbers of disabled and sick displayed a transforming optimism.

"The venerable instructor," continued the Assistant, "has set up a veritable workshop here for the restoration of the spirit. After enough years of purgation, and upon showing that they now have an edifying purpose for their life, former exponents of pride, who used to aggrandize themselves in vanity and crime, receive shelter here, where they reorganize

their sentiments and moral values on the pathway to the future. Countless rectifying reincarnations proceed from here, as well as from other institutions of the same type located in the expiatory realms. Cipriana's basic plan is for them to forget about evil and to value the good from now on in the light of hope in God. In the beginning, the organization cost her a lot of sacrifice in terms of the time and rights that her personal merit had earned for her. However, over the course of the years, members whom she herself had prepared began managing and maintaining the endeavor."

I was contemplating the goodness and wisdom of that valiant missionary who was ready for any type of service of a higher nature and was recalling my own particular case involving my demented grandfather entangled in the darkness, when we entered the sanctuary where her voice would be heard in prayer. She was surrounded by several individuals known to her.

A visibly comforted gentleman spoke to her reverently:

"I have been following your advice, Sister, and I haven't had any more nightmares. I've changed my attitude toward my family: I have begun cooperating instead of fighting."

"Good for you!" Cipriana exclaimed happily. "The lasting good is the child of fraternal cooperation. You'll see a considerable difference regarding the happiness that will surround you."

"Sister," said a pleasant lady, "my situation is different now. I can see that the world was not created for me, and that I must fulfill my obligation to work on its behalf."

Cipriana displayed a beautiful expression and remarked:

"I can see you've made progress. Forgetting about our personal wants expands our understanding."

A shaky elderly man, with all the features of having recently discarnated, addressed her with tear-filled eyes:

"Sister," he babbled, sadly, "I'm still experiencing my old aches and pains. There are times when I feel like I'm falling, losing control of myself; and then I wake up feeling anxious."

Cipriana patted his shoulder and encouraged him:

"That's natural. You should know, however, that the situation will improve. Sometimes we spend many years storing up impressions and of course they're not going to fade away in just a few days."

Others approached with the obvious intention of talking to her, but when she saw us, she walked towards us with a smile on her face, addressing us kindly:

"Andre, our patient's problem has been addressed as for the particulars that can be solved immediately. Claudio will stay here until he shows enough progress to be moved to our regenerative institute. While here, he will prepare himself suitably for his return to the corporeal realm. Everything will proceed harmoniously. Also, our coworkers have been told about the help we owe Ismenia for the fulfillment of her ideals."

Amazed and touched, I thanked her and gave thanks to God. Our conversation did not last long. The signal for prayer called to us to the cheerful and sweet duty.

Ready to lead the prayer, Cipriana was accompanied by her direct coworkers.

She knelt down in soul and looked toward heaven, from where an intense light poured over her head ... From her chest, head and hands beamed radiant emissions of divine energies, of which she had become the visible intermediary for all of us.

These splendid rays flowing down from the higher realms through her sublime personality reached us and we felt soothed by unspeakable gentleness ...

I shed a river of tears as a harmonious choir of a hundred voices in perfect tune sang an unforgettable hymn of praise to the Supreme Father.

Immediately afterward, the instructor's moving words vibrated in the atmosphere, invoking the protection of Christ:

"Lord Jesus,
Constant inspiration on our pathways,
As always,
In your mercy,
Open the sublime doors
Of your immeasurable providence ...

Giver of Life,
Awaken our consciousness
So that we may sow resurrection
In the gloomy valleys of death;

Dispenser of the Highest Good,
Help us fight evil
With weapons of the spirit;

Prince of Peace,
Do not leave us indifferent
To the discord
That lashes the hearts
Of our suffering companions;

Master of Wisdom,
Drive far from us
The fatigue we feel
From the work
That we must render
To our ignorant brothers and sisters;

Emissary of the Divine Love,
Do not grant us peace
Until we conquer
The monsters of war and hatred
As we cooperate with you
In your august terrestrial endeavor;

Shepherd of Immortal Light,
Strengthen us
So that we may never become intimidated
By the anguish and despair of the darkness;

Distributor of Infinite Wealth,
Supply our hands
With your unlimited resources
So that we may be useful
To all beings on the pathway
Who are still feeling a lack
Of Your imperishable gifts;

Angelic Ambassador,
Do not abandon us to the desire
For undue rest,
And make us
Your humble servants
Wherever we may be;

Messenger of the Good Tidings,
Do not allow
Our ears to fall asleep
To the chorus of tears
Of those who weep for help
In the circles of suffering;

Companion of Eternity,
Bless our responsibilities and duties;
Do not abandon us to
Our continued imperfection!

Grant us, beloved Jesus, the favor of serving you.
May the Supreme Lord of the Universe glorify you
Forever.
So be it!"

The sanctuary had become resplendent. Then, through a thick veil of tears, I saw that a marvelous crown of diamonds briefly glittered over the head of that venerable missionary of the good, as if suddenly placed there by invisible hands …

At the end of the meeting, Cipriana came to say goodbye with remarkable simplicity.

Why not admit it? My eyes were covered in tears, and I wanted to follow her as a son indebted to her forever – such was the wisdom and love overflowing from her glorified spirit.

Calderaro was the first to embrace me and wish me a good trip. Stifled by intense emotion, I couldn't respond. All the others greeted me tenderly. Finally, Cipriana held me tight, gave me a motherly kiss and said with tearful eyes:

"May the Father bless you. Never forget the good as you fulfill any obligation."

And perhaps because she saw that I was so deeply moved, she added:

"We shall be together in spirit."

I left her arms with the longing of a son, whose flame of gratitude is never extinguished in his inner sanctuary.

Returning to the work awaiting me, alone and touched, I smelled the scent of the clear night filled with marvelous messages from the sparkling stars …

"Merciful Lord," I pleaded mentally, "graciously bestow your blessing on the worm that I am!"

I had the impression of my heart beating large inside my chest. Constellations sparkled there before me, indicating glorious destinies in the unending future …

And silently pondering the greatness of God, I wept copious tears of jubilation, giving vent to the indefinable sensations that took over my soul, ecstatic and happy with renewed hope!

Publishing Committee:
Jorge Godinho Barreto Nery – President
Geraldo Campetti Sobrinho – Publishing Coordinator
Cirne Ferreira de Araújo
Evandro Noleto Bezerra
Maria de Lourdes Pereira de Oliveira
Marta Antunes de Oliveira de Moura
Miriam Lúcia Herrera Masotti Dusi

Publishing Producer:
Fernando César Quaglia

Translated by:
Darrel W. Kimble and Ily Reis

Cover:
Evelyn Yuri Furuta

Graphic Design and Layout:
Rones José Silvano de Lima – www.bookebooks.com.br

Photo of Chico Xavier:
Grupo Espírita Emmanuel (GEEM)

Cover Photo:
http://www.istockphoto.com / NH
http://www.dreamstime.com / Harlanov
http://www.dreamstime.com / Serp

Technical Standardization:
Library of Rare Works and Book's Patrimonial Documents

Printed in Great Britain
by Amazon

46416716R00148